LAW, BUREAUCRACY AND POLITICS

The Implementation of Title VI of the Civil Rights Act of 1964

Augustus J. Jones, Jr.

UNIVERSITY
PRESS OF
AMERICA

LANHAM • NEW YORK • LONDON

Library of Congress Cataloging in Publication Data

Jones, Augustus J.
   Law, bureaucracy, and politics.

   Bibliography: p.
   Includes index.
   1. Afro-Americans—Legal status, laws, etc. 2. Afro-
Americans—Civil rights. I. Title.
KF4757.J65   342.73'085   82–1852
ISBN 0–8191–2154–1   347.30285   AACR2
ISBN 0–8191–2155–X (pbk.)

For Diane, Juanita,
Shirley and Augustus Jones, Sr.

TABLE OF CONTENTS

ix

LIST OF TABLES

PREFACE

A 1981 survey found that a majority of Americans, mainly whites, believe that racially discriminatory practices in education, employment, and housing are largely non-existent in this country.* These views seem to be reflected well in the current posture of the Reagan Administration toward civil rights. But while the Administration stance mirrors popular sentiments, there remains sharp division and debate among academics who have researched this matter. Conclusions reached in a number of scholarly studies hold that despite exemplary governmental efforts, racial discrimination continues to persist in many areas including education, employment and housing. But evidence marshalled by other scholars suggests that racial discrimination has largely disappeared and that the "race" factor per se has greatly declined in significance. References to these and similar studies are found throughout the volume.

The focus of this study, however, is not directed primarily to this on-going controversy. Rather, the central purpose here is to critically analyze one segment of this general debate, viz; the efficacy of legislative efforts to overcome and to redress racial discrimination and inequities. More specifically, this study examines the actors and dynamics involved in the implementation of Title VI of the Civil Rights Act of 1964. This 1964 measure was by far the most comprehensive civil rights legislation to pass the Congress since Reconstruction. In general, Title VI makes it illegal to discriminate on the basis of race, color, and national origin in the administration of federally assisted programs, and authorizes agencies to terminate funds to programs found guilty of non-compliance. At the time of its passage, many civil rights advocates hailed this "fund termination" provision as the impetus needed to effectuate compliance with federal law. Overall then, while not focusing directly on the debate over whether or to what extent racial discrimination has been overcome, a study of the implementation and enforcement of

---

*Washington Post / ABC News Poll, "Blacks, Whites Agree Blacks have Gained, Differ on What's Ahead," March 24, 1981, p. 1A.

Title VI is of obvious importance and relevance to this on-going controversy.

A word about the organization and development of this study. My reasons, approach, and methodology for doing this project may be found in Chapter I. Chapters II and III delineate the political-social context in which Title VI enforcement takes place. Chapter IV-VI consist of in-depth analyses of each of the agencies selected for study. The analysis of each agency considers such factors as: 1) the attitudes and conflicting objectives of individuals who are responsible for enforcing Title VI; 2) the resources (e.g., staff, compliance instruments) the agency has at its disposal; 3) the conditions under which agencies have used or are subject to use various enforcement methods; and 4) the impact of clientele, constituency, congressional, executive, and judicial pressures on agency enforcement operations. In the final chapter (VII), we summarize our major findings and relate these findings both to earlier studies and to the future study of racial discrimination and public policy.

There are many people who contributed to the development of this study, but some contributed more than others and merit special mention. First and foremost, I humbly thank the Supreme Being for giving me the opportunity and the fortitude to complete this work. Second, I am indebted to Professors Lucius Barker, James Davis, and Barbara Salert of Washington University (St. Louis) for their valuable comments, criticisms, guidance and insights. Particular thanks to Professor Barker, a splendid friend and teacher, who inspired me to undertake this project and offered exceptionally helpful suggestions for developing and organizing it.

Third, I am indebted to the library staff of the Civil Rights Commission and to civil rights officers at the Departments of Health, Education, and Welfare; Housing and Urban Development; Labor; and Justice. Without these officials cooperation in interviews and their support in aiding me to locate relevant government documents, records, and reports, this book would not have been possible.

Fourth, I am grateful to the Brookings Institution for awarding me a Research Fellowship which allowed me to conduct this study in Washington, D. C.

Finally, I owe special thanks to Judy Rogers for doing a superb job in typing this manuscript.

While it is true that many people contributed to the development of this book, I alone take full responsibility for errors which may appear in this volume.

November 1981   Augustus J. Jones, Jr.

Chapter I

SOME NECESSARY BEGINNINGS

There are several reasons for undertaking this study. Much of my interest has been spurred by findings in the implementation literature. It is, of course, commonplace, as that literature makes clear-- that once a law is passed its enforcement does not automatically follow. However, what strikes me as particularly intriguing in the literature is the finding that the implementation of law is affected by the interplay of various policy actors--judges, bureaucrats, legislators, and the executive. Consequently, I felt it would be extremely fascinating to examine a law and analyze how the enforcement/ implementation of that law is shaped by the inter-actions of various policy actors--judges, bureaucrats, legislators, the executive.

Another reason for conducting this study is that, as far as I can determine, few if any, implementation studies have used a comparative framework in describing how and why two or more agencies have carried out a law or program in a particular fashion. Interestingly enough, the few works conducted with respect to federal officials enforcement of Title VI have either generally described what agencies have done in regard to meeting their Title VI responsibilities, or have sought to explain why a particular agency has taken certain actions in regard to the enforcement of this statute.

Several such studies have been made by the U. S. Civil Rights Commission. These studies generally describe actions agencies have taken or have failed to take in meeting Title VI obligations, and have gener-ally concluded that most agencies have neglected to meet such responsibilities. However, while the Commission reports draw such conclusions, they do not attempt to explain why some agencies tend to meet their Title VI duties better than others. To be sure, the Commission suggests a number of reasons why most agencies have not effectively carried out their Title VI responsibilities. These reasons include: "1) the reluctance of agencies to terminate funds of non-complying recipients; 2) inadequate resources; 3) poor procedures and mechanisms utilized to detect discrim-ination; and 4) lack of executive (presidential) leadership."[1] Again, however, we do not get any

1

explanation of why some agencies more vigorously enforce Title VI than do some others. Nor does the Civil Rights Commission consider the extent to which enforcement practices of the agencies might be influenced by such factors as the attitudes and the competing and conflicting objectives of agency officials, constituency and clientele influence, and congressional pressures.

There have, of course, been other studies with respect to agency implementation/enforcement of Title VI which have focused on some of the factors with which this thesis will be concerned. In the main, however, these works have been case studies of particular agencies and lack the comparative dimension that might shed light on the central question of this thesis; viz; why some agencies seem to be more vigorous (successful) in meeting their Title VI responsibilities than others. In one such study, Gary Orfield examines the Title VI enforcement operation of the Office of Education and explains how this agency (office) overcame numerous internal and external obstacles in its efforts to enforce Titel VI. Specifically, Orfield analyzes how the Office of Education coped successfully with internal office disputes and external political pressures from special interest groups and conservative members of Congress. Orfield contends that "the Office of Education overcame these obstacles because its top administrators were personally committed to the enforcement of Title VI."[2] In brief, Orfield's study indicates how such factors as administrators' attitudes, special interest groups and congressional pressures influenced the Office of Education's Title VI enforcement efforts.

By contrast, another study of the Title VI enforcement effort of the Law Enforcement Assistance Administration has shown how that agency has neglected to enforce Title VI despite the fact that the agency's own staff and court decisions have found non-compliance with Title VI. This study argues that LEAA's failure could be attributed to its having been granted excessive discretion in an area peripheral to its chief concern--law enforcement. Specifically, the contention is made that "the discretion conferred by Title VI permits an agency to prolong efforts to obtain compliance indefinitely."[3] As a consequence, the LEAA has abused such discretion by steadfastly refusing to set compliance deadlines for federal programs, some of which were found three or four years ago, to be operating in violation of Title VI. Again, however, the

2

limited scope of the LEAA study, just as the other studies mentioned above, did not allow it to address the central question with which this thesis will be concerned. Nonetheless, these earlier studies, especially when viewed collectively, should prove quite useful and instructive in organizing and carrying out my work.

It is true, of course, that there have been other implementation studies of a more general nature. For example, in their celebrated work, Implementation,[4] Pressman and Wildasky analyze the Economic Development Administration's efforts to implement a redevelopment program in Oakland, and pinpoint the multiple difficulties that that agency had to grapple with in seeking to put the particular program into effect. The authors contend that the major factor which militated against the smooth implementation of the redevelopment program was that before any action on the program could be initiated, the consent of a large number of actors involved with the implementation of the redevelopment project had to be obtained.

In their study,[5] Bailey and Mosher illuminate the efforts of the Office of Education to implement the Elementary Secondary and Education Act of 1965. This measure provides federal assistance to elementary and secondary school districts serving low income children. Specifically, the authors show how the Office of Education had to reorganize its structure to implement the Elementary and Secondary Act and how conflicts among local, state and federal educational officials, responsible for implementing this statute, hindered effective enforcement of this law.

Eugene Bardach, in his treatise The Implementation Game: How a Bill Becomes a Law,[6] generally discusses the difficulties in implementing mental health legislation in California and specifically highlights an array of implementation games engaged in by policymakers to further their objectives. Of the twenty implementation games the author considers, the most striking is "keeping the peace." In this particular game, interests who sought unsuccessfully to block the adoption of a law or program at the policy enactment stage seek to prevent the enforcement of this law or program at the policy implementation level by swaying executive officials responsible for writing regulations and guidelines.

Finally, in their edition <u>The Politics of Implementation</u>, Nakamura and Smallwood synthesize the implementation literature and "spell out the political dimensions of the policy implementation process by analyzing the complex types of linkages and inter-relations that characterize the policy system."[7] Utilizing such examples as Mayor Daley's political bout with the Johnson Administration over school desegregation and President Carter's battles with the Corps of Engineers over water projects, the authors make prominent the complex political bureaucratic linkages between policy makers (e.g., "the president, congress, governors, state legislators, interest groups and powerful constituents");[8] policy implementers (e.g., policy makers formal implementers, intermediaries, administrative lobbies, powerful individuals, policy recipients or consumers, the mass media, and other interested parties");[9] and professional evaluators (people from outside of the government who are hired by "policy makers or implementing agencies expressly to conduct evaluations that require their special skill or expertise").[10] By doing this, Nakamura and Smallwood accentuate how politics and bureaucratic skills fundamentally color the attitudes, behavior and environments of the aforementioned actors.

In general, however, the implementation studies by Pressman and Wildasky, Bailey and Mosher, Bardach, and Nakamura and Smallwood lack a comparative base. By contrast this study utilizes a comparative approach and seeks to explain the behavior of three agencies in attempts to meet their Title VI enforcement responsibilities. This should permit us to more fully delineate the various factors and conditions which affect the implementation of a given law in the context of several enforcement agencies. This study should then broaden and deepen our understanding of the dynamics of policy enforcement and implementation.

The Agencies Involved: Hypotheses and Data Collection

The three agencies with which this study is concerned are the Office of Investigation and Compliance of the Department of Labor; the Office of Civil Rights of the Department of Health, Education and Welfare;* and the Office of Program Compliance of

---

*With the creation of the Department of Education in 1979, the Department of Health, Education and Welfare

4

the Department of Housing and Urban Development. Previous studies have concluded that these agencies show marked differences in the extent to which they enforce Title VI. Specifically, in this study, I postulate that agency enforcement of Title VI varies because of: 1) the attitudes and the competing and conflicting objectives of individuals who are responsible for enforcing Title VI: 2) the pressure brought to bear on agencies by the executive, legislative, and judicial branches; 3) the influence of clientele and outside groups on agencies; and 4) the resources (e.g., staff, compliance instruments) agencies have at their disposal. The number of agencies chosen, and their apparent differences in enforcement patterns, should permit a richer context in which to address the question of why agencies might differ in their enforcement/implementation efforts.

Methdology

I primarily relied on interviews to test the validity of the hypotheses put forth above. Specifically, I conducted extensive interviews with relevant officials in the Department of Health, Education, and Welfare; Housing and Urban Development; and Labor. I interviewed officials not only in Washington, but I also talked with officials responsible for Title VI enforcement at the agencies' regional offices in Philadelphia and their local offices in Washington, D.C., and Baltimore, Maryland.[11]

In addition, I interviewed various Washington based or represented groups that are concerned with Title VI enforcement. Also, I talked with members of Congress who exercise influence in the agency, as for example through the budget process. Other officials in the Justice Department (Federal Programs Section) and the Commission on Civil Rights were also interviewed.

I also spent some time in and around the agencies involved so that I might get a better feel and "on the spot" view of the agency resources and their Title VI

---

has been renamed the Department of Health and Human Services. The present study, however, was generally conducted prior to this reorganization.

enforcement operations. Furthermore, I examined various government documents with respect to laws, directives and regulations concerning the Title VI enforcement efforts of administrative agencies, and a host of other materials including agency brochures, handbooks, and guidelines, and compliance and review reports.

More About Title VI

It might be useful here to make some general observations regarding the enactment of Title VI, and the nature of its provisions, especially those relating to enforcement procedures. There are several reasons why Title VI was passed by Congress, but surely one of the chief reasons why the statute was enacted was that civil rights lobbyists convinced the White House and Congress to take action to ban racial discrimination in federally subsidized programs. Indeed, in proposing Title VI for enactment, and in the legislative debate regarding this statute, it was constantly stressed that civil rights groups protests had shed light on the fact that blacks were being excluded from federally funded programs because of racially discriminatory acts, and that federal action was essential to rectify this discrimination. Thus, the need to extirpate racial discrimination in federally funded programs was the major force which led to congressional enactment of Title VI of the Civil Rights Act of 1964. And the provisions of the law were broadly drawn. Indeed, "federal financial assistance covered by Title VI is extended through more than 400 programs totalling as estimated 100 billion dollars annually."[12] These programs are administered by thirty-three agencies which are themselves responsible for Title VI enforcement. Some of the agencies with Title VI responsibilities are: The Department of Agriculture; Health, Education and Welfare; Housing and Urban Development; Interior; Justice; Transportation; and the Environmental Protection Agency.

Title VI grants agencies a choice of three sanctions to utilize when they discover non-compliance by recipients of federal funds.[13] These sanctions are: 1) voluntary compliance, 2) fund termination, or 3) any other means authorized by law. Under this "any other means" provision, agencies can use two other sanctions in implementing Title VI.[14] They are: 1) referral of a case to the Justice Department and 2) fund-deferral.

Hence, overall agencies with Title VI responsibilities have four sanctions that they can employ: 1) voluntary compliance, 2) fund termination, 3) fund-deferral, and 4) referral of a case to the Justice Department. My preliminary analysis of how these sanctions have been used by the three agencies involved in this study reveals some interesting variations. For example, the Office of Civil Rights of the Department of Health, Education and Welfare has utilized the sanctions granted it under Title VI more frequently than any of the agencies under investigation. Specifically, it has terminated funds 200 times, deferred funds 180 times, referred 80 cases to the Justice Department and utilized 480 times the voluntary compliance sanction.

Of the two remaining agencies, the Program Compliance Office of the Department of Housing and Urban Development has applied Title VI sanctions more frequently than the Department of Labor. Specifically, the Program Compliance Office has terminated funds one time, deferred funds six times, and has employed one hundred times the voluntary compliance sanction.

The Office of Compliance and Investigation of the Department of Labor has utilized Title VI sanctions less frequently than any of the agencies under investigation. Specifically, the Office of Compliance and Investigation has never terminated funds or deferred funds, and never referred a case to the Justice Department, but it has used one hundred and fifty times the voluntary compliance sanction.

The utilization of Title VI sanctions as a measure of enforcement may be viewed as follows:

Fund Term(FT)	Fund Def(FD)	Case Ref(CR)	Vol Comp(VC)
Office of	Office of		Office of
Civil Rights	Program		Compliance and
	Compliance		Investivation

Strong		Weak
HEW	HUD	Labor

Obviously, how the agencies have used these sanctions must be viewed only as gross indicators of their enforcement practices. The fact that a particular agency has used a certain sanction may not accurately portray the overall behavior pattern of the agency. In short, attention is given to the role and inter-relation between symbolic and actual behavior practices. Indeed, there are a number of other factors in addition to the use of Title VI sanctions that must be addressed in order to gain a more complete picture of the enforcement behavior of a particular agency.

The Department of Justice's Federal Program Section is primarily responsible for coordinating the federal government's enforcement of Title VI. The FPS was created in 1965 and in 1981 operated with a staff of twelve persons. The chief function of the FPS is to ensure that agencies with Title VI duties develop uniform guidelines and procedures for enforcing Title VI and make sure that they (Title VI agencies) apply Title VI sanctions upon uncovering acts of discrimination. In order to accomplish this objective, the FPS periodically examines federal agencies' Title VI operations and recommends ways in which they might improve them. Two points need to be made here regarding the FPS. First, while the FPS has investigated a number of agencies' Title VI enforcement operations, it has never studied HEW's operations, which is the largest Title VI enforcement office in the federal government. FPS officials generally contended that they had never scrutinized HEW's Title VI operations because of a shortage of staff and because HEW is too large. As one FPS official put it:

> a lack of manpower combined with HEW's hugeness has prevented us from probing HEW's Title VI operations.
> . . . HEW is a very large agency and we simply lack the staff to determine if it (HEW) is meeting its Title VI duties.
> . . . while two or three FPS staff persons could investigate HUD or Labor's Title VI programs, it would take the entire FPS staff to investigate HEW. Consequently, staff limitations have forced the Federal Programs Section to make a difficult decision. The choice for us is studying one agency or a number of agencies. Obviously, our decision has been to study a number of agencies.[15]

This particular viewpoint was shared by various officials in the FPS office. A second point concerning the FPS's operations is that though it recommends ways

in which Title VI agencies can improve their enforcement programs, these agencies oftern disregard such
recommendations. It was repeatedly emphasized that
time and again the FPS had recommended that agencies
like Labor and HUD adopt policies to improve their
enforcement of Title VI, but these agencies had
ignored such recommendations.[16] However, when Title VI
agencies disregarded the FPS's civil rights recommendations, FPS officials lobbied the White House, Congress,
and the civil rights clienteles of the various agencies
in an attempt to exert pressure on Title VI agencies to
adopt those recommendations.

Besides the Federal Programs Section, the Civil
Rights Commission, which was established by Congress
in 1957 primarily to appraise federal laws and
policies with respect to equal protection of the laws,
is another governmental agency which investigates
Title VI agencies' enforcement operations and recommends ways in which they can ameliorated their
operations. Over the years, the Commission has probed
the Departments of Agriculture, Health, Education and
Welfare, Interior, Justice, Labor, and Transportation's
Title VI programs. The Commission has detected flaws
in these agencies' programs, and has suggested ways of
rectifying these flaws. But the Commission's Title VI
recommendations, like those of the FPS, have generally
been disregarded by Title VI agencies. To cope with
this problem, the Commission, like the FPS, has urged
the White House and Congress to compel Title VI
agencies to adopt recommendations necessary to bring
about vigorous enforcement of Title VI.

A final general observation about Title VI is
that when Congress enacted this statute, it inserted
provisions in the law affording the president,
congress, the courts and agency officials the opportunity to shape the direction of Title VI enforcement.[17]
Relevant provisions of Title VI states that regulations
regarding Title VI can only become effective after the
president has approved them; that before agencies with
Title VI responsibilities can terminate the funds of
non-complying recipients, they must obtain the consent
of the House and Senate Committees having jurisdiction
over them; that agencies action regarding Title VI is
subject to judicial review; and that agency officials
can use the voluntary compliance sanction as long as
they think necessary to bring about compliance with
non-discriminating provisions of Title VI.

Consequently, it is clearly apparent that in enacting Title VI, Congress not only reserved unto itself the clout to affect Title VI enforcement, but also provided that the implementation of the law could be affected considerably by the president, courts, and by agency officials themselves. This leads us to the next chapter where we discuss the political-social context in which Title VI enforcement takes place.

[1]U. S. Commission on Civil Rights, The Federal Civil Rights Enforcement Effort--1970 (Government Printing Office, 1970), pp. 990-1038. Also, see U. S. Commission on Civil Rights, The Federal Civil Rights Enforcement Effort: Seven Months Later--May 1971 (Government Printing Office, 1971), pp. 70-75.

[2]Gary Orfield, The Reconstruction of Southern Education: The Schools and the 1964 Civil Rights Act (New York: Wiley, 1969), p. 48.

[3]Note, "Enforcing A Congressional Mandate: LEAA and Civil Rights," Yale Law Journal 85 (1976), 721.

[4]Jeffrey L. Pressman and Aaron Wildasky, Implementation (Berkeley: University of California Press, 1973), p. 79.

[5]Steve K. Bailey and Edith K. Mosher, ESEA: The Office of Education Administers a Law (Syracuse: Syracuse University Press, 1968), p. 101.

[6]Eugene Bardach, The Implementation Game (Cambridge, Mass.: M. I. T. Press, 1977), p. 56.

[7]Robert T. Nakamura and Frank Smallwood, The Politics of Implementation (New York: St. Martin's Press, 1980), p. 179.

[8]Ibid., p. 22.

[9]Ibid., p. 46.

[10]Ibid., p. 72.

[11]Officials in the agencies' regional and local offices were contacted for interviews because they are responsible for carrying out Title VI activities on a day-to day basis. For example, officials in the agencies' regional offices conduct Title VI complaint investigations and compliance reviews, and officials in the local (or area) offices monitor the activities of the agencies' recipients to determine if they are abiding by the provisions of Title VI.

Also, the agencies' regional offices in Philadelphia and their local offices in Baltimore and

Washington, D. C., were selected for analysis because officials in the agencies under study indicated that these particular offices were generally representative of their daily Title VI operations.

Finally, the offices above were chosen for analysis because of their proximity to Washington, D. C., the site from which I conducted the overall analysis of the agencies' Title VI enforcement effort.

[12]U. S. Commission on Civil Rights, The Federal Civil Rights Enforcement Effort--1974, Volume VI: To Extend Federal Financial Assistance (Washington: Government Printing Office, November 1975), p. 1.

[13]Title VI of the Civil Rights Act of 1964 states: "[n]o person in the United States shall, on the ground of race, color, or national origin, be excluded from participation in, be denied the benefits of, or be subjected to discrimination under any program or activity receiving Federal financial assistance. . . .Each Federal department and agency which is empowered to extend Federal financial assistance to any program or activity, by way of grant, loan, or contract other than a contract of insurance or guaranty, is authorized and directed to effectuate the provisions of section 601 with respect to such program or activity by issuing rules, regulations, or orders of general applicability which shall be consistent with achievement of the objectives of the statute authorizing the financial assistance in connection with which the action is taken. No such rule, regulation, or order shall become effective unless and until approved by the President. Compliance with any requirement adopted pursuant to this section may be effected (1) by the termination of or refusal to grant or to continue assistance under such program or activity to any recipient as to whom there has been an express finding on the record, after opportunity for hearing, of a failure to comply with such requirement, but such termination or refusal shall be limited to the particular political entity, or part thereof, or other recipient as to whom such a finding has been made and, shall be limited in its effect to the particular program, or part thereof, in which such noncompliance has been so found, or (2) by any other means authorized by law: Provided, however, That no such action shall be taken until the department or agency concerned has advised the appropriate person or persons of the failure to comply with the

12

requirement and has determined that compliance cannot be secured by voluntary means. In the case of any action terminating, or refusing to grant or continue, assistance because of failure to comply with a requirement imposed pursuant to this section, the head of the Federal department or agency shall file with the committees of the House and Senate having legislative jurisdiction over the program or activity involved a full-written report of the circumstances and the grounds for such action. No such action shall become effective until thirty days have elapsed after the filing of such report." If Congress does not block an agency's effort to terminate the funds of a recipient guilty of violating Title VI, that recipient still can seek to halt such efforts by lobbying the Federal courts.

[14] Ibid.

[15] Statement by Theodore Nickens, Deputy Director of the Department of Justice's Federal Programs Section, in a personal interview, Washington, D. C., January 13, 1979.

[16] Ibid.

[17] See footnote 13.

Chapter II

THE POLITICAL-SOCIAL CONTEXT: PRESIDENTIAL ACTIVITY AND TITLE VI ENFORCEMENT

In this chapter, we focus attention on the political-social environment in which Title VI enforcement takes place. The present chapter concerns the impact of presidential activity on Title VI enforcement. In the next chapter, we consider how Congress, the courts, bureaucratic officials, interest groups and public opinion may influence the environment in which this statute is implemented.

The Impact of Presidential Activity on Title VI Enforcement

Certainly, the president is one major policymaker who can affect the enforcement of Title VI. The president's varied roles and vast powers afford him multiple opportunities to shape and influence the implementation of any law including Title VI. As the chief law enforcement officer of the nation, the president interprets the meaning of law and decides the level and nature of enforcement. With respect to Title VI this means that the president's attitude and posture toward Title VI can surely influence how this law is implemented. For example, a president who calls for vigorous enforcement of civil rights laws and takes action to engender compliance with these laws may foster a milieu conducive to civil rights enforcement. By contrast, a chief executive who does not call for the vigorous enforcement of civil rights statutes and takes steps to retard the implementation of these laws may make it difficult to enforce anti-discriminatory laws like Title VI. Specific examples will be cited later to illustrate how the president's statements and actions regarding Title VI can significantly affect HUD's, HEW's or Labor's Title VI operations. Again, the major goal here is simply to delineate in a general fashion how the president's vast powers afford him the choice to exercise influence over the implementation of Title VI.

The president's powers to appoint and remove executive officials also afford him the chance to influence the implementation of Title VI. As chief

executive of the nation, the president has the power
to appoint agency directors who are responsible for
implementing Title VI. Surely, in making such appointments, the president can select agency officials who
are either supportive or non-supportive of civil rights
enforcement. A president who appoints agency heads
supportive of civil rights enforcement may facilitate
the enforcement of Title VI. By contrast, a chief
executive who appoints agency directors opposed to the
vigorous enforcement of civil rights statutes may
hamper Title VI enforcement.

The president's power to dismiss or remove may
also influence the implementation of Title VI. By
dismissing agency officials who have opposed efforts
to implement Title VI, the president might foster the
vigorous enforcement of Title VI. On the other hand,
by firing officials who have generally endorsed
efforts to forcefully implement Title VI, the president
might hinder the implementation of Title VI.

In addition, the president can exercise influence
on the enforcement of Title VI through his indirect
control over the budgets of Title VI agencies. While
the Congress appropriates money for Title VI enforcement programs within given agencies, it is the
president via the Office of Management and Budget who
recommends to the Congress how much money a Title VI
agency should receive. Given the fact that Congress
seriously weighs the president's budget recommendations, it stands to reason that the president through
his Title VI budget requests can affect whether or not
an agency can effectively fulfill its civil rights
responsibilities.

Thus far, we generally have focused on how presidential activity can affect Title VI agencies'
enforcement operations. Let us now take a closer look
with respect to the impact of such activity on Title VI
agencies' civil rights enforcement efforts. Specifically, an attempt is made here to assess whether the
statements and actions of the president including
Johnson, Nixon, Ford, Carter, and Reagan have facilitated or inhibited agencies' Title VI programs. In
making this assessment, I analyzed the statements and
actions of the various presidents with respect to
civil rights and civil rights enforcement generally.
In addition, I examined their attitudes toward the
poor and the bureaucracy to determine if such attitudes
appear to have had any bearing on agencies' Title VI

operations. However, the extent to which actid
various presidents have affected the Title VI e
ment operations of the agencies with which this
is concerned--HUD, HEW, and Labor--is reserved ᵢₒᵣ
discussion in the context of chapters dealing with the
particular agency.

Lyndon Johnson

Lyndon Johnson became President in 1963 after the
assassination of President John F. Kennedy. Johnson,
a Southerner, assumed the responsibilities of the
presidency at a time when the American people were
grieving Kennedy's death and when blacks were demon-
strating throughout the South--seeking economic,
political and social equality. Civil rights groups,
for the most part, were suspicious of Johnson because
of his Southern background and his conservative voting
record in the Congress. They wondered whether Johnson
as president would push for the passage of the civil
rights bill that Kennedy had proposed, or whether he
would simply let that bill die in a Congressional
committee as had been the fate of so many civil rights
measures. In short, civil rights groups were concerned
about how Johnson as president and as a Southerner,
would perceive his civil rights role. But that concern
was short-lived. Indeed, in a 1966 press conference
Johnson summarized how he viewed his civil rights role
in the three years he had been president. Responding
to the questions as to what should be the government
role in the civil rights field, Johnson said:

> I think the Federal government must be
> a leader in this field and I have--the three
> years I have been President--tried, by word
> and action, to do everything I could to
> bring about equality among the races in this
> country and to see that the Brown decision
> affecting our schools was carried forward
> expeditiously and in accordance with the
> law.[1]

Clearly, Johnson believed that as president, he should
lead the nation in the civil rights field and he did.
Only six days after the assassination of Kennedy,
Johnson, in his first address to Congress, urged that
legislative body to move expeditiously in enacting the
civil rights bill proposed by Kennedy. Johnson said
he could think of no better way to honor his

predecessor.

> No memorial oration or eulogy could
> more eloquently honor President Kennedy
> than the earliest possible passage of the
> civil rights bill for which he fought so
> long . . . I urge you . . . to enact a
> civil rights law so that we can move for-
> ward to eliminate from this nation every
> trace of discrimination and oppression
> that is based upon race or color.[2]

Johnson not only urged Congress to pass the 1964 Civil
Rights Bill, he also took steps to secure the passage
of this measure. He collaborated with civil rights
groups in mapping a strategy to insure Congressional
passage of the civil rights bill, and he used the
media to emphasize the importance of enacting this
bill. Johnson's efforts proved successful for in July
1964 Congress passed the Civil Rights Act of 1964.[3]
This particular act, as noted earlier, barred discrimination in public accommodation, barred unequal
application of voting registration requirements,
struck down employment discrimination based on race,
sex, color, or national origin; established the
Community Relations Service to assist communities in
grappling with discriminatory practices based on race,
color, sex, religion, or national origin; and, of
course, it prohibited discrimination on the basis of
race, color, and national origin in federally assisted
programs.

After the passage of the Civil Rights Act of
1964, Johnson continued to push for equality among the
races. In 1965[*] he proposed and successfully pushed
for the passage of the Voting Rights Act.[4] This
legislation outlawed discriminatory devices (such as

---

*To further combat discrimination, Johnson in
1965 issued Executive Order 11246 which led to the
Department of Labor's development of preferential
hiring requirements on the basis of race and sex in
the construction industry. The order is commonly
viewed as creating affirmative action programs,
programs to compensate blacks and women for past
discrimination.

the literacy test and the grandfather clause) which had been used by states to ban blacks from becoming registered voters. In his efforts to secure Congressional passage of the Voting Rights Act, Johnson personally lobbied members of Congress to gain their support, met regularly with civil rights and labor group leaders to make sure that they were exerting pressure on legislators, and used the media to drum up public support for this voting rights proposal.

After the passage of the Voting Rights Act of 1965, Johnson continued to strive for racial equality. In 1966, he proposed an open-housing law to end racial discrimination in housing. Civil rights groups responded favorably to Johnson's proposal and cooperated with him in seeking Congressional support. However, Congress rejected Johnson's open-housing bill. In spite of this defeat, Johnson did not give up. In 1967 he again asked Congress to enact a fair housing law. Again, Congress refused. Still unwilling to accept defeat, Johnson asked Congress again in 1968 to enact an open-housing law. However, this time[*] Congress responded favorably to Johnson's request by enacting the Open Housing Act of 1968 (a.k.a. Civil Rights Act of 1968) which prohibited discrimination in the sale or rental of about 80 percent of all housing.[5]

Basically, Johnson adopted a forceful and positive attitude toward civil rights enforcement. Admittedly, he did order HEW to fund Chicago's racially segregated schools, which seemed to have been a blatant violation of Title VI. Even so, however, the preponderance of the evidence indicates that Johnson generally had a positive attitude toward civil rights enforcement. He not only called for vigorous enforcement of civil rights laws, but overall his actions indicated that he was committed to ensuring their implementation. For example, in 1966, when Southern Congressmen urged Johnson to revoke HEW's Title VI guidelines on the ground that they were illegal, he refused to do so, contending that HEW guidelines were legal and he supported them.

---

[*]A change in the political climate, specifically the brutal assassination of Dr. Martin Luther King, seemed to prompt Congress to enact the Open Housing Act of 1968.

Civil rights leaders unanimously agreed that
Johnson was genuinely concerned about enforcing civil
rights laws. Whitney Young, former Director of the
Urban League, stated, "Johnson was fully committed to
civil rights even is it would put him at a political
disadvantage."[6] In addition, President Johnson
adopted the attitude that he had a special responsibility to assist the poor. Addressing the Congress in
1964, he declared:

> The President of the United States is
> the president of all the people in every
> section of the country. But this office
> holds a special responsibility to the
> distressed and disinherited, the hungry
> and the hopeless of this abundant nation.[7]

Johnson's words were backed up by his actions. In
1964 he urged Congress to pass the Economic Opportunity
Act, which he asserted, "strikes at the causes, not
just the consequences of poverty."[8] Also, Johnson
emphasized that if enacted "the Economic Opportunity
Act would give the entire nation the opportunity for a
concerted attack on poverty through the establishment,
under my direction, of the Office of Economic Opportunity, a national headquarters for a war against
poverty."[9] Civil rights groups endorsed Johnson's
proposal and contended that it offered great potential
for aiding the poor. They also lobbied Congress
stressing the need for the passage of the Economic
Opportunity Act.

Congress enacted the Economic Opportunity Act on
August 20, 1964. This legislation established an array
of programs to help the impoverished. There was a
community action program to assist local groups to
combat poverty, a work-training program for the long-
term unemployed (Job Corps), a loan program for poor
farmers, and a work-study program for college students.
Interestingly enough, after Congress passed the Economic Opportunity Act, Johnson lobbied Congress each
year to insure that adequate funds would be provided
for the Office of Economic Opportunity.

Johnson and the Bureaucracy

Basically, Johnson had an ambivalent attitude
toward the bureaucracy. He "thought highly of some
bureaucracies but lowly of others."[10] Stephen Hess,

in his study <u>Organizing the Presidency</u>, writes that while Johnson thought highly of the Departments of Health, Education and Welfare; Housing and Urban Development; and Labor, he did not think highly of the Departments of Agriculture or Defense. Exactly why Johnson felt this way about the agencies or departments mentioned above is never specifically spelled out by Hess. Nevertheless, Hess does suggest that Johnson's attitude toward the various bureaucracies was predicated on whether or not he liked the secretary who directed the agencies. In any event, Johnson held a favorable attitude toward the bureaucratic leadership of the agencies under discussion in this study.

Richard Nixon

Richard Nixon captured the office of the presidency by a slim margin in 1968. He became president at a time when the country was bitterly divided over the Vietnam conflict, when the nation's inflation rate had skyrocketed to seven percent and when public opinion polls showed that "a majority of Americans felt the government should play a less active role in civil rights matters."[11] Civil rights groups, commenting on the new president in 1968, felt that unlike his predecessor, Nixon would not be a leader in the civil rights sphere. In fact, many of these groups "believed Nixon would move slowly and cautiously on civil rights concerns."[12] These feelings and beliefs about Nixon were underscored by his campaign statements and actions. As a candidate for the presidency in 1968, Nixon ignored the black vote and concentrated on capturing Southern and suburban white votes. In seeking the votes of Southerners and suburbanites, Nixon called for "law and order" and emphasized that the government should play a less active role in civil rights matters. He made it perfectly clear during the presidential campaign on 1968 that the federal government should not impose its civil rights will on the states. Even more striking, he suggested that the federal government should not withhold funds as a means of pressuring segregated schools to desegregate. For example, in a 1968 interview in Charlotte, North Carolina, Nixon responded to questions of whether the withholding of funds under HEW guidelines was a valid weapon. Said he:

> I think that the use of power on the
> part of the federal government to force

the local community to carry out what a
federal administrator or bureaucrat. . .
may think is best for that local community,
I think that is a doctrine that is a very
dangerous one. It is one that I generally
would not approve. . . .I want to make it
clear that I supported the actions of the
Eisenhower Administration in this field.
I believe that the Supreme Court decision
was a correct decision, that is <u>Brown</u> vs.
<u>Board of Education</u>. But on the other
hand, while that decision dealt with
segregation and said that we would not
have segregation, when you go beyond that
and say that it is the responsibility of
the federal government and federal courts
to, in effect, act as a local school
district in determining how we carry that
out, then to use <u>the power of the federal
treasury to withhold funds in order to
carry it out, then I think we are going
too far. In my view that kind of activity
should be very scrupulously examined and
in many cases should be rescinded.</u>[13]

This statement by Nixon in the midst of the 1968
presidential campaign was widely interpreted as a sign
that: 1) Nixon would not push vigorously for civil
rights as Johnson had; and that 2) "Nixon had developed
a Southern strategy [and] that, as president, [he]
would not cut off funds to segregated school
districts."[14]

Surely, it can be argued that Nixon's statement
in Charlotte was made in the heat of a close presidential contest and was more a reflection of his
desire to maximize votes than an indication of his
genuine feelings about civil rights. In short, Candidate Nixon's concept of the government role in the
civil rights field might not be President Nixon's view
of the government role in this particular sphere.
While the argument above can be made, the facts show
that Candidate Nixon and President Nixon viewed civil
rights matters in the same light. In short, as
president, Nixon "adopted an ambivalent attitude
toward civil rights."[15] Consider, for example, the
comments he made at a press conference in 1969. When
asked what role he would play in the field of civil
rights, Nixon responded:

It seems to me that there are two
extreme groups. There are those who want
instant integration and those who want
segregation forever. I believe we need
to have a middle course between those two
extremes.[16]

Clearly, Nixon believed that as president he should
take the "middle-of-the-road" approach in grappling
with civil rights concerns.

In general, Nixon's assertions and actions in
regard to civil rights reflected his "middle-of-the-
road" philosophy. On some occasions, he indicated
support for civil rights, but, on other occasions, his
statements and actions indicated non-support. For
example, Nixon's efforts to get blacks into predominantly white construction unions indicated support for
civil rights. Under Nixon's Philadelphia Plan,
federal contractors were required to work toward hiring
a certain guota of minority employees on federal
construction projects. In proposing the Philadelphia
Plan, Nixon stated:

It is essential that black Americans,
all Americans, have an equal opportunity
to get into the construction unions. . . .
The interest of the nation requires this,
apart from the matters of simple justice
which are involved.[17]

Nixon backed up his words with action. When a
number of Congressmen in 1969 sought to persuade their
colleagues not to support his (Nixon's) Philadelphia
Plan, Nixon personally lobbied Congressmen to support
his plan. His efforts proved successful when Congress
passed the Philadelphia Plan in 1969.

Nixon's statements and actions regarding the need
to assist minority businesses also exemplified his
support for civil rights. Nixon observed:

We need to remove commercial obstacles
which have too often stood in the way of
minority group members--obstacles such as
the unavailability of credit, insurance
and technical assistance.[18]

Not only did Nixon talk about assisting minority
group businessmen, but he backed up his words with

23

actions. During his tenure as president, federal out-
lays for minority business enterprise programs
increased from $459 million in fiscal year 1971 to
$1,202 million in fiscal year 1975. In general civil
rights groups applauded these actions of the president.

On the other hand, however, certain statements and
actions of the president indicated his non-support for
civil rights. For example, efforts to halt busing was
a sign of non-support for civil rights. Though the
Supreme Court and a number of federal courts held that
busing was and is a legitimate tool for ending segregation in public schools, Nixon opposed busing
contending, "I am against forced busing."[19]

Not only did Nixon oppose busing, he also took
action to halt it. In a speech in March, 1972, Nixon
said that the time had come to stop busing. Specifically, Nixon stated:

> What we need now is not just speaking
> out against busing. We need action to stop
> it. . . .What we need is action now--not
> action 2, 3, or 4 years from now. And
> there is only one way to deal with the
> problem now. That is for Congress to act.
> That is why I am sending a special message
> to Congress tomorrow urging immediate
> consideration and action. . . .I shall
> propose legislation that could bring an
> immediate halt to all new busing orders.[20]

Civil rights groups sharply criticized Nixon's busing
statement emphasizing that the President was failing
to uphold the law of the land.

In addition, Nixon's veto of HUD's efforts to
integrate the suburbs was another sign of his non-
support for civil rights. In 1971, George Romney,
Secretary of Housing and Urban Development, adopted a
housing policy to integrate the suburbs. Under Romney's
policy, suburban communities would either have to
accept the construction of low-income subsidized
housing in their districts or risk the loss of federal
funds. Civil rights groups praised Romney's policy as
an effective means of opening up the suburbs to
minorities. Nixon, however, opposed Romney's plan to
integrate the suburbs, and promised that "the federal
government would not impose federally assisted housing
programs on communities which did not want them."[21]

Civil rights groups attacked Nixon's position a
that it "served to reinforce the racial exclusi
policies and practices of many suburban communi

Overall, the evidence indicates that Nixon nad an
ambivalent attitude toward civil rights. In short, he
was a zigzagger when it came to civil rights. On some
occasions, his assertions and actions exemplified
support for civil rights. On other occasions, however,
his statements and actions indicated non-support for
civil rights.

Basically, Nixon adopted a hostile attitude toward
civil rights enforcement. While he issued a few policy
statements calling for the enforcement of civil rights
laws, for the most part, he openly defied civil rights
laws and took steps to block the vigorous enactment of
these laws. In 1969, for example, Nixon openly defied
Title VI of the Civil Rights Act of 1964 when he
ordered the Department of Health, Education, and
Welfare to fund school districts which has been guilty
of racial discrimination. He justified his order on
the grounds that the withholding of funds for a school
district was not a victory for integration but a
defeat for education. Specifically, Nixon stated:

> I do not consider it a victory for
> integration when the federal government
> cuts off funds for a school and thereby,
> for both black and white students in that
> school, denies them the education they
> should have. This is not a victory for
> anybody. It is a defeat for education.[23]

Civil rights groups, commenting on Nixon's decision
not to terminate the funds of segregated school
systems, charged that the President had blatantly
violated Title VI and had adopted a hostile attitude
toward civil rights enforcement.

Moreover, Nixon's firing of Leon Panetta, HEW's
Director of Civil Rights, was interpreted by many as
further evidence of Nixon's hostile attitude toward
civil rights enforcement. Panetta, a staunch backer
of school desegregation, had pushed vigorously for
integrating the South's segregated school system.
Southern Congressmen were irritated by Panetta efforts
to integrate schools in the South. As a result, they
requested him to slow down the pace of school desegregation in the South. Panetta refused to do so, and
President Nixon dismissed him.

· Civil rights groups contended that Nixon's decision to dismiss Panetta indicated that the President was not concerned about civil rights enforcement. Senator Edward Brooke (R-Mass), commenting on the dismissal of Panetta, charged that "the Nixon Administration had made a cold, calculated political decision to shun the needs of blacks in America in favor of pursuing a Southern strategy to win re-election in 1972."[24]

Nixon's Attitude Toward the Poor

Nixon also had an ambivalent attitude toward the poor. On one hand, he took action which could be construed as helping the poor. On the other hand, however, he took actions which might be interpreted as hurting the poor. Nixon's Family Assistance Plan, though never adopted, was viewed as an instrument to assist the poor. "The Family Assistance Plan would have guaranteed a federal payment of $1,600 a year to a family of four with no income."[25] Families with earnings--the so called working poor--"also would have been eligible for payment, but on a decreasing scale until the earning reached $3,920 a year."[26] Though at first the Family Assistance Plan was lauded by liberals, conservatives, civil rights, and public interest groups as an excellent means for assisting the poor, all of these groups eventually opposed the plan, and Congress never adopted it. The Family Assistance Plan was not adopted because after it went through a series of compromises, "liberals and civil rights groups thought the plan did not go far enough, while conservatives felt the plan went too far."[27]

Nixon's efforts to dismantle the Office of Economic Opportunity was interpreted by civil rights groups and others as reflecting an unsympathetic attitude toward the poor. In 1973, Nixon sought to abolish the Office of Economic Opportunity because "it [the OEO] had failed to assist the poor."[28] Civil rights groups disagreed with Nixon's assessment of the Office of Economic Opportunity. They emphasized that while OEO had not operated as effectively as it could, it had assisted the impoverished. Also, civil rights groups charged that Nixon was seeking to abolish the OEO because "[Nixon] was insensitive to the needs of the poor."[29]

Nixon's decision to place a moratorium on the construction of subsidized housing programs for low and moderate income families was similarly viewed as another sign of the president's unsympathetic attitude toward the poor. In 1973 Nixon halted the construction of subsidized housing programs because "those programs had failed to assist the poor."[30] But once again civil rights groups disagreed. They maintained that the subsidized housing programs had significantly helped low and moderate income families. Furthermore, they contended that "Nixon's housing moratorium had disastrous effects on the availability of housing for low and moderate income persons, many of whom were minorities and women."[31]

Nixon and the Bureaucracy

Basically, "Nixon distrusted the bureaucracy."[32] He distrusted the bureaucracy because: 1) as a conservative he was opposed to big government;[33] 2) he realized that the bureaucracy was controlled by the Democrats and believed they would not support his policy objectives;[34] and 3) he felt that his cabinet officers were spokesmen for their agencies rather than for the White House.

Gerald Ford

Gerald Ford, a former Republican leader of the House of Representatives, became the first non-elected president of the United States in 1974 after Richard Nixon resigned because of his involvement in Watergate. Ford became chief executive of the nation when public trust in the federal government was extremely low, when the nation was confronted with the twin problems of high unemployment and inflation, and when blacks and whites continued to hold opposing viewpoints on such controversial issues as busing and affirmative action. Aware of the problems he had to grapple with, Ford promised to restore public faith in the government, to reduce unemployment and inflation, and to "be the president of all Americans--blacks, whites, browns, and reds."[35]

Civil rights groups were generally skeptical of Ford's pledge to be the president of "all" Americans because as a Congressman he did not support the Civil Rights Act of 1964 until after it became apparent that a majority of Congressmen would endorse the legislation. In addition, these groups were suspicious of Ford because as the Republican leader in the House of Representatives, he had supported Richard Nixon's attempts to retard the enforcement of civil rights laws and had stated categorically that he opposed court-ordered busing, a means used by courts and supported by civil rights groups to eradicate racially segregated school systems.

As president, Ford essentially adopted an ambivalent attitude toward civil rights. On some occasions, his assertions and actions indicated support for civil rights, but on other occasions his statements and actions indicated non-support. For example, upon becoming president, Ford as noted above, pledged to be the president of black, brown, and white Americans, and promised to push for equal opportunity for all. On the one hand, Ford backed up his words with action. He did, for example, in 1974 lobby for Congressional extension of the Voting Rights Act of 1965[*], which barred discriminatory devices used mostly in Southern states to bar blacks from voting.

Civil rights groups praised Ford for supporting the extension of the Voting Rights Act and claimed that his actions indicated support for civil rights interests.

On the other hand, however, certain statements and actions of the president indicated his non-support for civil rights. For example, in spite of the fact that the Supreme Court and a number of other courts had ruled that busing was a legitimate technique for eliminating segregated school systems, Ford vigorously opposed busing, contending that "the courts have gone too far" and that he was opposed to "court-ordered busing."[36]

Ford not only opposed court-ordered busing but he endeavored to limit it. In 1976 Ford proposed the School Desegregation Standards and Assistance Bill, which was designed to restrict court-ordered busing. Civil rights groups charged that Ford's anti-busing statements and his proposal to check busing illustrated

---

[*]When congress enacted the Voting Rights Act in 1965, it stipulated that this law would have to be renewed every five years.

that he was not sensitive to the needs of civil rights interests.

In general, Ford, just as Nixon, adopted a hostile attitude toward civil rights enforcement. Though he made a few statements calling for enforcement of civil rights laws, by and large, Ford took steps which indicated non-support for civil rights enforcement.

Ford's effort to block the desegregation of suburbs was one sign of his hostile attitude toward civil rights enforcement. Though the Eighth Circuit Court of Appeals ruled that the federal district court judges "could order the construction of low-income housing for minorities in Chicago's white suburbs to relieve racial segregation in housing within the city of Chicago,"[37] Ford's Secretary of Housing and Urban Development, Carla Hill, under specific instructions from the White House, sought to convince the Supreme Court to overturn the ruling. However, the Supreme Court rejected the position of the Ford Administration and upheld the Court of Appeals.

Civil rights groups alleged that the Ford Administration efforts to block the desegregation of Chicago's suburbs indicated that "the president and his advisors had adopted an unfriendly attitude toward minorities and civil rights interests."[38]

In addition, Ford adopted a hostile attitude toward the poor. During his tenure as president, Ford consistently called for cutbacks in social welfare programs aimed at assisting the needy. For example, in his proposed budget for fiscal year 1977, Ford cut the federal budget by 1.7 billion dollars and the bulk of his proposed reductions were programs designed to aid the impoverished and elderly. Specifically, in his 1977 budget, Ford sought reduced funding for community health and mental centers, Medicare, food stamps, welfare, child nutrition programs, and federal pensions--all programs designed to help the poor and the aged. Commenting on Ford's proposed cutbacks in his 1977 budget, the Urban Coalition, an alliance of civil rights and public interest groups, alleged that "Ford's proposed cutbacks would be a disaster to blacks and other minorities as well as the nation's poor people."[39]

Furthermore, Ford, just like Nixon, disliked bureaucracy because he felt it was "too big and too costly and because it interfered unnecessarily in the lives of American citizens."[40]

Jimmy Carter

Jimmy Carter, a peanut farmer from Georgia, became President of the United States in 1976 after narrowly defeating the incumbent, Gerald R. Ford. Carter became president at a time when the nation was confronting spiraling inflation and unemployment and when blacks were charging that the federal government was intentionally disregarding their economic, political, and social problems. Civil rights groups, which generally endorsed Carter during the 1976 and 1980 presidential contests, repeatedly emphasized that they were supporting Carter not because he had an excellent civil rights record, but because his record on civil rights suggested that he would be more sympathetic and sensitive to their needs than his opponents, Gerald Ford and Ronald Reagan. Still, despite pledges by Carter that he would take action to ameliorate political and social conditions for black Americans, a number of civil rights groups expressed reservations about Carter's genuine commitment to achieve this goal. These groups had reservations about Carter because he had taken some ambiguous stances on civil rights issues during the course of the 1976 campaign. For example, though he stated during the campaign that the 1964 Civil Rights Act was the best thing that ever happened to the South and stressed that his administration would vigorously enforce all civil rights laws, he also indicated that his administration would do nothing to destroy the ethnic purity of neighborhoods. Carter's ethnic purity remark was widely construed in civil rights circles as indicating that he would take no action to dismantle racially segregated neighborhoods. Not surprisingly, Carter's ethnic purity remark upset major civil rights groups which had fought hard for the passage of the Open Housing Act of 1968. Indeed, civil rights groups were so irritated by Carter's ethnic purity statement that he called a meeting of civil rights leaders and assured them that he favored open housing and would push for vigorous implementation of the Open Housing Act. In spite of Carter's assurances, some civil rights leaders remained skeptical of Carter's support for civil rights policy goals. However, by and large, black leaders and the black populace apparently overlooked Carter's ethnic purity

remark and gave him over 90% of their vote in the
and 1980 presidential elections.

As president, Carter too adopted an ambivalent
attitude on civil rights. Some of his statements and
actions had been construed as indicating support for
civil rights but others had been interpreted as
suggesting non-support. Carter's endorsement of
affirmative action was viewed as an indication of
support for civil rights. At a presidential press
conference in 1977, Carter underscored the fact that
he supported efforts to compensate minorities for past
acts of discrimination, when he stated:

> I think it is appropriate for both private
> employers, the public governments, and
> also institutions of education, health,
> and so forth, to try to compensate
> minorities as well as possible for past
> discrimination and also take into
> consideration the fact that many tests
> that are used to screen applicants quite
> often are inadvertently biased against
> those whose environment and whose training
> might be different from white majority
> representatives of our society.[41]

Carter backed up his words with action. For example,
in the Bakke case where the legality of a university's
special admissions program for minorities was being
challenged in the Supreme Court, the Carter Administration filed an amicus brief with the Court defending the
constitutionality and necessity of race conscious
measures to undo effects of discrimination.* In
general, civil rights groups applauded the pro-affirmative action stance adopted by the Carter Administration
in Bakke and contended that by taking such a stance the
Administration had displayed its commitment to equal
opportunity.

---

*The Carter Administration also filed amicus
briefs defending the constitutionality of affirmative
action measures in two other important Supreme Court
cases--United Steelworkers of America v Weber and
Fullilove v Klutznick.

·However, on the other hand, Carter's ambivalent stance on anti-busing amendments was viewed as an indication of non-support for civil rights. To be sure, in December 1980 Carter vetoed a congressional measure that would have prohibited the Department of Justice from initiating litigation to require busing for school integration since he felt this measure to be "an unprecedented prohibition on the ability of the president and attorney general to enforce constitutional rights."[42] Nonetheless, in 1977 and 1978, President Carter remained silent when Congress enacted busing bills which prohibited HEW from using busing, pairing or clustering as tools for dismantling segregated school systems. In effect, these anti-busing amendments banned HEW from ordering segregated schools to bus school children in order that they (the school districts) could comply with Title VI. Civil rights groups, which generally opposed the busing amendments, charged that Carter's failure to take a position on the amendments strongly suggested non-support of civil rights interests.

Carter also adopted a somewhat ambivalent attitude toward civil rights enforcement. On some occasions, his statements and actions indicated support for civil rights enforcement, but on other occasions, his assertions and actions indicated non-support. For example, Carter's strong endorsement of Title VI, together with the Justice Department's effort to coordinate the federal government's Title VI operations, indicated support for civil rights enforcement. As the chief executive of the country, Carter directed federal officials not to tolerate discrimination in any of their programs. In his strongly worded memorandum to the Heads of Executive Departments and Agencies on Title VI, Carter stated:

> The government of all the people should
> not support programs which discriminate
> on the grounds of race, color, or national
> origin. There are no exceptions to this
> rule; no matter how urgent the goals,
> they do not excuse violating any of our
> laws--including the laws against
> discrimination.[43]

Responding to the president's strong statement on Title VI, the Justice Department brought together <u>for the first time</u> "the civil rights staff of all major agencies to discuss the development of stronger and more uniform enforcement standards throughout the government."[44] Civil rights groups commended the president for his Title VI memorandum and also praised the Justice Department efforts to implement Title VI.

On the other hand, "Carter decisions to block HEW's efforts to cut-off the North Carolina University System federal funds was an indication of non-support for civil rights enforcement."[45] Though HEW officials as far back as 1970 had determined that the North Carolina University System was blatantly disregarding the anti-discriminatory provisions of Title VI, and though these officials have endeavored unsuccessfully for nine years to persuade university officials to take steps to comply with Title VI, when they attempted to cut-off funds to the university system, President Carter prevented them from doing so. Civil rights groups charged that "the fact that President Carter had prevented HEW officials from enforcing Title VI in North Carolina signified the president's non-support for civil rights enforcement."[46]

Carter essentially adopted an ambivalent attitude toward the poor. On some occasions, Carter exhibited a sympathetic attitude toward the impoverished, but, on the other occasions, he manifested an unsympathetic attitude. Carter's 1981 budget, which called for increased funding for the construction of low-income housing and for over two billion dollars for job training programs for disadvantaged minority youth, was viewed as a manifestation of his sympathetic attitude toward the poor.[47] Many low-income organizations praised Carter's 1978 and 1979 budgets in that they reflected the president's concern for poor people.

On the other hand, Carter's "lean and austere" 1980 and 1981 budgets which called for reduced funding for programs that assist the needy were perceived as signals of the president's unsympathetic attitude toward the poor. In his budgets, Carter proposed that Congress reduce funding for 1) the low income subsidized housing program; 2) the Comprehensive Employment and Training Program (which grants jobs to the hard-core unemployed); and 3) the Social Security Program (which aids the aged and the impoverished). Carter's justification for requesting cutbacks in these programs was that they were "too costly and inflationary."[48] Civil rights, labor, and public interest groups and their allies in Congress alleged that "Carter's proposed cutbacks in social welfare programs

33

were unfair to the poor, the black, the young . . . the aged and the disadvantaged."[49]

In addition, Carter adopted an ambivalent attitude toward the bureaucracy. On some occasions, his statements and actions indicated a friendly attitude toward the bureaucracy, but, on other occasions, his assertions and actions suggest an unfriendly attitude. For example, the fact that Carter proposed and supported the establishment of the Department of Energy and the Department of Education suggested that he had a friendly attitude toward the bureaucracy. But on the other hand, certain statements and actions by Carter indicate an unfriendly attitude toward the bureaucracy. The fact that Carter called for less federal spending (or a balanced budget), and proposed cutting back on and in some cases terminating federal programs suggests that he had an unfriendly attitude toward the bureaucracy.

In general, however, two points concerning Carter's civil rights record need to be stressed here. First, he appointed more blacks to federal posts (particularly the judiciary) than any other president; and second, after ignoring civil rights groups' pleas that he heartily endorse a congressional measure to strengthen the Open Housing Act of 1968, Carter supported this measure in 1980, calling it the most important piece of civil rights legislation in years.

Ronald Reagan

Ronald Reagan was sworn in as president of the United States in January 1981 after decisively defeating former President Carter in the 1980 election. Reagan assumed the presidency at a time when the American people were coping with double-digit inflation and high unemployment, when public opinion polls showed that "white Americans generally felt that the federal government was doing too much for blacks,"[50] and when there was "near hysteria in the black community that a Reagan presidency would mean a retreat from efforts toward progress for blacks."[51] Aware of the problems that beset him, Reagan pledged to take steps to improve the economy, promised "to get the federal government off the American people's backs,"[52] and declared that he was "heart and soul in favor of things done in the name of civil rights and desegregation."[53]

34

Most civil rights groups genuinely doubt
statement about being "heart and soul" in fav
civil rights since he had previously opposed
civil rights measures. These groups noted th
opposed the Civil Rights Act of 1964.[54] More...,
during the 1980 campaign, Reagan not only supported a
constitutional amendment to ban busing for desegregation purposes; but he also made clear his opposition
to racial quotas in education and employment, quotas
designed to compensate minorities and women for past
and current discrimination.

In addition, civil rights groups were uneasy
about Reagan's commitment to civil rights because of
the strong endorsement he received from the white
supremacist Ku Klux Klan organization in the 1980
election. Though Reagan repudiated the Klan's
endorsement and some civil rights leaders applauded
his actions, most civil rights groups still viewed the
Klan endorsement as an omen that Reagan would be no
vigorous supporter of civil rights causes.

As president, Reagan, just as his predecessors
Carter, Ford and Nixon, has also adopted an ambivalent
attitude on civil rights. Some of his assertions and
actions have been interpreted as indicating support
for civil rights, but others have been construed as
suggesting non-support. For example, President Reagan
has declared that his administration will "maintain
our national commitment to battle against discrimination."[55] Reagan apparently has backed up his word
with action. Though he initially expressed support
for amending the Voting Rights Action of 1965* (a
measure designed to ban discriminatory practices

---

*Key provisions of the Voting Rights Act will
lapse in 1982 unless there is some favorable action by
Congress and the Reagan Administration. Most critical
among these provisions is a requirement that covers
nine states--Alabama, Alaska, Arizona, Georgia,
Louisiana, Mississippi, South Carolina, Texas and
Virginia--and several other states must gain the
approval from the Justice Department for all election
law and districting changes. President Reagan was
contemplating supporting a measure extending these
provisions to all fifty states.

eventing blacks and Hispanics from exercising their
franchise), Reagan subsequently came out in favor of
this law without amendment,[56] contending that altering
this statute would significantly impair its effectiveness.

Civil rights groups unanimously agreed with
President Reagan's stance on the Voting Rights Act.
In fact, most civil rights organizations, which had
always maintained that amending this act would render
it ineffective, viewed the president's stance as being
supportive of civil rights interests. However,
despite all of this, many civil rights organizations
remain skeptical not only about President Reagan's
position on the Voting Rights Act, but his position on
civil rights in general.

Indeed, Reagan's opposition to busing for school
desegregation purposes has been viewed as an indication
of non-support for civil rights. Despite the fact that
federal courts have ruled that busing is the most
effective remedy for eliminating racially segregated
schools, President Reagan and United States Attorney
General Smith have made it abundantly clear that they
oppose busing because it has been "a failure"[57] and
has been "overused."[58] Consequently, both the president and his attorney general have moved to restrict
the use of busing by supporting congressional legislation that would prohibit the Department of Justice
from pursuing cases that could lead to busing for
desegregation and by emphasizing voluntary integration
plans (e.g. Chicago, Houston, Seattle and St. Louis)
as the most effective strategy for ending racially
segregated schools. Civil rights groups have sharply
criticized both President Reagan and Attorney General
Smith for their stance on busing and have charged
that both men are skillfully seeking to turn back the
clock of civil rights progress.

In addition, Reagan's opposition to affirmative
action plans that purport to compensate minorities for
past discrimination has also been viewed by civil
rights groups as a sign of non-support for civil
rights. Both President Reagan and Attorney General
Smith have made public pronouncements indicating that
they oppose affirmative action plans, especially those
involving quotas because such plans discriminate
against non-minorities and have been overused.
Indeed, in his first press conference at the White
House in January 1981, Reagan suggested that his

36

administration would not strongly support affirmative action. Responding to a query as to whether there will be a retreat in the federal government's advocacy of affirmative action programs, Reagan said:

> No. There will be no retreat . . . I think we have made great progress in the civil rights field. I think there are some things, however, that have been but may not be as useful as they once were, or that may even be distorted in the practice, such as affirmative action programs becoming racial quotas systems. I'm old enough to remember when quotas existed for the purpose of discrimination. And I don't want to see that happen again.[59]

Similarly, in a major speech in May 1981, Attorney General Smith made it quite clear that the Reagan Administration would be no ardent advocate of affirmative action in the employment area. "We have come perilously close in recent years to fostering discrimination by establishing racial quotas in various areas,"[60] said Smith, and the "Reagan Administration will not vigorously pursue racial quotas in employment discrimination cases."[61]

Civil rights spokesmen have charged that the Reagan Administration policy on affirmative action (particularly as applied to "goals" and "timetables") signals a retreat in the federal government's advocacy of equal opportunity and "sends a clear message to the enemies of equal opportunities for women and minorities that they can feel free to evade [anti-discriminatory] laws."[62]

Moreover, the "cool reception" President Reagan received when he addressed the 1981 annual convention of the National Association for the Advancement of Colored People (NAACP) was viewed as another sign of how blacks and others view the president's attitude toward civil rights. Nonetheless, in his speech to the NAACP convention, Reagan strongly affirmed that his budget cuts in social welfare programs will not hurt blacks. He also highlighted his opposition to busing by asserting that "a black child need not be seated next to a white child in order to learn."[63] But these fundamental policy disagreements between the Reagan Administration and the NAACP did not come as a surprise to anyone. They were anticipated. Indeed,

NAACP Chairperson Margaret Bush Wilson, in introducing
the president to the convention, craftily observed to
the cheering delight of the delegates that "the NAACP
does not necessarily subscribe to the views that are
about to be expressed."[64] Though not surprised by
President Reagan's defense of his economic program or
his general anti-busing statements, NAACP members
expressed disappointment that the president seemed bent
on endorsing economic and civil rights policies that
will adversely affect poor people and civil rights
interests.

Overall, Reagan has essentially adopted a hostile
attitude toward civil rights enforcement. While
asserting that he is "heart and soul in favor of the
things done in the name of civil rights,"[65] for the
most part, Reagan has projected an unfriendly attitude
toward civil rights enforcement. The president's
proposal to relax anti-discrimination rules for federal
contractors has been viewed by civil rights groups as
clear evidence of his anti-civil rights posture. To
be sure, in August 1981, the Reagan Administration
proposed that three-fourths of the companies doing
business with the federal government would no longer
be required to submit affirmative action goals or
plans, detailing their efforts to recruit minorities
and women and outlining the racial and sexual composition of their staffs. The administration contended
that this particular proposal would "cut down on the
burdensome affirmative action paperwork for employers
and would get the federal government off their
backs."[66]

Civil rights, labor, and women groups, have
sharply criticized the Reagan Administration's
affirmative action recommendation. Eleanor Smeal,
President of the National Organization for Women
charged that the "Reagan Administration's affirmative
action proposal would not only cut back on paperwork
but would also cut back on justice for minorities and
women."[67] Similarly, William Pollard, Director of
the Department of Civil Rights of the AFL-CIO,
suggested that the administration's decision indicates
that President Reagan in leading the retreat against
discrimination. Specifically, Pollard pointed out
that

> Affirmative Action guidelines are designed
> to eliminate discrimination against minor-
> ities and women. No president until now

has tried to weaken them. President Reagan
is saying discrimination is over, just like
that. He is wrong. The government ought
to lead the way against discrimination, not
the retreat.[68]

In addition, Reagan's decision to trim the budgets
of major civil rights agencies has also been viewed
as further manifestation of his unfriendly attitude
toward civil rights. Under Reagan's fiscal year 1982
economic package, nearly twenty percent of the
budgets* will be cut for the Equal Employment Opportunity Commission (which enforces civil rights laws
in the employment area), the Department of Labor's
Office of Federal Contract Compliance (which implements anti-discrimination laws in organizations
working under federal contracts), and the Department
of Health and Human Services' Office for Civil Rights
(which enforces non-discriminatory laws in schools,
colleges, and other institutions that receive federal
funds). Spokesmen for these agencies have argued
that the president's budget cuts will mean that their
agencies "will be scaling back the level of services
for people seeking protection from discrimination."[69]
And civil rights and women organizations contend that
cutting the budgets of civil rights enforcement
agencies will severely impede the federal government's
efforts to ensure quality and justice for all American
citizens.

Reagan's Attitude Toward the Poor

The Reagan Administration also has projected an
unsympathetic attitude toward the poor. In his fiscal
1982 budget,* Reagan proposed--and the Congress voted--
massive reductions in programs designed to assist the

---

*The Reagan Administration has slated even deeper
cuts in these civil rights agencies' budgets for fiscal
year 1983. See, "Budget Cuts Constrain Major Civil
Rights Agencies" Washington Post March 12, 1981, p. 7A.

*David Stockman, President Reagan's Director of
the Office of Management and Budget asserted in August
1981 that the Reagan Administration is determined to
make further cuts in social welfare programs for
fiscal year 1983.

poor. These programs include welfare, food stamps, child nutrition, low-income subsidized housing, public service jobs and unemployment compensation. Reagan claimed that such cuts were necessary to help make the economy flourish and would not hurt the "truly needed."[70] The Congressional Budget Office, which has thoroughly examined how the president's budget cuts will affect the poor, has come up with evidence that disputes Reagan's claim. Indeed, the Congressional Budget Office has estimated that "up to 25 million people, most of them poor, would lose benefits because of projected cuts in just four social welfare programs--welfare, food stamps, public service jobs, and housing subsidy programs."[71]

Reagan and the Bureaucracy

Reagan, just like Ford and Nixon, has projected a hostile attitude toward the bureaucracy. In his inaugural address, Reagan pledged "to curb the size and influence of the federal establishment."[72] Keeping his promise, Reagan has moved to abolish the Departments of Education and Energy by instructing his cabinet secretaries who direct these agencies to dismantle them.

Furthermore, Reagan's negative posture toward "big government" was reflected in his 1982 fiscal budget. The Reagan budget proposed--and the Congress approved--major spending cuts in all federal agencies, except the Department of Defense.* Also, in his efforts to reduce the influence of the federal government, the President has proposed to eliminate federal regulations concerning anti-discrimination protections for blacks, women, and the handicap; food labeling; occupational and health standards; and noise and pollution levels. Reagan's position is that these regulations should be discarded because they are "burdensome, costly and unnecessary."[73]

---

*As of September 1981, the Reagan Administration was planning to cut the budget of all federal agencies including defense for fiscal year 1983.

Presidents, Civil Rights
and Title VI: A Summary View

This chapter has highlighted the fact that the president's assertions and actions may affect civil rights enforcement. Indeed, in the discussion above, it was stressed that the president's public pronouncement and his powers to appoint and remove agency heads and his control over civil rights agencies' budgets afford him various opportunities to influence how civil rights laws will be enforced. More specifically, our discussion above has shown that no president (including Johnson, Nixon, Ford, Carter and Reagan) has expressed unequivocal support for Title VI enforcement. Certain actions of each president have been perceived as indicating non-support for Title VI. However, the evidence does show that some presidents generally have been more supportive than others in endorsing efforts to implement this law. For example, President Johnson, for the most part, strongly supported the vigorous implementation of Title VI, while President Carter was somewhat supportive of efforts to enforce this particular statute. However, Presidents Nixon, Ford, and Reagan exhibited little or no support for efforts to aggressively implement Title VI. Let us now examine how other institutional factors and forces may shape the political-social milieu in which Title VI enforcement takes place.

FOOTNOTES

[1] U. S., President, Public Papers of The Presidents: Lyndon B. Johnson, 1965, Volume II (Washington: Government Printing Office, 1966), p. 742.

[2] U. S., President, Public Papers of The Presidents: Lyndon B. Johnson, 1963-1964, Volume I (Washington: Government Printing Office, 1964), p. 9.

[3] Civil Rights Act (1964), 42 U. S. C. 2000d-4 (1970).

[4] Voting Rights Act of 1965 (S1564-PL89-110).

[5] Open Housing Act of 1968 (HR2516-PL90-284).

[6] Civil Rights Progress Report, 1979, Congressional Quarterly (Washington: Congressional Quarterly Inc., 1971), p. 14.

[7] Public Papers of the Presidents: Lyndon B. Johnson, 1963-1964, Volume II, op. cit., p. 114.

[8] Ibid.

[9] Ibid.

[10] Stephen Hess, Organizing the Presidency (Washington: Brookings Institute, 1973), p. 13.

[11] Richard Dawson, Public Opinion and Contemporary Disarray (New York: Harper and Row Publishers, 1973), p. 42.

[12] New York Times, December 8, 1969, p. 15, col. 3A.

[13] Rowland Evans and Robert Novak, Nixon in the White House: The Frustration of Power (New York: Random House, 1971), pp. 140-141.

[14] Ibid.

[15] Statement by Brad Patterson, Special Assistant to President Richard Nixon, in a personal interview, Washington, D. C.: October 19, 1978.

[16]Evans and Novak, op. cit., p. 133.

[17]U. S., President, Public Papers of The Presidents: Richard Nixon, 1969 (Washington: Government Printing Office, 1971), p. 197.

[18]Ibid.

[19]U. S., President, Public Papers of The Presidents: Richard Nixon, 1972 (Washington: Government Printing Office, 1974), p. 430.

[20]Ibid.

[21]U. S., President, Public Papers of The Presidents: Richard Nixon, 1971 (Washington: Government Printing Office, 1973, pp. 721-735.

[22]U. S. Commission on Civil Rights, The Federal Civil Rights Enforcement Effort--1974, Volume VII: To Preserve, Protect and Defend the Constitution (Washington: Government Printing Office, June 1977), p. 29.

[23]U. S., President, Public Papers of The Presidents: Richard Nixon, 1969 (Washington: Government Printing Office, 1971), p. 750.

[24]Congressional Quarterly, Civil Rights Progress Report, 1970, op. cit., p. 20.

[25]Public Papers of The Presidents: Richard Nixon, 1969, op. cit., p. 351.

[26]Ibid.

[27]Evans and Novak, op. cit., p. 162.

[28]Congressional Quarterly, March 10, 1973, p. 635.

[29]Ibid., p. 636.

[30]Ibid., p. 637.

[31]The Federal Civil Rights Enforcement Effort--1974, Volume VII: To Preserve, Protect and Defend the Constitution, op. cit., p. 29.

[32]Richard P. Nathan, The Plot That Failed: Nixon and the Administrative Presidency (New York: John Wiley and Sons, 1975), pp. 36-37.

[33]Ibid., p. 38.

[34]Ibid., p. 40.

[35]U. S., President, Public Papers of the Presidents: Gerald R. Ford, 1974 (Washington: Government Printing Office, 1976), p. 13.

[36]The Federal Civil Rights Enforcement Effort-- 1974, Volume VII: To Preserve, Protect and Defend the the Constitution, op. cit., pp. 68-69.

[37]New York Times, April 9, 1975, p. 87, Col 1A.

[38]Ibid.

[39]Ibid., Feb. 4, 1975, p. 21. col. 5A.

[40]Congressional Quarterly, Gerald Ford, 1974, p. 69.

[41]U. S., President, Weekly Compilation of Presidential Documents, News Conference Volume XIII, No. 31 (July 28, 1977), p. 1126.

[42]"Anti-Busing Rider Draws Veto of Justice Bill," Congressional Quarterly Almanac XXXVI, 1980, p. 210.

[43]U. S., Presidents, Public Papers of The President: Jimmy Carter, 1977 (Washington: Government Printing Office, 1978), p. 1293.

[44]Statement by Glendora Sloane, Chairperson for the Leadership Conference on Civil Rights, in a personal interview, Washington, D. C.: January 10, 1978.

[45]Statement by Joseph Rauh, NAACP Attorney and Chairman of Americans for Democratic Action, in a personal interview, Washington, D. C.: April 16, 1978.

[46]Ibid.

[47]Note that as of March 1980, Carter had reduced funding for job training programs and civil rights organizations had severely criticized him for doing so.

44

[48] Den Kemp, "The 1981 Budget," *Time Magazine*, March 20, 1980, p. 37.

[49] William C. Freund, "The Politics of Austerity," *Time Magazine*, January 29, 1979, p. 21.

[50] "Race Issue: Cutting Edge in 80 Elections," *New York Times*, October 10, 1980, Section D, p. 15.

[51] "NAACP Leaders Express Concerns About Reagan," *New York Times*, November 23, 1980, p. 27.

[52] "President Reagan's Inaugural Address," *Congressional Quarterly*, January 24, 1981, p. 187.

[53] "Reagan Supports Measure to Curb Suits on Busing," *New York Times*, November 19, 1980, pp. 1 and 30.

[54] Charles Moran *Current Biography 1967/1968* (New York: H. W. Wilson Co., 1967), p. 340.

[55] "All the People," *National Journal*, July 11, 1981, p. 1261.

[56] "Reagan Favors Voting Rights Act Extension," *Washington Post*, August 6, 1981, p. 1.

[57] "U. S. Changes School, Job Bias Policy," *Washington Post*, May 23, 1981, p. 1A.

[58] Ibid.

[59] "President Reagan's Press Conference Text," *Congressional Quarterly*, January 31, 1981, p. 239.

[60] "U. S. Changes School, Job Bias Policy," op. cit.

[61] Ibid.

[62] "Proposal to Ease Job Bias Rules," *Washington Post*, August 26, 1981, p. 1A.

[63] "All the People," *National Journal*, op. cit.

[64] Ibid.

[65] "Reagan Supports Measure to Curb Suits on Busing," *New York Times*, op. cit.

[66]"U. S. Easing Rules on Discrimination by its Contractors," New York Times, August 25, 1981, p. 1.

[67]CBS Evening News, August 26, 1981.

[68]"U. S. Easing Rules on Discrimination by its Contractors," New York Times, op. cit.

[69]"Budget Cuts Constrain Major Civil Rights Agencies," Washington Post, March 12, 1981, p. 7A.

[70]"Safety Net Not Much Help, Critics Charge: What Reagan's Budget Cuts Would Do To The Poor," Congressional Quarterly, April 18, 1981, pp. 665-666.

[71]Ibid.

[72]"President Reagan's Inaugural Address," op. cit.

[73]Ibid.

CHAPTER III

FURTHER REFLECTIONS ON THE
POLITICAL-SOCIAL CONTEXT: CONGRESS,
THE COURTS, INTEREST GROUPS,
BUREAUCRATIC OFFICIALS, PUBLIC
OPINION, AND TITLE VI ENFORCEMENT

Our analysis of Title VI in Chapter II indicated that presidential activity had affected the political-social environment in which this law is implemented. This chapter considers how that environment may be shaped by Congress, the courts, interest groups, bureaucratic officials, and public opinion.

Congress and Title VI Enforcement

This particular section considers the impact of congressional activity on Title VI enforcement. Specifically, this section generally analyzes how the powers of Congress to appropriate, legislate, and investigate, afford Congress opportunities to affect the enforcement of Title VI.

1. The Power to Appropriate

The appropriation power gives Congress the chance to exercise considerable influence over an agency's budget. Agencies, including those with Title VI responsibilities, appear before the House and Senate Appropriation Committees annually in efforts to convince legislators to approve their budget requests. This congressional decision can significantly affect an agency's performance. If Congress generally approves their requests, "agencies are in a position to operate just about as they had planned."[1] By contrast, should Congress significantly reduce or deny their budget requests, agencies' operations can be severely hampered. How the appropriation process has affected HUD's, HEW's, and Labor's Title VI enforcement operations is discussed in subsequent chapters dealing with each of these agencies.

2. The Power to Legislate

Legislation is another means by which Congress may exercise influence over the implementation of Title VI. Under its power to enact legislation,

Congress can pass measures to facilitate or inhibit
any agency including a Title VI one from meeting its
responsibilities. This matter is also addressed in
this study. At any rate, it seems appropriate here
to note that Congress's support for civil rights has
fluctuated over the years, and this becomes quite
manifest when examining legislation Congress enacted
between 1964 and 1981. In 1964 Congress passed a very
comprehensive Civil Rights Act, and in 1965 Congress
enacted the Voting Rights Act. Congress also moved
to end discrimination in the field of housing when it
enacted the Open Housing Act of 1968. Thus, during
the 1960's Congress exhibited a strong civil rights
posture.

However, in the 1970's Congress's attitude toward
civil rights, as expressed through its enactment of
legislation, has been fairly mixed. In short, in some
instances, Congress has expressed support for civil
rights, but on other occasions it has expressed non-
support. Between 1970 and 1973, Congress exhibited
support for civil rights by enacting various anti-
discriminatory statutes aimed at banning discrimination
based on sex, physical or mental handicap, and race.
In 1972, for example, Congress passed Title IX of the
Education Amendments, which required an end to sex
discrimination in schools receiving federal aid. In
1973, Congress enacted Section 504 of the Rehabilitation Act, which forbade discrimination against people
with mental or physical handicaps in programs receiving
federal aid. Also in 1973 Congress passed the Comprehensive Employment and Training Act, which prohibited
discrimination based on race, color, national origin,
sex, or mental or physical handicap in all employment
training programs receiving federal funds.

Finally, in 1975, Congress enacted the Aged
Discrimination Act which proscribes discrimination
against the elderly in federally assisted programs.

Despite its support for civil rights between
1970-1973, congressional attitude toward civil rights
seemed to change during the time period 1974-1981.
Indeed, during this period Congress adopted a number
of measures prohibiting busing, a means used by
federal courts and supported by civil rights groups
to dismantle segregated school systems. To be sure,
Congress did exhibit support for civil rights in
1979 when it voted down a constitutional amendment
to halt court-ordered busing. But, during the time

48

period 1974-1981, Congress, by and large, took action to halt racial change by adopting a number of anti-busing laws which have made it difficult to integrate racially segregated educational institutions. In 1974 Congress adopted the Esch Amendment, which "prohibited any Federal agency from ordering the implementation of a desegregation plan requiring the transportation of students beyond schools closest or next closest to their homes that provide the appropriate grade level and type of education for those students."[2] In 1975 and 1976 Congress adopted the Byrd Amendment which went beyond the Esch Amendment by forbidding "the use of appropriated funds, directly or indirectly, to require the transportation of any student to a school other than that one which is nearest the students' homes and offers the courses of study pursued by the student."[3] And in 1977, 1978, and 1979 Congress adopted the Eagleton-Biden Amendment, which "forbids HEW to require, directly or indirectly, the transportation of any students to any paired or clustered schools.[4]

Essentially, these anti-busing amendments restricted the desegregation techniques that HEW could utilize in its effort to dismantle racially segregated school systems. Specifically, the anti-busing amendments banned HEW from ordering the busing of school children past their neighborhood schools and banned it from transporting students to paired or clustered schools for desegregation purpose. The Civil Rights Commission charged that "the anti-busing amendments removed HEW's authority to terminate funds to school districts not in compliance with Title VI where compliance would have required transportation beyond the nearest schools."[5] Because HEW could not act, the Commission observed, these cases had to be referred to the Department of Justice for litigation. However, in 1980 and 1981, Congress moved to stop the Department of Justice from pursuing cases that could lead to court-ordered busing. For example, in 1980, Congress enacted a law forbidding the Department of Justice from bringing lawsuits that could lead to school busing for desegregation. This statute, however, was vetoed by then President Carter. In any case, the House of Representatives for July 1981 re-enacted the same anti-busing measure that Carter had vetoed; and the Senate, which is currently (October 1981) considering this anti-desegregation measure, is expected once again to approve it.

· Senator Lowell Weicker, a liberal Republican from Connecticut and an opponent of the measure to prevent the Department of Justice from bringing lawsuits leading to court-ordered busing, warned his colleagues that is they adopt this measure they would "send a message to the entire country that we no longer value the concept of equality in education, that civil rights is an issue of the past."6

Congress's negative posture toward civil rights was not only reflected in anti-busing measures, but it was also mirrored in legislation concerning affirmative action, open housing, and voting rights. Let us first consider congressional actions regarding affirmative action. Certainly, Congress displayed support for civil rights in 1977 when it enacted the minority business enterprise (MBE) provision of the Public Works Employment Act which required the Department of Commerce to set aside 10% of all federal contracts for minorities--blacks, Spanish-speaking, Orientals, Indians, Eskimos, and Aleuts. Nevertheless, the fact remains that Congress, for the most part, has attacked affirmative action efforts designed to compensate minorities for past discrimination. For example, in 1977, 1978, 1979, 1980, and 1981, the House of Representatives passed the Walker Amendment which bars the use of numerical requirements to promote hiring of minorities; however, during the period 1977 to 1980, the Senate refused to endorse this amendment.

Congress's refusal in 1980 to strengthen HUD's ability to implement the Open Housing Act of 1968 was also perceived as a signal of its unfriendly attitude toward civil rights. Under the Open Housing Act (which bans discrimination on the basis of race, color, religion and sex) HUD can uncover racially discriminatory practices in housing, but lacks the clout to penalize parties who engage in these practices. Indeed, where HUD finds violations of the Open Housing Act, it only can conciliate or mediate with the parties violating this statute. If conciliation or mediation fails, HUD can then refer the cases to the Department of Justice which often will file suits against the parties practicing discrimination.

Aware of HUD's inability to aggressively implement the Open Housing Act, the House of Representatives, under pressure from civil rights groups, passed a fair housing bill giving HUD the direct authority to pass sentence upon individuals or groups who disobey this particular act. However, a Senate filibuster led by conservative Senators Orrin Hatch of Utah and Strom Thurmond of South Carolina killed this fair housing measure.

The debate in the 97th Congress concerning the extension of the Voting Rights Act of 1965 (which will expire in 1982) may also be viewed as a manifestation of Congress's unfriendly attitude toward civil rights. As pointed out earlier, the landmark Voting Rights Act "prohibited the use of literacy test or similar devices that had been used to disqualify black voters, gave the Justice Department the power to send federal examiners into areas with low voting participation by blacks and established criminal penalties for interference with voting rights."[7] The focal point of the controversy over extension of the Voting Rights Act concerns the pre-clearance section of this statute. This section requires six southern states (Alabama, Georgia, Louisiana, Mississippi, South Carolina and Virginia), Alaska and parts of four other states to get Justice Department approval before changing any election laws. Critics--primarily conservative members of Congress from the South and West--charge that the pre-clearance provision is unnecessary because southern states' voting procedures no longer discriminate against blacks, and is unfair because it applies only to the South, not the nation as a whole.

Conversely, supporters--mainly the congressional Black Caucus, congress persons from the Northeast and leaders of civil rights organizations--have taken issue with those who oppose the extension of the pre-clearance provision. They maintain that extending the pre-clearance provision of the Voting Rights Act is necessary because subtle and sophisticated forms of discrimination persist. Specifically, they contend that "while obvious barriers to voting, such as poll taxes, may be gone, more subtle and sophisticated methods of discrimination have surfaced, such as gerrymandering election districts, holding at-large elections, and annexation of predominantly white areas to dilute minority voting strength."[8]

As for the opposition's contention that the pre-clearance provision should apply nationwide, not only to the South, those who support the Voting Rights Act without amendment argue that the federal government should continue to apply this provision primarily to the South because voting discrimination practices

continue predominantly in that region. To apply the
provision nationwide, they charge, would be a waste of
limited resources and would cripple the Justice Department's efforts to enforce the Voting Rights Act.

Whether or not Congress extends the Voting Rights
Act without amendment is difficult to predict. But
what is certain is that those who seek to extend the
law without amendment, must somehow overcome opposition
from powerful members of Congress. Indeed, both Strom
Thurmond of South Carolina and Orrin Hatch of Utah have
made it clear they will fight the re-enactment of the
Voting Rights Act every step of the way, at least as
the law is presently structured.

3. The Power to Investigate

Congress's power to conduct investigations or
hold oversight hearings also provides it with the
opportunity to shape and influence the implementation
of Title VI. After a law is passed, Congress may
periodically conduct investigations or hold oversight
hearings to assess how an agency has undertaken to
implement that law. Such investigations as hearings
are not only conducted to determine how an agency has
sought to enforce a particular statute, but they are
also used by members of Congress either to induce an
agency to vigorously enforce a law or to discourage
that agency from forcefully implementing it. With
respect to Title VI, our primary concern will be
1) has Congress held any hearings regarding the
Title VI agencies under study--HUD, HEW, and Labor--
and 2) if it has, have those investigations or
hearings been employed by Congress to encourage or
discourage these agencies from vigorously meeting
their Title VI responsibilities? These are questions
that are addressed later in this study.

In general, the evidence indicates that over the
years legislative support for civil rights has fluctuated. In the 1960's Congress expressed its support
for civil rights through the enactment of various
anti-discriminatory measures including the 1964 Civil
Rights Act, the 1965 Voting Rights Act, and the 1968
Open Housing Act. In the 1970's Congress continued to
pass legislation which banned discriminatory practices
regarding sex, the aged, the handicap. At the same
time, however, Congress also passed a number of
anti-busing amendments that adversely affected HEW's
Title VI operations. Finally, in the 1980's, Congress,

just as other federal institutions, seems to be retreating in the civil rights field. This is evidenced by several indicators including the failure in 1980 to strengthen the enforcement of the Fair Housing Act, and the surfacing of influential congressional opposition with respect to extending the Voting Rights Act of 1965. Let us now consider how judicial activity may affect the enforcement of Title VI.

The Impact of Judicial Activity on Title VI Enforcement

Federal courts may also influence the implementation of Title VI. Under Title VI, federal courts have been granted the authority to review the actions of agencies to determine whether their actions have been in conformity with Title VI. Put another way, federal courts have the power to determine the legality of guidelines, procedures, and regulations of agencies subject to Title VI. In making such determinations, federal courts are in the position of either helping or hindering Title VI agencies' enforcement programs. For example, if federal courts uphold forceful actions taken by agencies to implement Title VI, it might be said that they are encouraging such agencies to vigorously enforce this statute. By contrast, if federal courts declare illegal those aggressive actions taken by agencies to implement Title VI, it might be said that they are discouraging these agencies from forcefully implementing Title VI. How and in what manner particular court decisions have affected particular Title VI operations of the various agencies is reserved for later discussion. In this section, we discuss several major decisions that generally impact on how Title VI agencies such as HUD, HEW, and Labor meet their Title VI responsibilities. These cases are Washington v Davis,[9] The Board of Regents of the California University System v Bakke,[10] United Steelworkers of America v Weber,[11] and Fullilove v Klutznick.[12] In the case of Washington v Davis, Davis et al., a group of blacks who sought unsuccessfully to become members of the District of Columbia Police Department, brought suit against the District of Columbia government officials, charging that "the police department recruitment procedures, including a written personnel test, were racially discriminatory and thus violated the Due Process Clause of the Fifth Amendment."[13] They specified that four times as many blacks as whites failed the test administered by the

District of Columbia government and that such a
disproportionate impact amounted to a constitutional
violation. A federal district court ruled against the
plaintiffs. However, the Federal Court of Appeals
ruled in the plaintiffs' favor. As a result, city
officials (Mayor Walter Washington et al) appealed the
case to the Supreme Court. The Supreme Court overturned the ruling of the Court of Appeals and thus
held no violation had occurred. The Court reasoned
that it does not follow that a law or an official's
act is unconstitutional solely because it has a
racially disproportionate impact. In effect, the
Supreme Court was telling Davis et al that in order
to prove that they were discriminated against, they
would not only have to show the test administered by
the District of Columbia Police Department had a
disproportionate impact on blacks, but would also have
to demonstrate that the person or persons who authored
the test purposely designed it to discriminate against
them (blacks). In short, the Court told Davis et al.
that in order to show that they had been discriminated
against, they had to prove discriminatory intent.

In the celebrated case of The Regents of the
University of California v Bakke, a fragmented Supreme
Court ruled that a particular university's special
admission (or affirmative action) program for minorities discriminated against non-minorities on the basis
of race and thus violated Title VI. But the Court
also ruled that race was among the factors that could
be considered in a university's admission policies.
In rendering these rulings, the Supreme Court upheld
the contention of Allen Bakke, a thirty-eight year old
white engineer who had charged that the University of
California at Davis affirmative action program was
illegal because it discriminated against non-
minorities, specifically white Americans. But by
upholding race as among factors that universities may
legitimately consider in admissions, the Court also
gave support to pro-affirmative action interests.

In the instance of United Steelworkers of
America v Weber, the Supreme Court ruled that
"employers and unions could establish voluntary
(affirmative action) programs, including the use of
quotas, to aid minorities and women in employment."[14]
Such programs were legal, the court held, even where
there was no evidence of previous discrimination by
employers. In handing down this particular ruling,

the court rejected the challenge of Brian Weber, a
white worker at the Kaiser Aluminum plant who had
challenged the program as being illegal.

Finally, in the case of <u>Fullilove</u> v <u>Klutznick</u>,
the Supreme Court upheld the power of Congress to make
some limited use of racial quotas to remedy past
discrimination against black businessmen. Specifically, the Court held that "Congress did not violate
the constitutional guarantee of Equal Protection when
it set aside for minority businessmen 10% of federal
funds for local public works projects."[15] In
rendering this ruling, the Court rejected the claim
of Fullilove, a white businessman who not only
contended that Congress lacked the authority to
establish racial quotas for minorities in government
contracts, but also that these quotas violated his
and other white businessmen constitutional right of
equal protection.

Given the fact that Title VI agencies like HUD,
HEW, and Labor have required that certain recipients
adopt affirmative action programs and given the fact
that these agencies have been and are engaged in the
business of documenting purposeful discrimination, it
seems reasonable to hypothesize that the Supreme Court
cases cited above may have had some impact on the
agencies' Title VI enforcement efforts. This particular hypothesis will be tested and evaluated in the
chapters that focus directly on the agencies discussed
in this study. Let us now consider how bureaucratic
activity may influence the enforcement of Title VI.

The Impact of Bureaucratic
Activity on Title VI Enforcement

Agency officials also affect the implementation
of Title VI. Indeed, under the provisions of Title VI,
agency officials can influence the enforcement of
Title VI by formulating and implementing Title VI
guidelines and regulations and by exercising their
power to employ whichever Title VI sanction they deem
necessary in enforcing this law. After Congress
passed Title VI, it charged various agency officials
with the responsibility of formulating and implementing
guidelines and regulations necessary for enforcing
Title VI. In their efforts to meet this task, agency
officers have drawn up Title VI guidelines and regulations and, in some instances, have taken action to

implement them. By carrying on these activities, officials can certainly affect the enforcement of Title VI. Indeed, vague and poorly drafted guidelines and regulations or laxly enforced Title VI procedures may result in non-vigorous enforcement of Title VI. On the other hand, clear and uniform Title VI guidelines and regulations or forcefully enforced Title VI procedures may result in vigorous implementation of Title VI.

Agency officials can also affect the implementation of anti-discriminatory provisions of Title VI by exercising their discretionary powers over the usage of Title VI sanctions--voluntary compliance, referral of a case to the Justice Department, deferral of funds, and termination of funds. Agency officials who opt to employ the termination of funds sanction-- the most stringent sanction--are likely to have a more positive impact on Title VI enforcement than those employing less stringent sanctions. At least this is the position taken by the Civil Rights Commission, which has contended that the termination of funds sanction is the most effective sanction for bringing about compliance with Title VI.

On the other hand, agency officials who decide only to use voluntary compliance, the weakest sanctions under Title VI are likely to have a little or no positive effect on Title VI enforcement. Again, the Civil Rights Commission has argued that voluntary compliance is the least effective sanction for inducing non-complying recipients to abide by the provisions of Title VI.

How agency behavior specifically affects the implementation of Title VI will be discussed in subsequent chapters that focus on particular agencies.

The Impact of Interest
    Group Activity on Title VI Enforcement

Interest group activity also affects the political-social context in which Title VI enforcement takes place. In this particular section, we generally consider the political techniques--lobbying, propaganda and electioneering--employed by interest groups to affect the enforcement of Title VI, and identify the major groups which have endeavored to shape and influence the implementation of Title VI. By lobbying agency officials, whether directly or indirectly, interest groups seek to affect the enforcement of Title VI. Direct lobbying by interest groups includes such activity as telephoning, writing, and urging Title VI officers to take certain actions regarding Title VI. Indirect lobbying by interest groups encompasses such activities as urging the Office of Management and Budget to increase or decrease Title VI agencies' budgets, testifying before Congressional Committees urging them to put pressure on Title VI agencies, and taking Title VI agencies to court.

Propaganda is another technique used by interest groups to affect the implementation of Title VI. By preparing and publicizing reports and studies regarding Title VI, interest groups seek to drum up public support for their positions regarding Title VI and seek to get Title VI officers to take certain actions regarding Title VI.

Electioneering is another means used by interest groups to affect the implementation of Title VI. By seeking to elect candidates who share their policy views regarding Title VI, interest groups attempt to put in office officials who will use their powers to affect Title VI enforcement in a particular fashion.

There are, to be sure, several interest groups which have undertaken to shape and influence the implementation of Title VI, and some have been very active in seeking to accomplish this task. These more active groups include the National Association for the Advancement of Colored People, the Leadership Conference on Civil Rights, the Council of Chief State School Officers, the National School Board Association, the National Committee Against Discrimination in Housing, the Center for National Policy Review, and the Center for Law and Social Policy. The specifics of how these groups have attempted to influence Title VI enforcement is reserved for discussion in the context of chapters that focus on particular agencies. But it may be useful here to briefly identify these groups and their objectives.

The National Association for
 The Advancement of Colored People

Founded in 1909, the National Association for the Advancement of Colored People is one of the oldest and largest civil rights organizations in the United

States. The primary objectives of the Association
(hereafter referred to as NAACP) "is to ensure the
economic, educational, political, and social equality
of Negro citizens."[16] In its efforts to achieve this
objective, the NAACP lobbied Congress to enact the
Civil Rights Act of 1964, the Voting Rights Act of
1965, and the Open Housing Act of 1968. And since
congressional enactment of these statutes, the NAACP
has followed up on their implementation.

Leadership Conference
on Civil Rights

Formed in 1949, "the Leadership Conference on
Civil Rights is a coalition of 145 national civil
rights, labor, religious, and civic organizations
dedicated to the achievement of equal opportunity and
the advancement of civil rights."[17] In its efforts
to achieve equal opportunity and advance civil rights,
the Leadership Conference lobbied Congress to pass the
Civil Rights Act of 1964 and subsequently has sought
to influence the implementation of this statute.

Council of Chief State
School Officers

Known as one of the most potent education interest
groups in the United States, the Council of Chief
State School Officers, which was established in 1929,
is an independent organization of fifty state superin-
tendents and commissioners of education. The major
objectives of the Council are "(1) to resist the
development of guidelines, rules and regulations
deleterious to state education agencies; (2) to work
for the establishment of a cabinet level Department
of Education; (3) to establish and maintain a working
relationship with members of Congress and (4) to keep
the United States Office of Education informed
regarding the positions of the chiefs."[18] To fulfill
its objectives, the Council of Chief State School
Officers (hereafter referred to as the CCSO) has
called for more federal aid for education; has continually emphasized the need for less federal paperwork,
procedures, and regulations regarding education; and
has lobbied for the creation of a cabinet level
Department of Education.

The National School
Boards Association

The only major education organization representing
school board members is the National School Boards
Association (hereafter referred to as the NSBA). The
NSBA, which was established in 1936 and which has
80,000 members, "is a federation of state school
boards association, constituted to strengthen local
lay control of education and to work for the improve-
ment of education."[19] To achieve its objectives, the
NSBA, among other things, has lobbied for less federal
paperwork, guidelines, and regulations that affect the
authority of its member boards.

National Committee Against
Discrimination in Housing

The National Committee Against Discrimination in
Housing (hereafter referred to as the NCADH) is the
only national civil rights group solely dedicated to
civil rights aspects of housing and urban development.
"Started in 1950, the NCADH is a nonprofit, civil
rights organization working with 47 national, civil
rights, religious, and civic organizations to achieve
a 'slum-free' America in which all persons are able
to obtain decent housing without discriminatory limitations."[20] In its efforts to combat discrimination in
housing, the NCADH lobbied for the passage of the 1964
Civil Rights Act and the 1968 Open Housing Act. Not
only did NCADH push for the passage of these laws, but
as we discuss later, the organization has taken an
interest in how the legislation has been implemented.

Center for National
Policy Review

Established in 1970, the Center for National
Policy Review, which has a staff of ten, is "a non-
partisan research organization which investigates and
reviews national issues with urban and racial implications."[21] The Center's primary objective is to aid
civil rights and public interest groups in representing
and presenting the concerns of their membership before
federal administrative agencies and judicial bodies.
In its efforts to accomplish this task, the Center for
Policy Review has conducted various studies on racial
segregation in education, employment and housing which

have been widely cited by civil rights groups in their
testimony before Congress's Civil Rights oversight
committees.

Center for Law and
Social Policy

Founded in 1969, the Center for Law and Social
Policy is essentially a group of 14 public-interest
lawyers who have dedicated themselves to employing
litigation as a major means of pressuring governmental
agencies to implement civil rights laws guaranteeing
equality for blacks and women. Just as with the other
groups, how the Center has specifically endeavored to
affect HUD's, HEW's, and Labor's Title VI is discussed
later in this study. Let us now examine how public
opinion may shape the implementation of Title VI.

The Impact of Public Opinion
on Title VI Enforcement

We all know how the president, Congress, the
courts, bureaucratic officials, and interest groups
may fundamentally color the political-social milieu
of Title VI enforcement. Let us now pinpoint how
public opinion may affect that environment. Certainly,
pollsters, pundits, and political scientists generally
have concurred that public opinion can and sometimes
does influence major policymakers including the
president, Congress, judges, and agency officials.
This is highly significant because the vast powers of
these policymakers afford them the opportunity to
shape and influence the implementation of law.
Because of this, it seems important to consider public
opinion toward civil rights from 1964 to 1981. (See
Fig. 3.1, p. 61.) The public's attitude toward civil
rights has fluctuated over time. In short, over the
years the American public has exhibited high concern
or support for civil rights on some occasions, but low
regard or little support on other occasions. Public
opinion polls in 1964 and in 1965 revealed that 52% or
a majority of Americans supported the federal government's effort to combat racial discrimination and
considered the race issue the most important question
before the country. This support for racial equality
came in response to civil rights groups' boycotts,
sit-ins, and demonstrations which dramatized the fact
that blacks were victims of blatantly discriminatory

60

Figure 3.1. Trends in the Public's Perceptions of Race as the Most Important Problem Confronting the Country*

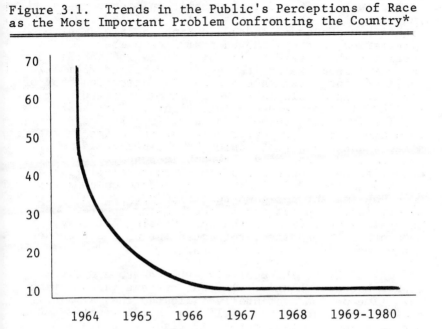

*Sources: Gallup Poll Index (1978) Report No. 160,
              p. 23.
            Lucius J. Barker and Jessie J. McCorry, Jr.,
              Black Americans and the Political System
              (Mass.: Winthrop Publishers, 1976), p. 37.
            Gary Orfield, Must We Bus? (Washington:
              The Brookings Institution, 1977), p. 110.
            ABC/Washington Post Poll "Blacks, Whites
              Agree Blacks Have Gained, Differ on What's
              Ahead," Washington Post, March 24, 1981,
              p. 1A.

customs, laws, and practices. Seemingly, public
support for civil rights also influenced Congress's
behavior. In 1964 Congress enacted the comprehensive
Civil Rights Act of 1964, which among other things
banned discrimination on the basis of race, color, and
national origin in federally-funded programs. And in
1965 Congress passed the Voting Rights Act which in-
validated discriminatory techniques employed to
prevent blacks from voting.

Between 1966 and 1968, public opinion surveys indicated that the public's attitude toward civil rights had changed. Indeed, during the aforementioned time period, surveys showed that "the number of Americans who viewed racial discrimination as the most important issue before the country declined from 52% to 9%"[22], and these same surveys indicated that 65% of the American people felt the government was pushing too fast in the field of civil rights. This sharp decline in public support for civil rights "came in response to growing public concern over crime in the streets and urban riots which heightened racial tensions."[23] Seemingly, low public support for racial change shaped Congress's posture toward civil rights. In 1966 and in 1967, Congress refused to enact an Open Housing Act designed to strike down racially discriminatory practices in the housing sphere. Congress's rejection of the Open Housing Act, many commentators suggested, reflected the nation's conservative mood toward civil rights.

As of 1968, the public's attitude toward civil rights had not changed. Indeed, surveys taken during this time period continually indicated that a majority of Americans, about 65%, felt that civil rights groups were pushing too fast for civil rights and also believed that the federal government should play a more passive role in the civil rights field. Perhaps taking note of the public mood, Richard M. Nixon, the Republican nominee for President in 1968, promised to slow down the enforcement of civil rights laws and pledged to appoint conservative justices (or strict constructionists) to the Supreme Court, replacing liberal justices who had played a major role in furthering racial change. Nixon's campaign pitch proved fruitful for he won the 1968 presidential contest and thus became the chief executive of the United States.

Throughout the 1970's the American public has continued to express little interest in or concern for civil rights. A national study of the "hopes and fears of Americans in 1971 found that only one person in ten rated settlement of racial problems as a hope for the nation, down substantially from earlier measures in 1959 and 1964."[24] Similarly, the problems of black Americans received low priority in a 1972 public ranking of national matters of concern. "On a list of twenty-seven issues, [they] the public ranked solving problems of blacks twenty-fourth."[25]

Since 1972 the American public has continued to express little concern or support for civil rights. For example, a survey of public attitudes in 1974 found that Americans concern for civil rights had plunged to an all time low. Specifically, "a study of public attitudes in 1974 found that the problems of black Americans ranked lowest among thirty issues studied."[26] Issues deemed more important than the problems of blacks were inflation, violence, and crime. Many political analysts have suggested that the public has displayed less and less concern for civil rights in the seventies because they generally believe that blacks are no longer the victims of discrimination. Specifically, many analysts have argued that a majority of Americans, specifically white Americans, firmly believe that civil rights statutes, enacted in the sixties, eradicated racial discrimination in the United States and consequently they feel that the country no longer has a race problem.

Public opinion surveys conducted between 1976 and 1981 lend support to the argument that a majority of white Americans believe that blacks no longer have to grapple with discrimination in areas such as education and employment. "Polls conducted by Louis Harris in 1976 and 1977 found that a 75-7% majority of white Americans believed that blacks were not discriminated against in public education."[27] Similarly, a public opinion poll conducted by George Gallup in 1978 discovered that while a majority of blacks (65%) felt that they did not have as good a chance as whites to obtain jobs for which they were qualified, a majority of whites (68%) felt differently. This particular Gallup poll also found that "while 65% of white Americans believed that blacks were treated the same as whites"[28] in white communities, only 30% of black Americans shared this view. Gallup findings were confirmed by a 1981 Washington Post/ABC News Survey which showed that blacks and whites still disagree as to whether blacks still must cope with discrimination in education, employment and housing. Specifically, this survey found that while a majority of blacks (66%) contended that they must grapple with racially discriminatory practices in education, employment and housing, a majority of whites (66%) disagreed with this contention. Surely these polls suggest that while a majority of black Americans believe that they are still the victims of discrimination, a majority of white Americans disagree with this viewpoint.

Given the fact that a majority of Americans believe that racial discrimination no longer exists and given the fact that policymakers including the president, the Congress, the courts, and agency officials ofttimes heed public opinion, it might be that these policymakers, responding to the public mood, might not use their positions of influence to push for the forceful implementation of the anti-discriminatory provisions of Title VI.

Of course, specific attention will be given in specific chapters to whether the public mood toward civil rights has had any impact on agency implementation of Title VI.

<u>Summary</u>

Overall, this chapter has considered the general political and social milieu of Title VI enforcement. Specifically, it has generally delineated how the powers of the Congress, the courts, and agency officials afford them the opportunity to shape and influence the implementation of Title VI. Also, we have identified those interest groups that seek to influence the enforcement of Title VI and have generally commented on the state of public opinion toward civil rights from 1964 to 1981. In the chapters that follow, we attempt to illustrate specifically how these institutions, groups, and public opinion may affect or influence the Title VI enforcement operation of HUD, HEW, and Labor.

[1]James W. Davis, An Introduction to Public Administration: Politics, Policy and Bureaucracy (New York: The Free Press, 1974), p. 192.

[2]U. S. Commission on Civil Rights, A Report of the United States Civil Rights Commission: The State of Civil Rights 1977 (Washington: Government Printing Office, 1977), p. 11.

[3]Ibid.

[4]Ibid.

[5]U. S. Commission on Civil Rights, The State of Civil Rights: 1979 (Washington: Government Printing Office, 1980), pp. 17-18.

[6]"Reagan Supports Measure To Curb Suits on Busing," New York Times, November 19, 1980, p. 30.

[7]"110 Years of Voting Rights Legislation," Congressional Quarterly Weekly Report, April 11, 1981, pp. 633-636.

[8]Ibid., p. 633.

[9]Washington v Davis 425 U. S. 229 (1976).

[10]Regents of The University of California v Bakke 98 S. Ct. 2733 (1978).

[11]United Steelworkers of America v Weber 99 S. Ct. 2721 (1979).

[12]Fullilove v Klutznick 65 L. Ed. 2d 902 (1980).

[13]Washington v Davis, op cit., p. 229.

[14]United Steelworkers of America v Weber, op cit., p. 2721.

[15]Fullilove v Klutznick, op cit., p. 902.

[16]Statement by Stan Polypous, Attorney for the National Association for the Advancement of Colored People, in a personal interview, Washington, D. C., February 23, 1979.

[17]Statement by Glendora Sloane, Chairperson for The Leadership Conference on Civil Rights, in a personal interview, Washington, D.C.; January 10, 1978.

[18]Based on personal correspondence between Dan Patter, Public Affairs Officer for the Council of Chief State School Officers, and the writer, February 8, 1979. Also, information presented here was taken from a pamphlet distributed by the Council of Chief State School Officers entitled "The Role, Scope, and Function of the Council of Chief State School Officers."

[19]Based on personal correspondence between Jack Keleman, Public Affairs Officer for the National School Board Association, and the writer, February 7 to February 10, 1979.

[20]Statement by Martin Sloane, General Counsel for the National Committee against Discrimination in Housing in a personal interview, Washington, D. C., September 7, 1978.

[21]Statement by William Taylor, Director of the Center for National Policy Review, in a personal interview, Washington, D. C., August 15, 1978.

[22]Gary Orfield, Must We Bus? (Washington: The Brookings Institution, 1977), p. 110.

[23]Ibid.

[24]Ibid.

[25]Ibid.

[26]Ibid., p. 111.

[27]Ibid.

[28]Gallup Poll Index (1978) Report No. 160. (New Jersey American Institute of Public Opinion) p. 23.

CHAPTER IV

THE HUD EXPERIENCE:
"AFRAID TO ACT"

In the last two chapters we have focused on the
political-social context of Title VI enforcement.
This chapter examines how the Department of Housing
and Urban Development has undertaken to implement
Title VI of the Civil Rights Act of 1964. As will
become apparent in the pages that follow, HUD has
been very apprehensive about utilizing stringent sanctions in implementing this law. More will be said
about this later. Here we discuss: 1) the resources
(e.g., staff and compliance instruments) that HUD has
at its disposal; 2) the attitudes and objectives of
HUD officials who are responsible for enforcing Title
VI; 3) the impact of executive, legislative and judicial activities on HUD's Title VI enforcement effort;
and 4) the influence of clientele and interest group
activities on HUD's Title VI enforcement operations.

Established by the Housing and Urban Development
Act of 1965, the Department of Housing and Urban
Development is the major agency with responsibilities
"for improving housing conditions in this country and
assisting the president in achieving maximum coordination of various federal activities which have a major
effect upon urban, suburban, or metropolitan development."[1] In meeting its overall objectives, HUD
"employs 16,000 workers who assist in administering
insurance programs that help families to become
homeowners; a rental subsidy program for low income
families who otherwise could not afford decent housing;
and programs that aid neighborhood rehabilitation and
the preservation of American urban centers from blight
and decay."[2] HUD also has an array of civil rights
responsibilities. These responsibilities are included
in various federal statutes and executive orders that
ban discrimination in federally assisted and federally
subsidized programs against persons on account of race,
sex, religion, and physical and mental impairment.
For example, the Civil Rights Act of 1968 prohibits
discrimination in the sale and rental of housing
because of race, color, religion, or national origin;
Executive Order 11063, issued in 1962, which requires
nondiscrimination in the sale and rental of federally
subsidized and insured housing; and the Housing and
Community Development Act of 1974 bans sex

67

discrimination in the sale and rental of housing. And, of course, Title VI of the Civil Rights Act of 1964 forbids discrimination on the basis of race, color, and national origin in federally assisted projects. To be sure, these various governmental actions have been in response to the pervasive racism and invidious discrimination suffered by minorities and others in the housing sphere. The history of racism and discriminatory practices in this field has been well-documented elsewhere and need not be repeated here.[3] What should be stated here is that all three branches of government-executive, legislative and judicial branches have taken steps to end racial discrimination in housing. Yet, as recent as March 1980, a Civil Rights Commission study concluded that though illegal, racial discrimination in housing still exists.[4] It becomes obvious then that implementation problems exist. Let us then focus on what HUD has done in this regard with respect to its Title VI responsibilities.

HUD's Title VI Organizational Structure

At the top of HUD's Title VI organizational structure is the Secretary of Housing and Urban Development, "who has the duty to administer and enforce the provisions of Title VI in all HUD programs except those programs which HUD assistance is extended by way of contract or guaranty."[5] However, as of 1971, the bulk of the responsibility for administering Title VI was delegated from the Secretary to the Assistant Secretary for Fair Housing and Equal Opportunity. Consequently, since 1971, the Assistant Secretary for Fair Housing and Equal Opportunity "has been acting as the responsible Department official in all matters related to carrying out the requirement set forth in HUD's regulations implementing Title VI."[6] While it is true that the Assistant Secretary for Fair Housing and Equal Opportunity is primarily responsible for enforcing Title VI, it should be noted that the secretary can veto any decision made by the Assistant Secretary in regard to Title VI.

Within the Fair Housing Equal Opportunity Office, there are three other offices which are responsible for compliance and enforcement activities under Title VI. HUD's Office of Program Compliance, which is generally viewed as the national headquarters for Title VI activities, is one such office. Since August 1975 this particular office has been

responsible for providing policy direction to regional
offices which are responsible for conducting compliant
investigations and compliance reviews. It should be
emphasized here that the Program Compliance Office
does not conduct Title VI complaint investigations or
compliance reviews; rather, it establishes guidelines
for regional offices to conduct investigations and
reviews. In short, the Program Compliance Office has
little or no involvement with day-to-day Title VI
enforcement activities. Nonetheless, this particular
office is powerful. In cases where noncomplying
recipients refuse to comply with Title VI, the Program
Compliance Officer can initiate Title VI enforcement
proceedings against them, which can result in the
termination of funds.

Inside the Program Compliance Office is the
Program Compliance Division, which monitors and
assists regional equal opportunity staffs as they
(regional office staffs) conduct compliance reviews
and investigate complaints. The division also
prepares Title VI and other handbooks, reviews final
investigation reports, and prepares material necessary
to initiate administrative proceedings under Title VI.

The Office of Management and Field Coordination
is another sector of The Fair Housing Equal Opportunity Office, which helps in the enforcement of Title
VI. This particular office "prepares and administers
the fair housing and equal opportunity budget and
coordinates the collection, tabulation and preparation
of reports on the racial and ethnic characteristics of
applicants, recipients, and participants in HUD
assisted programs."[7] Within the Office of Management
and Field Coordination is the Field Support and
Evaluation Division, "which evaluates the overall
performance of regional equal opportunity
operations."[8] More specifically, the Field Support
and Evaluation unit receives annual reports from the
regional offices in which regional officials responsible for Title VI outline how many Title VI
complaints they received, how many complaints they
have investigated, the number of Title VI backlog
cases, the number of compliance reviews that have
been conducted, and problems that affected their
Tite VI enforcement operations.

The Program Standards Division, a subdivision of the Office of Management and Field Coordination, "develops appropriate requirements, supportive of all equal opportunity authorities, for HUD assistance,"[9]

The Fair Housing Equal Opportunity staff at HUD's ten regional offices investigates Title VI complaints and conducts compliance reviews. Each of the regional offices has an assistant regional administrator for equal opportunity who reports to the regional administrator, acts as the principal adviser on all equal opportunity matters at the regional level, and has responsibility for ensuring that all departmental policies and procedures relating to equal opportunity are carried out.

Also, each regional office contains an Evaluation and Support Division, which has responsibility for monitoring and providing technical assistance and training in support of equal opportunity programs and requirements in HUD area (or local) offices. With respect to HUD regional office, it is interesting to note that the Assistant Secretary for Fair Housing and Equal Opportunity has no line authority over regional office's operations. The regional administrator is appointed by the Secretary of HUD, and the Regional Administrator appoints the Assistant Regional Administrator for equal opportunity.

To get a better feel of the nature and operations of HUD's regional offices, I visited the regional office in Philadelphia. This particular office was established in 1970, and is responsible for ensuring that Title VI is enforced in the District of Columbia and in four states. They are Pennsylvania, Virginia, West Virginia, and Maryland. Also, the Philadelphia office is responsible for providing technical assistance and training in equal opportunity to area (or local) offices in Pittsburgh and Philadelphia; the District of Columbia; Richmond, Virginia; Charleston, West Virginia; and Baltimore, Maryland. Currently, the Philadelphia regional office has a staff of 200. Of that 200, six are responsible for Title VI enforcement.

In addition to the regional offices, HUD also has thirty-nine offices which are responsible for Title VI enforcement. Each of the area offices has an equal opportunity division whose director reports to the area director or manager. The equal

opportunity division's Title VI responsibilities
include routine monitoring of HUD's recipients,
conducting pre-award reviews, and providing technical
assistance to program recipients.

To get a closer look at HUD's area offices,
particular attention was given to the offices in
Washington, D. C. and Baltimore, Maryland. Both of
these area offices were established in 1972, and both
are responsible for ensuring that 600 recipients of
federal funds adhere to Title VI. This is done by
monitoring these recipients' activities. As of
October 1978 there were three persons on the equal
opportunity staff in the District of Columbia area
office and two persons on that staff in the Baltimore
area office.

Overall, HUD's Title VI organizational structure
may be graphically illustrated as follows:

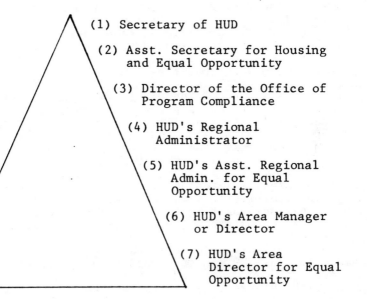

(1) Secretary of HUD

(2) Asst. Secretary for Housing
and Equal Opportunity

(3) Director of the Office of
Program Compliance

(4) HUD's Regional
Administrator

(5) HUD's Asst. Regional
Admin. for Equal
Opportunity

(6) HUD's Area Manager
or Director

(7) HUD's Area
Director for Equal
Opportunity

These then are the organizational units used by HUD to carry out its Title VI responsibilities. In the next section we describe the various compliance instruments and their relative effectiveness in combatting discrimination in HUD funded projects.

HUD's Compliance Instruments: Nature and Operations

1. _The handbook situation_. Basically, HUD has used a number of instruments in its efforts to enforce Title VI. First, it has issued a Title VI handbook which establishes uniform procedures for Title VI enforcement and provides policy direction to officials responsible for enforcing this statute. More specifically, the Title VI handbook 1) delineates the major duties of HUD officials who are responsible for Title VI enforcement; 2) the procedures and techniques for conducting Title VI complaint investigations and compliance reviews; 3) the types of documentation which are essential for proving a recipient has violated Title VI; and 4) the conditions under which HUD officials may use Title VI sanctions. The handbook points up the fact that HUD employs uniform procedures to enforce Title VI. However, it is interesting to note that these uniform guidelines were not begun until 1974, almost a decade after Title VI was enacted. Why did it take HUD officials almost a decade to develop regularized and systematic procedures for enforcing Title VI? When this question was put to HUD officials, they gave various responses. Some contended that "the fact that HUD is basically a new agency may explain why it took so long to institute uniform Title VI procedures."[10] Specifically these officials pointed out that "HUD was established one year after Title VI was enacted, and that it took HUD a great deal of time to organize, recruit personnel, and formulate uniform Title VI regulations."[11]

Other officials believed and stressed "that the reason it took HUD almost a decade to establish uniform Title VI procedures reflects HUD's indifference about Title VI."[12] These officials pointed out that "there was and is an attitude at HUD that housing production is more important than implementing Title VI."[13] This attitude, officials charged, "delayed the establishment of regularized and systematic procedures for enforcing Title VI."[14]

Still other HUD officials maintained "that HUD's failure to institute swiftly uniform and systematic procedures for enforcing Title VI was due to the fact that prior to 1972, HUD had no centralized Title VI office."[15] Specifically, these officials observed "that before 1972, HUD's Title VI program was highly fragmented."[16] Each program administrator was delegated the responsibility for enforcing Title VI, and each basically developed his or her own procedures for enforcing Title VI. With no centralized office to coordinate Title VI activities, officials emphasized, uniform and systematic procedures for enforcing Title VI were not established.

2. <u>Assurance pledges</u>. HUD's policy that all federally assisted programs must annually file documentation that they are complying with Title VI is another instrument that HUD utilizes to gain compliance with Title VI. Under this policy, all federally assisted program recipients must file forms with HUD's area offices indicating that they (the recipients) are obeying Title VI. If an area office discovers that a particular recipient repeatedly has not presented sufficient proof that it is obeying Title VI, the area office can recommend that that particular recipient no longer receive federal funds.

Though HUD's policy of requiring recipients to show proof that they are abiding by Title VI is ideally an excellent mechanism for ensuring Title VI enforcement, the fact is that this particular policy has not been vigorously enforced. Equal opportunity officials in HUD's area offices stated that when they recommended that certain recipients no longer receive financial assistance because of their failure to abide by Title VI or because these recipients failed to present sufficient proof of Title VI compliance, their recommendations were ignored. These officials charged that "the area office director consistently disregarded their recommendations that recipients be penalized for repeated violations of not presenting sufficient proof of Title VI compliance."[17] They believed that "the area manager had rejected their recommendations because he was more concerned about housing production than Title VI enforcement."[18] More specifically, these officials reasoned that:

> The area manager is a Civil Service appointee, and is primarily evaluated by the number of houses that are produced.

73

> . . . If the area manager backed our
> recommendations that funds not be granted
> to recipients (who are responsible for
> constructing housing), this would slower
> housing production. . . . Because the area
> office manager's livelihood depends on
> housing production, he will take no action
> to retard production.[19]

However, area office managers in Washington and
Baltimore disagreed with the charge that they had
administratively overridden their (equal opportunity
officials) recommendations because they were solely
interested in housing production. Both area managers
stressed that "they had seldom vetoed suggestions of
equal opportunity officials, and noted that on those
occasions where they had vetoed those suggestions,
they did so mainly because equal opportunity officials
lacked the evidence to show that a particular recipient had violated Title VI."[20]

In general, there seems to be some credence to
the positions of both the area managers and HUD
officials. At least, this seems to be the conclusion
of a Justice Department study that investigated HUD's
Title VI enforcement operations. Specifically, the
Justice Department found that area managers did
indeed often ignore equal opportunity officials
recommendations, despite the fact that these officials
had presented substantial proof that recipients "had
violated Title VI or had continually failed to supply
adequate proof that they were obeying Title VI."[21]
At the same time, however, the Justice Department
study also found that area office managers were
ofttimes justified in vetoing equal opportunity
officials recommendations because there was insufficient evidence to support such recommendations."[22]

3. Complaint investigations. HUD officials also
utilize complaint investigations to determine if its
recipients are obeying Title VI. These investigations
are triggered by persons who complain that their
rights under Title VI have been violated. Basically,
a complaint investigation is an agency inquiry into
one or more of its recipients' activities to determine
if those activities violate Title VI. Usually, an
agency begins an investigation when any person or
class of persons charges that he/she has been
subjected to discrimination banned by Title VI.

HUD's Tilte VI handbook not only outlines who may file Title VI complaints, but also describes how, when, and where to do so. According to HUD's handbook, "any person or any specific class of persons who believe that he/she has been subjected to discrimination prohibited by Title VI and HUD's implementing procedures may personally, or by a representative, file a complaint."[23]

With respect to how, when, and where to file a Title VI complaint, HUD's handbook states that "all complaints under Title VI must be submitted in writing and filed with HUD not later than 180 days from the date of alleged discrimination, unless the time for filing has been extended by the Assistant Secretary for Fair Housing and Equal Opportunity."[24] In addition, the handbook specifies that Title VI complaints should be sent to the Area Regional Administrator for Fair Housing Equal Opportunity for the state in which the agency identified in the complaint is located."[25] Alternatively, Title VI complaints may be directed to the Assistant Secretary for Fair Housing Equal Opportunity Office of HUD's area offices.

HUD's Title VI handbook also describes what should take place once relevant HUD officials receive a complaint. The handbook indicates that when the Fair Housing and Equal Opportunity staff in a HUD central, regional, area, or insuring office receives a Title VI complaint, they should make note of the date the letter-complaint was received and immediately send a letter of acknowledgment to the complainant.

After the above procedures are taken, the regional Fair Housing Equal Opportunity Compliance Staff, which is responsible for conducting Title VI investigations, should take appropriate action to dispose of the case. Such action usually includes informing a recipient that it is under investigation.

Table 4.1 (p. 76) indicates for fiscal years 1965 through 1980 the number of Title VI complaints HUD received, the number it investigated, HUD's carryover complaints, and its findings of noncompliance. With respect to the number of complaints HUD has received, Table 4.1 shows figures only for fiscal years 1969 through 1980. Figures are not presented for fiscal years 1965-1968 because Title VI records for this period were not kept. Larry Pearl, Director of HUD's Title VI office, and his Deputy Assistant,

Table 4.1.[*] Title VI Complaints and the Department of Housing and Urban Development (1965-1980)

Fiscal years	Number of complaints received	Number of complaints investigated	HUD carryover complaints	Findings of non-compliance
1965	-	-	-	-
1966	-	-	-	-
1967	-	-	-	-
1968	-	-	-	-
1969	115	-	-	-
1970	150	-	-	-
1971	431	-	-	-
1972	345	-	-	-
1973	292	-	-	-
1974	235	85	203	48
1975	265	80	200	42
1976	116	75	180	16
1977	87	14	180	6
1978	70	20	140	3
1979	72	27	130	4
1980	70	26	136	3

[*]Data were taken from U. S. Congress, House, Committee on Appropriations, Subcommittee on Appropriations, Hearings, 95th Congress, 1st Session, March 24, 1977 (Washington: Government Printing Office, 1977), pp. 700-726; U. S. Congress, House, Committee on Appropriations, Hearings, 94th Congress, 1st Session, April 17, 1975 (Washington: Government Printing Office, 1975) pp. 955-60; United States, Congress, House, Committee on Appropriations, Subcommittee on Appropriations, Hearings, 93rd Congress, 2nd Session, March 30, 1974 (Washington: Government Printing Office, 1974), pp. 1337-1361; U. S. Congress, House, Committee on Appropriations, Subcommittee on Appropriations, Hearings, 92nd Congress, 1st Session, April 28, 1971 (Washington: Government Printing Office, 1971),

Mildred Morse both stated "that from 1964 to 1968 officials responsible for keeping Title VI records did not do so."[26] Even more striking, Pearl and Morse stated that prior to 1974, "inadequate and sometimes no Title VI data files had been kept by HUD officials."[27] At any rate, it still seems important to analyze the data that are available. As already mentioned, Table 4.1 lists the number of complaints HUD received from fiscal years 1969 through 1980. An examination of Table 4.1 reveals that HUD received 115 complaints in fiscal year 1969, 150 in 1970, 431 in 1971, 345 in 1972, 292 in 1973, 235 in 1974, 265 in 1975, 116 in 1976, 87 in 1977, 70 in 1978, 72 in 1979, and 70 in 1980. Overall, Table 4.1 indicates that the number of complaints HUD received fluctuated from 431 in fiscal year 1971 to 70 in fiscal year 1980. Two questions come to mind: 1) why has HUD received so few complaints and 2) why has the number of Title VI complaints been decreasing? When HUD officials were asked "why has HUD received so few complaints," most stressed that "HUD had received a small number of complaints because the average citizen was unaware of his or her rights under Title VI."[28] Specifically, these officials observed that "the average citizen does not realize that he or she can file a Title VI complaint when discriminated against on the basis of race, color, or national origin in federally assisted programs."[29]

When HUD officials were asked "why has the number of Title VI complaints declined," most asserted that "they did not know;"[30] however, they did speculate. One group of officials speculated "that the decrease in Title VI complaints was due to the public's realization that HUD simply takes too long to process a complaint."[31] Specifically, these officials asserted:

> It may take seven or eight months to process a complaint and the general public is simply not willing to wait that long for a remedy.[32]

There is evidence to back up these officials' assertion. A Justice Department study which investigated

---

pp. 891-894. Also, data were obtained from The Department of Justice's Title VI Forum Report 1979, p. 2A.

HUD's Title VI enforcement operations found that "the length of time taken to investigate complaints may explain, in part, why there has been a decrease in the number of Title VI complaints."[33]

Other officials contended that "the decline in Title VI complaints might reflect a growing awareness among aggrieved parties that they have more to gain by using other civil rights remedies."[34] To support their contention, these officials pointed out that "Title VI does not afford victims of discrimination an opportunity to obtain monetary compensation for discriminatory acts, but they observed that Title VIII does."[35] Because aggrieved parties may have realized this, officials explained, "they may have opted to utilize Title VIII rather than Title VI."[36]

While these officials did not present any hard evidence to support their argument, they did note that "the Title VIII complaints have increased while Title VI complaints have decreased."[37]

It is worth noting here that though a majority of HUD's ten regional offices have reported a decrease in the number of Title VI complaints, HUD's regional office in Philadelphia has reported an increase in Title VI complaints. Equal opportunity personnel at the Philadelphia Regional Office reported that "the number of Title VI complaints have increased from ten in 1975 to forty in 1980."[38] The Equal Opportunity personnel attributed the increase in Title VI complaints to the fact that "minorities are becoming better informed about their rights under Title VI."[39]

It may be useful here to describe the type of persons who file Title VI complaints. In short, what are the racial and ethnic characteristics of such persons. Attention is centered upon the racial and ethnic characteristics of persons filing complaints from 1974 to 1976 because prior to this time, HUD did not collect racial or ethnic data. Also, as of September 1980, HUD had not published a breakdown of the racial and ethnic characteristics of persons filing Title VI complaints for 1977 through 1980.*

---

*While HUD had not published data regarding the racial and ethnic characteristics of persons filing complaints from 1977 through 1980, Title VI officers

Table 4.2 (p. 79) gives a racial and ethnic breakdown of persons filing Title VI complaints with HUD from 1974-1976. A study of Table 4.2 reveals that of the 243 complaints filed with HUD in 1974, ten were filed by whites, 178 were filed by blacks, 29 were filed by other minorities (Spanish speaking Americans and Orientals), and the racial or ethnic identity of thirty-five persons filing complaints is unknown.

Table 4.2.* HUD Complaints Filed By Race and National Origin (1974-1976)

	1974	1975	1976
TNC	243	222	93
W	10	6	0
B	178	134	56
OM	29	29	8
NA	35	66	29

TNC denotes total number of complaints
B denotes Blacks
W denotes Whites
OM denotes Other Minorities
NA denotes Not Available

*Data were taken from the 1976 Statistical Yearbook of The Department of Housing and Urban Development, p. 29; the 1975 Statistical Yearbook of the Department of Housing and Urban Development, p. 33; and the 1974 Statistical Yearbook of the Department of Housing and Urban Development, p. 37.

at HUD asserted most of the complaints received during this period came from blacks.

For calendar year 1975, Table 4.2 shows that HUD received a total of 222 complaints. Of these Title VI complaints, six were filed by whites, 134 were filed by blacks, twenty-nine were filed by other minorities (Spanish speaking Americans and Orientals), and the racial or ethnic identity of sixty-six persons filing complaints is unavailable.

Table 4.2 also indicates that HUD received 93 Title VI complaints in 1976. Of the 93 complaints filed with HUD in 1976, none were filed by whites, fifty-six were filed by blacks, eight were filed by other minorities (Spanish speaking Americans and Orientals), and the racial or ethnic identity of twenty-nine persons filing Title VI complaints is not available.

Overall, Table 4.2 shows that the vast majority of Title VI complaints filed with HUD from 1974 to 1976 came from blacks. Next to blacks in terms of Title VI complaints filed were Spanish speaking Americans and Orientals. Whites, by and large, filed fewer Title VI complaints than any other racial or ethnic group.

With respect to the number of Title VI complaints HUD investigated for fiscal years 1965 through 1980, Table 4.1 shows figures for only fiscal years--1974, 1975, 1976, 1977, 1978, 1979 and 1980. The reason for this is that HUD officials did not maintain data files concerning the number of complaints HUD investigated for fiscal years 1965 through 1973. As previously stated, Table 4.1 indicates the number of complaints HUD investigated from fiscal years 1974 through 1980. An examination of Table 4.1 reveals that HUD investigated eighty-five complaints in fiscal year 1974, eighty in 1975, seventy-five in fiscal year 1976, fourteen in 1977, twenty in 1978, twenty-seven in fiscal year 1979, and twenty-six in fiscal year 1980.

A comparison of the number of complaints received (Table 4.1) with the number investigated for fiscal years 1974, 1975, 1976, 1977, 1978, 1979 and 1980 reveals that HUD did not investigate all of the complaints it received for fiscal years 1974 through 1980. Indeed, an examination of Table 4.1 shows that of the 235 complaints HUD received in fiscal year 1974, 85 were investigated. Of the 265 complaints HUD received in fiscal year 1975, 80 were investigated. Of the 116 complaints HUD received in fiscal year 1976, 75 were investigated. Of the 87 complaints HUD received in 1977, 14 were investigated. Of the 70 complaints HUD received in fiscal year 1978, 20 were investigated. Of the 72 complaints HUD received in fiscal year 1979, 27 were investigated. And of the 70 complaints received in fiscal year 1980, 26 were investigated. Lack of manpower seems to be the major reason why all complaints were not investigated. Equal opportunity officials in HUD's central office in Washington and in its regional office in Philadelphia both emphasized the understaffing problem."[40]

In regards to HUD's carryover complaints for fiscal years 1965 to 1980, Table 4.1 only indicates the number of carryover complaints for fiscal years 1974 through 1980. HUD officials did not maintain data files concerning carryover complaints from fiscal years 1965 through 1973. At any rate, it is still important to study the little data that are available. As previously stated, Table 4.1 lists the number of carryover complaints for fiscal years 1974, 1975, 1976, 1977, 1978, 1979 and 1980. These data reveal that HUD had 203 carryover complaints in fiscal year 1974, 200 in 1975, 180 in 1976, 180 in 1977, 140 in 1978, 130 in 1979, and 136 in 1980. According to HUD officials, "the department has a large Title VI backlog because its equal opportunity divisions are understaffed and cannot process Title VI complaints in an expeditious manner."[41] Also, HUD officials maintained that they did not investigate all complaints because many times complainants neglected to present adequate proof of discrimination."[42]

With respect to findings of noncompliance for fiscal years 1965 through 1980, Table 4.1 presents HUD's findings of noncompliance for fiscal years 1974 through 1980. Again, the reason for this is that HUD officials did not maintain data files in regard to HUD's findings of noncompliance for fiscal years 1965 through 1973. Nevertheless, it is still important to examine the data that are available. As previously stated, Table 4.1 presents HUD findings of noncompliance for fiscal years 1974 through 1978. An examination of Table 4.1 reveals that HUD found that forty-eight of its recipients had violated Title VI in 1974, forty-two had violated Title VI in 1975, sixteen had violated Title VI in 1976, six had violated Title VI in 1977, three had violated Title VI in 1978, four had violated Title VI in 1979, and three had violated Title VI in 1980.

4. <u>Compliance reviews</u>. Besides complaint investigations, another method used by HUD officials to
ensure that its recipients are complying with Title VI
is the compliance review. "A compliance review is the
in-depth examination of all facets of the operations
of a local agency to assure that a HUD aided program
at the local level is conducted in full accord with
Title VI and department regulations and requirements."[43] Basically, there are three types of compliance reviews. They are single agency compliance
reviews, community-wide compliance reviews, and
follow-up reviews. According to HUD's Title VI
handbook, "a single agency compliance review is an
in-depth examination of an agency which receives
HUD financial assistance to determine whether its
programs and activities are administered and operated
in compliance with Title VI."[44] A community-wide
compliance review, the HUD handbook specified, "is an
in-depth examination of all agencies which receive
HUD financial assistance in a clearly defined area or
locality to determine whether their HUD assisted
programs or activities are administered and operated
in compliance with Title VI."[45]

A follow-up review is an examination of specific
aspects of the administration and operation of a HUD
financially assisted agency to determine whether the
said agency is complying with special requirements and
procedures designed to improve a HUD recipient Title
VI posture."[46]

There are a number of factors that HUD officials
are to consider in selecting a recipient for a compliance review. More specifically, the selection of
a particular recipient for a compliance review should
be based on, but not limited to, the following factors:

(1) an increase in complaints of
discrimination based on race, color,or
national origin in HUD programs: (2)
statistical data which indicates that
any particular minority group is not
benefiting from or participating in HUD
programs to an extent indicated by the
number of each minority group eligible
to participate or benefit in HUD programs;
(3) community patterns of discrimination
in programs covered by Title VI; (4)
failure of a recipient to file adequate

compliance reports; (5) indication of
discrimination in HUD programs; (6) or
the need for a periodic assessment of
compliance.[47]

It seems appropriate here to examine HUD's record
with respect to compliance reviews. Table 4.3 (p. 84)
lists for fiscal years 1965 through 1980 the number
of compliance reviews conducted by HUD. An examination
of Table 4.3 reveals that the number of compliance
reviews conducted by HUD are listed only for fiscal
years 1970 through 1980. The reason for this is that
HUD officials did not record the number of compliance
reviews for fiscal years 1965 through 1969. Nonetheless, it is important to focus on the data that are
available. A study of Table 4.3 reveals that HUD
conducted 72 compliance reviews in 1970, 142 reviews
in 1971, 158 reviews in 1972, 100 reviews in 1973,
94 reviews in 1974, 125 reviews in 1975, 108 reviews
in 1976, 219 reviews in 1977, 180 reviews in 1979, and
196 reviews in 1980.

Overall, Table 4.3 indicates that for fiscal
years 1970 through 1980, HUD never conducted over 219
compliance reviews in any one year. This should be
placed in the broader context that HUD funds approximately 14,000 recipients. In short, the evidence
suggests that HUD conducts an extremely small number
of compliance reviews and may have no notion of whether
the vast majority of its recipients are obeying
Title VI. A question that immediately arises is why
has HUD conducted such a small number of compliance
reviews. According to HUD officials, there are two
basic reasons for this situation. First, some
officials pointed out that "HUD had conducted only a
small number of compliance reviews because it lacked
the money and the staff to conduct a larger number
of reviews."[48] Officials also stressed that HUD had
done a small number of reviews because equal opportunity officials responsible for conducting Title VI
reviews lacked that expertise essential for doing
good reviews. As one official put it, "the regional
offices' equal opportunity staffs simply do not know
how to conduct good compliance reviews."[49] This
official added:

To do a good compliance review one
needs a background in urban planning,
budget analysis or public policy. People

83

Table 4.3.*   Compliance Reviews Conducted by HUD
(1965-1980)

Fiscal years	No. of Reviews
1965	-
1966	-
1967	-
1968	-
1969	-
1970	72
1971	142
1972	158
1973	100
1974	94
1975	125
1976	108
1977	219
1979	180
1980	196

*Data were taken from U. S. Congress, House, Committee on Appropriations, Subcommittee on Appropriations, Hearings, 95th Congress, 1st Session, March 24, 1977 (Washington: Government Printing Office, 1977), pp. 700-726, U. S. Congress, House, Committee on Appropriations, Subcommittee on Appropriations, Hearings, 94th Congress, 1st Session, April 17, 1975 (Washington: Government Printing Office, 1975), pp. 955-960, and U. S. Congress, House, Committee on Appropriations, Subcommittee on Appropriations, Hearings, 93rd Congress, 2nd Session, May 30, 1974 (Washington: Government Printing Office, 1974), pp. 1337-1361. Also data appearing above were obtained from Larry Pearl, Director of HUD's Title VI program.

on our staff have little or no training
or background in these areas.[50]

A compliance review recently conducted by HUD's
regional office in Philadelphia lends support to the
argument that a background in public policy, budget
analysis and planning is essential for conducting a
good compliance review. The Philadelphia review was
very comprehensive. The equal opportunity staff
reviewed 24 city agencies to determine if there was
equal opportunity in participation and benefits in
those agencies funded by HUD. One official described
in some detail what had to be done in assessing
whether the City of Philadelphia was complying with
Title VI. This official stated:

> In conducting the Philadelphia review,
> we had to trace the money and examine how
> it was spent. We also had to determine who
> spent the money and analyze where it was
> spent. Further, we had to look at planning.
> Who did the planning? And, of course, we
> had to assess whether there was any dis-
> parity in the planning. We also had to
> examine whether planning favored non-
> minority impacted areas as opposed to
> minority impacted areas. To do this, we
> had to examine census tracts in order to
> identify minority impacted areas and non-
> minority impacted areas.[51]

Clearly, this official's description of the compliance
review in Philadelphia supports the point made earlier
that a background in public policy, budget analysis
and planning is essential for conducting a quality
review.

At this point, it seems appropriate to note that
while officials in HUD's national office complained
about regional officials' lack of expertise in conducting quality Title VI reviews, these same officials
(officials in the national office) have neglected to
conduct systematic Title VI training sessions, which
could assist regional officials gain the skills essential for conducting quality reviews. HUD has conducted
only one systematic Title VI training session for
regional equal opportunity staffers, and that session
was held in August 1975.

Enforcement Mechanisms

1. <u>Voluntary compliance</u>. So far, major
attention has been given to the compliance instruments
that HUD uses to detect discrimination. However, here
our discussion centers on what HUD does upon finding
discrimination. In short, what enforcement sanction
or sanctions are HUD officials subject to employ when
they find that their recipients are disobeying the
provisions of Title VI. As noted in Chapter I, the
Civil Rights Act of 1964 grants agencies four
sanctions to induce noncomplying recipients to adhere
to the law. These sanctions are 1) voluntary
compliance, 2) referring a case to the Justice
Department, 3) deferring funds, and 4) terminating
funds. Voluntary compliance refers to the efforts
of an agency to negotiate with or persuade a
noncomplying recipient to obey Title VI before the
agency resorts to other sanctions. If voluntary
compliance proves unsuccessful, for example, an
agency may opt to refer a case to the Justice Department. Referring a case to the Justice Department
usually indicates an agency's decision to file a
legal suit against a noncomplying recipient.

When an agency decides not to refer a case to
the Justice Department, it may defer a noncomplying
recipient's funds; that is, it might delay or postpone
a recipient's funds until the recipient takes steps
to rectify discriminatory actions.

Finally, an agency might opt to terminate funds
of a noncomplying recipient. Basically this means
withdrawing the funds of a program which violates
Title VI.

Obviously, of the four sanctions that an agency
has at its disposal, the least stringent is voluntary
compliance and the most stringent is fund termination.
The Civil Rights Commission has observed that "fund
termination is not only the most austere sanction an
agency can utilize, but it also is the most effective
means of compelling a noncomplying recipient to abide
by Title VI."[52] HUD's Title VI enforcement record
over the last ten years reveals that it (HUD) has
used voluntary compliance as the major enforcement
technique for gaining compliance with Title VI. This,
to be sure, does not indicate that HUD does not employ
other enforcement sanctions, for HUD has referred four
cases to the Justice Department, deferred funding

noncomplying recipients six times, and has terminated funds once. A Civil Rights Commission study sheds light on HUD's enforcement patterns. The Commission has observed that:

> When a recipient is found in noncompliance, HUD's actions are directed almost exclusively toward achieving voluntary compliance.[53]

Although the Civil Rights Commission report supports the contention that HUD, for the most part, has utilized voluntary compliance in seeking to fulfill the commands of Title VI, the report does not address the question regarding why HUD officials seem more inclined to use the voluntary compliance sanction as opposed to the other sanctions available. When this question was put to HUD officials, they gave various responses. Officials contended that "they used the voluntary compliance sanction more frequently than others because there was seldom a need to take Title VI enforcement proceedings beyond the voluntary compliance stage."[54] Specifically, officials explained that they seldom used stronger sanctions such as deferring funds or terminating funds "because noncomplying recipients usually opted to comply voluntarily with the law, rather than risk the chance of their funds being deferred or terminated."[55]

Two points should be stressed here. First, it is important to note that while HUD officials generally have relied on the voluntary compliance agreement (a.k.a. the voluntary compliance sanction) as the major instrument for enforcing Title VI, they have not monitored these agreements to determine whether recipients are abiding by them. Zina Greene, Equal Opportunity Specialist in HUD Program Compliance Office stated "we have convinced a number of noncomplying recipients to sign voluntary compliance agreements, but for the most part we have neglected to monitor them to assess whether recipients are adhering to them."[56] Similarly, Maxine Cunningham, Director of HUD's Equal Opportunity Division in Baltimore area office, stated:

> Voluntary compliance agreements are worthless if they are not monitored. Unfortunately, the department has not monitored the bulk of its compliance

agreements. Instead, the department has depended on verbal assurance as opposed to demonstrated results.[57]

Also, it is important to note that HUD utilizes the voluntary compliance approach even when it discovers that this particular approach does not prove successful in gaining compliance with Title VI. HUD's Title VI regulations state that if voluntary compliance proves unsuccessful after sixty days, HUD officials should use other sanctions--referring a case to the Justice Department, deferring funds or terminating funds--to secure compliance with Title VI. But HUD officials have not followed these regulations. For example, in fiscal year 1974, HUD found that 48 of its recipients had violated Title VI. It convinced 22 of the forty-eight noncomplying recipients to sign voluntary compliance agreements; in short, agreements that they would abide by Title VI. The remaining twenty-six noncomplying recipients refused to sign voluntary compliance agreements on the grounds that they had not violated Title VI. As of fiscal year 1980, ten of the twenty-six noncomplying recipients had still not signed voluntary compliance agreements. However, HUD continues to employ the voluntary compliance sanction as the sole means for gaining compliance with Title VI.

The other reason HUD officials have utilized the voluntary compliance sanction more frequently than other sanctions is "politics." A number of HUD officials stated quite candidly that "HUD had used the voluntary compliance sanction more frequently than other sanctions because of political consideration."[58] These officials explained that when they used the voluntary compliance sanction, congressmen generally have not sought to exert political pressure on their offices. However, when HUD opted to defer funds or terminate funds, congressmen have applied political pressure. One official put it this way.

Voluntary compliance does not get the department in trouble with Congress because using this sanction does not mean delaying or withholding the program funds of Congressmen's constituencies. But when you talk about terminating funds, you are talking about opening the door for some hostile confrontations with Congress.[59]

To be sure, there is evidence that when officials have sought to terminate funds, Congressmen have exerted political pressure to prevent them from doing so. Consider for example the case of Cheyenne, Wyoming. Here equal opportunity officials determined that Cheyenne was guilty of violating Title VI. As a result, HUD sought to persuade the city to sign a voluntary compliance agreement to abide by Title VI. When the city refused to do so, HUD officials initiated Title VI enforcement proceedings to terminate the city's model cities' funds. When HUD took this action, the Mayor of Cheyenne and Congressmen from the state attempted to influence HUD's Title VI enforcement operations. Larry Pearl, Director HUD's Program Compliance Office, described the tactics that the mayor and the Congressmen employed. According to Pearl, "the mayor and the Congressmen from the area called, wrote, and visited HUD's Secretary Lynn's office and the Assistant Secretary for Fair Housing to convince them to block any Title VI actions against the city of Cheyenne."[60] But it was reported that neither Secretary Lynn or the Assistant Secretary for Fair Housing and Equal Opportunity attempted to halt the Title VI enforcement actions against Cheyenne.

In general, however, it seems apparent that fear of political pressures affect the type of sanction that officials use in gaining compliance with Title VI. Consider, for example, the case of Boston, Massachusetts. HUD officials stated that in 1975 they uncovered widespread racial discrimination in the city of Boston. Yet officials noted that despite repeated efforts to persuade Boston to comply with Title VI, as of August 1978 city authorities have refused to adhere to the provisions of that law. When these HUD officials were asked why they had not terminated Boston's housing funds, they generally replied "that would be politically impossible."[61] One official explained it this way.

> Everybody in the department, including the Secretary (of HUD) knows that Boston has violated the law, but everyone is afraid to do anything. People are scared because if we threaten to terminate Boston's housing funds, we can expect enormous political pressure to be exerted on the department. Mayor White (the Mayor of Boston) would simply get on the phone to O'Neill (Speaker of the House of Representatives). O'Neill

would then get in touch with Carter. In
turn, Carter would get in touch with Pat
Harris (Secretary of HUD) and she would
get in touch with the fair housing division
to halt our Title VI proceedings.[62]

On the basis of the evidence, it seems clear that
political pressures do influence the type of sanction
that officials are likely to use.

2. Deferring funds and terminating funds.
Sanctions such as the deferral of funds and the termination of funds are rarely used because they run
counter to HUD's primary mission of disbursing funds
for housing production. HUD's equal opportunity staff
stated that when they recommended that funds of noncomplying recipients be deferred or terminated, their
recommendations were ignored. To them this occurred
because HUD's program officials and top administra-
tors--i.e., the Secretary of HUD, regional administrators, and the area managers--are primarily concerned
about housing production, not civil rights enforcement.
One equal opportunity staff member summed up the
situation this way:

> The name of the game here at HUD is
> housing production. As a result, program
> officials' major objective is to keep the
> money flowing so that more housing units
> will be constructed. . . .Efforts on the
> part of the equal opportunity staffs to
> delay or stop the flow of funds because
> of civil rights violations foster conflicts
> with program officials. Usually these
> conflicts are resolved by Secretary (of
> HUD), the Regional Administrator or the
> area manager, and usually these officials
> side with program officials. Why?
> Because the Secretary, the regional
> administrators and the area managers are
> production oriented.[63]

This view that HUD was and is chiefly concerned with
the production of housing and not civil rights
enforcement was widely shared by equal opportunity
officials in HUD's Program Compliance Office, in its
regional office in Philadelphia, and in its area
offices in the District of Columbia and Baltimore.

3. <u>Termination of funds: A closer look</u>. The fact that key officials in HUD's equal opportunity offices do not believe that the termination of funds sanction is an effective means to combat discrimination in federally assisted programs may explain why HUD seldom uses this particular sanction. These officials, the Assistant Secretary for Fair Housing and Equal Opportunity, the Deputy Assistant Secretary for Fair Housing and Equal Opportunity, the Director of HUD's Program Compliance Office, the Assistant Regional Administrator for Fair Housing and Equal Opportunity in Philadelphia, and the Director of the Equal Opportunity Divisions in the District of Columbia area office are concerned that the termination of funds was not an effective means to deter discrimination in federally assisted programs because "it impacts negatively on intended program beneficiaries."[64] They emphasized that the termination of funds sanction was not effective because "it ends a program, and the intended beneficiaries of that program are adversely affected."[65]

That key officials in HUD's equal opportunity offices believe that the termination of funds is not an effective means to deter discrimination in federally assisted programs is important since these officials, by virtue of their positions, have the authority and opportunity to veto attempts to apply the termination of funds sanction. But though most key officials in HUD's equal opportunity office expressed the view that terminating funds was not an effective means to deter discrimination in federally assisted programs, there were a few such officials who expressed the opposing viewpoint. For example, some officials, such as the Deputy Director of HUD's Program Compliance Office, the Assistant Title VI Branch Chief in HUD's regional office in Philadelphia, and the Director of the Equal Opportunity Division in Baltimore's area office "contended that terminating funds was an effective means to deter discrimination in federally assisted programs, because if imposed, recipients would be disinclined to discriminate for fear the government would terminate funds."[66]

The lengthy and cumbersome procedures for terminating funds are another reason why HUD officials seldom use the termination of funds sanction. Some officials indicated that the fact the department had terminated funds in only one instance was because the procedures for terminating funds are "slow, cumbersome and legalistic."[67] Indeed, the evidence supports HUD officials' contention that procedures for enforcing Title VI are lengthy, complicated and legalistic. Before equal opportunity officials can terminate funds, they must first negotiate with a noncomplying recipient for a period of sixty days. If after sixty days, equal opportunity officials have failed to convince a non-complying to abide by Title VI, they must then notify the recipient that the matter is being referred to the national fair housing office for formal enforcement proceedings. Once the case reaches the central office, it examines the case to assess whether there has been a violation of Title VI. If the national office determines that there has been a Title VI violation, this office may attempt once more to persuade the noncomplying recipient to comply voluntarily with Title VI. If these efforts at negotiation fail, the national office can request that a hearing be held. However, before a hearing can be held, officials in the national fair housing office must first obtain the consent of the Secretary of HUD. If consent of the Secretary is obtained, the fair housing officials must then get the consent of HUD's general counsel. If the general counsel agrees that there is sufficient evidence to go to a hearing, the recipient involved is notified and is given approximately twenty-eight days to prepare its case. The hearing is then held before an administrative judge. If the judge determines that the noncomplying recipient has violated Title VI, equal opportunity officials still cannot terminate funds. Rather, they must submit the findings of the administrative judge to the committees of Congress which have legislative jurisdiction over HUD. Thirty days after submitting the report to Congress, equal opportunity officials can then terminate funds. When reviewed in the overall context, it becomes quite apparent that the procedures for terminating funds are complicated and lengthy.

4. Referring a case to the Department of Justice. It seems important to emphasize here that HUD has only referred four cases to the Department of Justice. Given the large number of HUD recipients who have violated Title VI, the question arises as to why has HUD referred such a small number of cases to the Department of Justice. When this question was put to equal opportunity officers, most stated that the reason HUD had referred only a small number of cases to the Department of Justice was that the Justice Department simply takes too long to bring

action against noncomplying recipients. As one equal opportunity officer put it, "the department has been reluctant to forward cases to the Justice Department because it (DOJ) takes approximately a year-and-a-half before it begins considering Title VI cases that have been submitted."[68]

Impediments to HUD's
Title VI Enforcement Operations

HUD officials cited a number of problems that impeded their Title VI enforcement effort. Generally, however, they emphasized three problems: 1) inadequate staffing, 2) lack of department commitment to civil rights enforcement, and 3) politics.

Lack of staff. Officials in HUD's central, regional, and area equal opportunity offices emphasized that they could not effectively enforce Title VI because they lacked the staff. Larry Pearl, Director of HUD's Program Compliance Office, stated that his Office is responsible for ensuring enforcement of Title VI of the Civil Rights Act of 1964, Section 504 of the Rehabilitation Act of 1973, and Section 109 of the Community Development Act of 1974. But with only six people, Pearl stated that his office "cannot remotely do the job of overseeing Title VI enforcement with six people."[69] Similarly, Bob Myers, Branch Chief of HUD's Title VI office in Philadelphia, stressed that "because of a shortage of staff, we cannot investigate Title VI complaints which are piling up."[70]

Maxine Cunningham, Director of the Equal Opportunity Division in the Baltimore Area Office, also observed that "inadequate staffing had prevented the equal opportunity division in Baltimore from meeting its Title VI responsibilities."[71]

Lack of departmental commitment to civil rights. Equal opportunity officials stressed that when conflicts arose between HUD's chief mission housing production and civil rights objectives, civil rights tended to receive lower priority. This occurred, some officials contended, "because top officials including the Secretaries of HUD--Moon Landrieu, Pat Harris, Carla Hill and James Lynn--were and are not genuinely committed to seeing Title VI enforced."[72] These civil rights officers sought to substantiate their contention by emphasizing that "even when they found overwhelming evidence that HUD recipients were violating Title VI and subsequently attempted to take action against these recipients, the Secretaries of HUD--Landrieu, Harris, Hill, and Lynn generally blocked those efforts."[73]

This view that top officials including the Secretaries of HUD have generally not been supportive of efforts to implement Title VI was widely shared by civil rights officers in HUD national office in Washington and in its regional office in Philadelphia.

Politics. Civil rights officers at HUD also emphasized that politics had impeded their efforts to enforce Title VI. These officials explained that each time they attempted to investigate whether a particular recipient was complying with Title VI or undertook to take enforcement action against noncomplying recipients, Congressmen, mayors, or the White House would take action to prevent them from vigorously enforcing Title VI. A civil rights officer in HUD's regional office in Philadelphia described and explained what happened when she and other Title VI officers endeavored to assess whether the city of Philadelphia housing authorities were complying with the provisions of Title VI:

> We received numerous complaints from blacks in Philadelphia that Philadelphia's housing authorities were not abiding by the nondiscriminatory provisions of Title VI. Hence our task was to investigate whether there was concrete evidence to support these complaints or allegations. As soon as we started our investigation, the Mayor of Philadelphia (Rizzo) and the Congressmen from the area wrote and called us claiming there was no need to investigate housing officials in Philadelphia, because we surely ought to know that these officials were law abiding citizens. . . .Despite these pressures, we carried out the investigation and found that Philadelphia's housing officials were guilty of disobeying Title VI. Nevertheless, no strong Title VI enforcement action has been taken against these officials because the Mayor of Philadelphia and the Congressmen from the area have put pressure on Harris [Secretary of HUD] and the White

House not to penalize housing officers for disregarding Title VI. In fact, rumors are floating around here that Philadelphia's Congressmen threaten not to support President Carter's programs if action was taken against their constituents.[74]

Let us now examine the impact of presidential activity on HUD's Title VI operations.

The Impact of Executive Activity on HUD's Title VI Enforcement Operations

As in other areas, it seems clear that the attitude of the president has influenced Title VI enforcement operations. Let us take a closer look with respect to the impact of such activity on HUD's enforcement effort.

Johnson and Title VI Enforcement: A favorable climate. Lyndon Johnson, in large measure, projected a very strong and favorable posture toward civil rights and surely this posture was well known. But with respect to the bureaucracy, Johnson assumed an ambivalent attitude. He "thought highly of some bureaucracies but lowly of others."[75] The agency that Johnson thought particularly highly of was HUD. This was made manifest by the fact that he proposed the creation of HUD in 1965. In his request to Congress to establish the Department of Housing and Urban Development, Johnson asserted, "because our cities and suburbs are so important to the welfare of all of our people, we believe a department devoted to urban affairs should be added to the president's cabinet."[76] Congress granted the president his request in September 1965 when it enacted the Housing and Urban Development Act of 1965, which created HUD. In addition, the fact that HUD's budget increased substantially during the Johnson years reflected the president's high esteem for HUD. For example, during the Johnson years HUD's budget rose from 2.9 billion dollars in 1965 to 5.8 billion dollars in 1968.

The fact that Johnson pushed for the enactment of HUD's programs was another indication of his high regard for HUD. In 1966, for example, Johnson persuaded Congress to enact the Demonstration Cities and Metropolitan Act, which resulted in the establishment of the Model Cities Program. In 1968, Johnson convinced Congress to pass the Housing and Urban

Development Act of 1968, which created two subsidized housing programs for low and moderate income families.

In general, and on the basis of interviews with HUD officials, it seems apparent that Johnson's statements and actions penetrated the HUD bureaucracy. The President's posture created a favorable climate for civil rights enforcement generally, including Title VI.

Nixon, HUD, and Title VI. Richard Nixon, as reported in Chapter II, adopted an ambivalent attitude toward civil rights. On some occasions his assertions and actions indicated support for civil rights, but at other times his statements and actions indicated nonsupport. Overall, however, Nixon essentially adopted a hostile attitude toward civil rights.

Nixon was generally hostile toward the bureaucracy. It was not unexpected then that Nixon projected a hostile attitude toward HUD. In 1973, the President stated that "domestic agencies like HUD, HEW, and Transportation were too big, too bloated, and too expensive."[77] Further, he pointed out that many of the programs of these agencies could be trimmed down because they had failed.

And Nixon did take steps to trim HUD. He cut HUD's model cities budget in 1970, 1971, 1972, and 1973, charging that Model Cities was an utter failure. Also, in 1973, Nixon placed a moratorium on HUD's subsidized housing programs for the poor, contending they were "not working, too costly, and inflationary."[78]

Furthermore, there were conflicts between Nixon and the Secretary of HUD, George Romney. Nixon wanted to dismantle the Model Cities programs, but Romney did not. Romney's efforts to integrate the suburbs were vetoed by Nixon. The battles between the White House and Romney were so intense that one press account reported that Attorney General John Mitchell asked Secretary Romney to resign. Overall, the point is that Nixon did not have a good relationship with HUD.

This view was underscored by the perceptions which HUD officials had of Nixon and his posture toward Title VI enforcement. For example, when equal opportunity officials were asked if President Nixon's statements or actions had helped or hindered HUD's Title VI enforcement effort, most expressed the belief

that his actions and statements had inhibited rather
than facilitated Title VI enforcement. Perhaps the
most striking observations concerning the Nixon
Administration's impact on Title VI enforcement were
those of Samuel J. Simmons, HUD's Assistant Secretary
for Fair Housing and Equal Opportunity from 1969 to
1972. Simmons charged that "Nixon hampered rather
than helped HUD's Title VI enforcement efforts."[79]
He pointed out how the White House sought to prevent
him from obtaining the power to enforce Title VI.
Specifically, Simmons stated:

> When I became the Assistant Secretary
> for Fair Housing and Equal Opportunity in
> 1969, I lacked the power to act in regard
> to Title VI. . . .True, I had the power to
> investigate Title VI complaints, but lacked
> the power to conciliate with recipients or
> to compel them to obey Title VI. Realizing
> this, I set out to gain the power which
> would permit me to coerce recipients to
> comply with this law. Secretary Romney
> [Secretary of the Department of Housing
> and Urban Development] assisted me in my
> efforts. However, top White House aides
> sought to block my efforts every step of
> the way.[80]

This incident, according to Simmons, conveyed to him
that the White House was not solidly committed to
civil rights.

Also, Simmons observed that there was a feeling
at HUD that the Fair Housing staff was to grapple only
with crisis situations; in short, the Fair Housing
office was to cope only with cases which might result
in some political embarrassment for the White House.
Overall, Simmons contended that "there was a feeling
at HUD that the President did not care about civil
rights enforcement and that one did not have to do
anything as long as one did not get caught."[81]

Ford, HUD and the bureaucracy. In general, Gerald
Ford, just as Nixon, adopted a hostile attitude toward
civil rights enforcement. Though he made a few statements calling for enforcement of civil rights laws, by
and large, Ford, as pointed out in Chapter II, took
steps which indicated nonsupport for civil rights
enforcement. Also, Ford, like Nixon, projected a rather
hostile attitude toward HUD. Indeed, as president,

Ford proposed in fiscal years 1975, 1976, and 1977 that Congress significantly reduce funding for HUD's Community Development Bloc Grant Program. But perhaps most striking was the fact that Ford urged Congress to trim HUD's overall budget in fiscal years 1975, 1976, and 1977 in order to reduce inflation, and he promised to veto any legislation which disregarded his policy wish.

In general, civil rights officials at HUD contended that Ford had definitely not been supportive of their efforts to enforce Title VI. They noted that "Ford had refused to grant them the money and staff necessary for implementing Title VI,"[82] and that he had opposed the efforts of federal courts to eliminate racial segregation in Chicago's housing market. These actions, civil rights officials emphasized, made it difficult for them to vigorously enforce Title VI.

Carter, HUD, and the bureaucracy. Though more favorable than Nixon or Ford, Carter adopted an ambivalent attitude toward civil rights, the bureaucracy, and toward HUD. For example, after calling on Congress to increase funding for HUD's Community Development Bloc Grant and Low-Income Housing Programs in fiscal years 1977 and 1978, Carter urged Congress to decrease funding for these particular programs in fiscal years 1979, 1980, and 1981, contending the cuts were essential to balance the budget. This ambivalence in Carter was also reflected in the perceptions that HUD officials had of him. These HUD officials generally contended that "Carter's statements and actions had helped their Title VI enforcement operations in some instances, but had hurt in others."[83] They explained that Carter's Title VI memorandum calling for aggressive enforcement of Title VI had helped their civil rights operations because positive statements from the commander-in-chief make it easier to enforce anti-discriminatory statutes. On the other hand, however, these same officials emphasized that Carter had impeded their efforts to implement Title VI by refusing to grant them the staff and money needed for effective enforcement.

Reagan, HUD and Title VI Enforcement. For the most part, Reagan, just as his Republican predecessors Ford and Nixon, adopted an ambivalent attitude toward civil rights. On some occasions his assertions and actions indicated support for civil rights, but at other times his statements and actions suggested non-support. Overall, however, Reagan essentially adopted a hostile attitude toward civil rights enforcement.

Reagan has generally displayed an unfriendly attitude toward the bureaucracy. It was no surprise then that he projected an antagonistic attitude toward HUD. For example, Reagan succeeded at persuading Congress to substantially cut HUD's Community Development Bloc Grant, Subsidized Housing, Fair Housing and Urban Development Action programs in fiscal year 1982, contending the cuts were essential to balance the federal budget in 1984.

In general, civil rights officials at HUD charged that Reagan's statements and actions had not helped their Title VI enforcement effort. Specifically, these officials pointed out that by cutting their Title VI budgets, Reagan had made it more difficult for their regional offices, which conduct Title VI complaint investigations and compliance reviews, to fulfill their civil rights responsibilities.

Also, these officials explained that "Reagan's anti-busing statements and his opposition to affirmative action did not create a favorable environment in which to enforce any civil rights law including Title VI."[84]

Let us now analyze the impact of congressional bureaucratic activity on HUD's Title VI operations.

The Impact of Legislative-Bureaucratic Activity on HUD's Title VI Enforcement Operations.

This section attempts to describe how HUD's interactions with Congress may have helped or hindered its Title VI enforcement effort. Contact points which foster bureaucratic-legislative interaction include congressional control over agencies' budget, legislation, and oversight.

1. Appropriations. At this point, it seems appropriate to examine whether Congress's interactions with HUD via the appropriations process have helped or hindered HUD's Title VI operations. Put another way, has congressional funding facilitated or inhibited HUD from meeting its Title VI responsibilities? In order to assess the impact of congressional funding on HUD's Title VI enforcement effort, I studied HUD's Fair

Housing Equal Opportunity Office budget requests and congressional appropriations for fiscal years 1969 to 1978 to determine if Congress had generally allotted, substantially decreased or pointedly denied the Fair Housing Equal Opportunity Office (hereafter referred to as FHEO) funding requests. Also, I conducted interviews with HUD's FHEO staff to gain their perceptions of the impact of congressional funding on HUD's enforcement effort.

Table 4.4 (p. 101) lists the FHEO's initial and supplemental budget requests and congressional appropriations from fiscal years 1969 through 1980. An examination of Table 4.4 reveals that while Congress substantially reduced the FHEO's budget requests from fiscal years 1969 to 1971, it generally granted the FHEO its budgetary requests for fiscal years 1972 to 1980. Hence, overall Congress has generally honored the FHEO's budget requests.

Still, the question remains why did Congress drastically cut the FHEO's budget from fiscal years 1969 to 1971, but generally approved this office's requests from fiscal years 1972 to 1980. When asked this question, current and former FHEO officials emphasized that Congress had cut the FHEO's budget in earlier years because "we had no major supporters or lobbyists on the House Appropriations Committee."[85] However, they explained that Congress had not cut the FHEO's budget in recent years "because now we have lobbyists or supporters on the Appropriations Committee."[86] One FHEO official summed it up this way:

> Prior to 1972, we had no major supporters on the Appropriations Committee. In fact, during this period (from 1969 to 1972), the Committee was dominated by Southern congressmen who bitterly opposed civil rights and civil rights programs. . . .The chairman of the appropriations committee (Joe Evins of Tennessee) was a powerful Southern conservative who was hostile to civil rights, and he made this painfully obvious each time we appeared before the committee. . . .Our relationship with the appropriations committee was simply not good. The huge budget cuts reflect this fact. . . .However, in 1972, things began to change, the composition of the committee began to change. Congressmen

Table 4.4.* HUD's Fair Housing Equal Opportunity
Office Initial and Supplemental Requests and Congressional Appropriations for Fiscal Years 1969-1979.

Year	Budget Requested		Congressional Appropriations
1969	$11,100,00		-
	8,000,000	(1st Supp.)	$ 2,000,000
	2,000,000	(2nd Supp.)	-
1970	10,500,000		6,000,000
	412,000	(1st Supp.)	391.000
1971	11,000,000		8,000,000
1972	9,254,000		8,250,000
1973	9,489,000		9,546,000
1974	9,580,000		9,546,000
1975	11,900,000		11,735,000
1977	13,003,000		13,003,000
1978	13,500,000		13,500,000
1979	14,500,000		14,500,000
1980	15,000,000		15,000,000

*Data were obtained from Larry Pearl, Director
of HUD's Title VI Office, in a personal interview,
Washington, D. C., August 9, 1978 and in a telephone
interview on August 12, 1981.

Boland of Massachusetts, a liberal and a
supporter of civil rights, became chairman
of the Appropriations Committee. This
certainly helped our cause. . . .Also,
around that time Congresswoman Yvonne Burke
of California, and Congressman Louis Stokes
of Ohio (two members of the Congressional
Black Caucus) became members of the Appropriations Committee, and these two members
supported our budget requests. . . .Hence,
I would say that the elevation of

Congressman Boland to chairman of the
Appropriations Committee and the
addition of Representatives Burke and
Stokes in recent years have significantly
contributed to Congress appropriating the
funds that we have requested.[87]

However, it seems appropriate to note here that while
FHEO officials generally agreed that Congress had
given them the funds they had requested, they still
insisted that those funds were inadequate in meeting
their Title VI responsibilities. FHEO officials
explained their seemingly paradoxical contention this
way:

> Before we defend or justify our budget
> before Congress's Appropriations Committees,
> we must defend it first before the depart-
> ment's budget office and then before the
> Office of Management and Budget. Most times
> the department and OMB substantially cut our
> budget. Hence, the (FHEO) budget we present
> to Congress has been cut twice, and is inade-
> quate. . . .Yet we defend this budget because
> it is assumed that the Secretary and her
> assistants will support the President's
> budget.[88]

The Office of Management and Budget, and the budget
office for HUD confirmed the fact that OMB had cut
HUD's FHEO budget. However, the OMB budget examiner
reasoned that "FHEO's budget was cut because there is
no longer a pro-civil rights climate in this country
and [more importantly] because HUD gives low priority
to FHEO."[89] The examiner explained the latter point
this way:

> The United States government operates
> on a zero base budgeting system. Under this
> system, each agency, when it presents its
> budget to OMB, must rank its programs in
> terms of high or low priority. If an agency
> ranks a program high, OMB seldom cut that
> program's budget. However, if an agency
> ranks a program low, OMB usually cut its
> budget. . . .HUD usually designates the
> Fair Housing Equal Opportunity Office as
> low priority, and thus OMB has cut the Fair
> Housing Equal Opportunity Office budget.[90]

Two points should be emphasized here. First, it is important to note the process (and strategy) by which HUD has presented its FHEO budget to Congress. In the last ten years, FHEO's budget requests have been presented to Congress by various persons who have served in the position of Assistant Secretary for Fair Housing and Equal Opportunity. In their budget presentations to Congress, the Assistant Secretaries for FHEO have not requested funds specifically for Title VI, Title VIII or other civil rights activities, but have sought funds under the label "salaries and expenses" for the Fair Housing Equal Opportunity Office. Simply put, FHEO's budget is not broken down in terms of x dollars for Title VI activities, or x dollars for Title VIII activities. Rather, the FHEO budget lumps together Title VI and Title VIII activities under "salaries and expenses" for the FHEO. Most FHEO officials explained the situations by saying that HUD has sought funds for its civil rights activities in this manner because the Fair Housing Equal Opportunity Office was and is viewed as a division and not a program.[91] Ralph Carter, Director of the Fair Housing Equal Opportunity Budget Office, put it this way:

> The FHEO, for the most part, engages in equal opportunity activities; it does not administer housing programs or disburse funds or grants to states and local communities. Because the FHEO neither administers housing programs or disburses grants, it is looked upon as a division and not a program.[92]

Another fascinating aspect about the FHEO's budget presentations to Congress is that officials who have presented the FHEO budget to Congress have emphasized FHEO's Title VIII activities and have largely ignored its Title VI activities. A study of the FHEO's budget presentations to the Congress over the last eight years reveals that in their testimony before the House and Senate Appropriations Committees, the Assistant Secretaries for FHEO have accentuated FHEO's actions to 1) process Title VIII complaints in an expeditious manner; 2) eliminate the backlog of Title VIII complaints; and 3) make the Title VIII voluntary compliance program more effective. The Assistant Secretaries, for the most part, said little or nothing regarding the FHEO's efforts to 1) investigate Title VI complaints in a prompt fashion; 2) reduce the Title VI backlog; and 3) upgrade or make more effective the HUD Title VI's voluntary compliance program. Clearly, on the basis of the evidence, it is reasonable to infer that Title VI basically has been ignored by FHEO officials in their budget presentations.

HUD officials explained that they stressed Title VIII rather than Title VI activities because the FHEO was created by Civil Rights Act of 1968 and not Title VI of the 1964 Act. Also, officials contended that they emphasized "Title VIII rather than Title VI activities before the Appropriations Committees because Title VIII covers 80% of the nation's housing while Title VI covers less than 10% of all housing.[93]

While appropriation hearings are used as forums by executive agencies to defend, explain, and justify their budget requests, they may also be used by members of appropriation committees to exert pressure on agencies or to determine whether agency actions will adversely affect their constituents. Consider, for example, the exchange between Congressmen Lawrence Coughlin (Democrat of Philadelphia), a member of the Subcommittee on Appropriation for HUD, and Chester McGuire, Assistant Secretary for FHEO during HUD's appropriation hearings for fiscal year 1979.

> Mr. Coughlin: I know HUD is receiving a lot of press in my home town on charges that several of the programs favor Caucasians in violation of federal law (Title VI).

> Mr. McGuire: We have done an extensive analysis of the civil rights compliance activity of the City of Philadelphia. Right now, we are putting together final recommendations which would go the the city.

> Mr. Coughlin: Have you read the various accounts in the media?

> Mr. McGuire: Several of them.

> Mr. Coughlin: Do you expect your final report to be substantially similar to your preliminary report as reported in those press accounts?

> Mr. McGuire: I think the major findings will stand. Certainly anything that we have misinterpreted or misread would be either eliminated or changed. This is

what we are doing now.

Mr. Coughlin: Is HUD considering suspending Philadelphia's Community Development funding?

Mr. McGuire: No. I do not think we have to look forward to a situation where we go way down the road and actually terminate the benefits to the citizens.

Mr. Coughlin: As you know, I am a member of a minority in Philadelphia, too. Thank you.[94]

The exchange between Congressman Coughlin and Secretary McGuire is fascinating in that it illustrates that the Congressmen was implicitly using HUD's appropriation hearings to pressure the Assistant Secretary not to take action which would negatively affect his (the Congressman) constitutents. Also, the exchange between Congressman Coughlin and Secretary McGuire lend support to Wildavsky's observation that:

> Where their constituencies are affected, appropriation committee members use all the leverage over men and money which their positions give them to secure favorable outcomes.[95]

2. _Legislation_. Legislation is another factor which fosters bureaucratic-legislative contact. Over the years, Congress, by enacting legislation, has continued to show interest in HUD's civil rights enforcement effort. The question that arises is whether Congress via legislation has helped or hindered HUD's efforts to implement Title VI. By and large, the evidence seemingly suggests that Congress through the enactment of legislation has generally helped HUD in some instances, but has hurt in others. Congress generally seemed to help HUD's Title VI operations when it enacted the Open Housing Act of 1968 and the Housing Community and Development Act of 1974, two statutes which banned discrimination based on race, sex, religion and the handicap. However, Congress seemingly impeded HUD's Title VI operations when it failed in 1980 to pass a fair housing bill that would have strengthened HUD's ability to enforce the Open Housing Act of 1968. As expected, civil rights officials at HUD generally agreed that Congress via legislation had facilitated HUD's enforcement of Title VI when it passed the Open Housing Act of 1968 and the Housing and Community Development Act of 1974.

However, these officials stressed that Congress had not helped HUD's civil rights operations when it exhibited no support for civil rights by declining to pass the 1980 Fair Housing measure. By failing to pass this proposal, one official observed, Congress had created an environment that was not conducive for enforcing any civil rights law including Title VI.

3. Oversight hearings. Over the years Congress has continued to express an interest in HUD's implementation of Title VI. For example, in 1972 and in 1976, Congress's Civil Rights Oversight Committees conducted hearings concerning HUD's efforts to enforce Title VI. As these hearings, congressmen supportive of HUD's efforts to implement Title VI have urged HUD to vigorously enforce this statute by terminating the funds of housing officials guilty of violating this law. But congressmen opposed to HUD's endeavors to implement Title VI called on HUD not to aggressively enforce this statute. More specifically, at the hearing in 1972, Representative John Conyers (Democrat, Michigan, and a member of the Congressional Black Caucus) pointed out that the Civil Rights Commission Reports had repeatedly documented the fact that HUD had continually neglected to implement Title VI and urged the Secretary of HUD to take steps to ensure that Title VI would be vigorously enforced.

In direct contrast, at the hearing in 1976, Senator Harry Byrd of West Virginia noted that HUD was investigating housing officials in his district for violating Title VI, and called on HUD officials to cease their investigation. Byrd contended that he knew for certain that his constituents were abiding by the mandates of that law.

Generally, civil rights officials at HUD emphasized that Congress had helped their civil rights enforcement operations in some instances but had hurt in others. By enacting the Open Housing Act of 1968 and the Housing and Community Development Act of 1974, officials contended Congress had indirectly declared its support for their efforts to combat discrimination. However, these officials quickly stressed that Congress had impeded their civil rights operations by seeking to block their Title VI investigations. How have courts affected HUD's Title VI enforcement efforts? We address this question in the next section.

106

The Impact of Judicial Activity
On HUD's Title VI Enforcement Operations

By and large, there have been few cases concerning HUD's Title VI enforcement operations, and the court rulings have been mixed. Indeed, some court rulings have encouraged HUD to vigorously implement Title VI, while others have tended to impede enforcement. First let us look at cases that have called for vigorous Title VI enforcement. Consider, for example, the case of Hicks et al. v Weaver. In Hicks, a group of blacks sought to block the construction of federally assisted, low-rent public housing projects at various sites in Bogalusa, Louisiana "on the grounds that the sites selected for construction would perpetuate segregation, thus resulting in a violation of Title VI."[96] Specifically, Hicks alleged that HUD's Title VI policy forbids the construction of federally financed public housing in all black neighborhoods, but he stressed that the proposed locations for the housing projects in Bogalusa would violate Title VI in that the units were to be located in predominantly black neighborhoods. Further, Hicks charged that HUD officials were acutely aware of the fact that proposed public housing sites in Bogalusa woudl be constructed in all black neighborhoods, and consequently would violate Title VI.

Basically, there were two issues before the court: 1) would the proposed public housing sites perpetuate segregation and thus result in a violation of Title VI, and 2) were HUD officials cognizant of the fact that the proposed housing units would be located in predominantly black neighborhoods, thus violating HUD's Title VI policy. The court ruled that the proposed public housing sites would perpetuate segregation, thus violate Title VI. Also, the court held that HUD officials were aware of the situation in Bogalusa and knew that the construction of the proposed low-rent housing units in predominantly black neighborhoods would violate HUD Title VI policy.

As a result of its findings, the court ordered HUD to discontinue funding the proposed low-rent housing projects in Bogalusa. Clearly, the court in Hicks et al. v Weaver advocated that HUD vigorously enforce Title VI.

Gautreaux et al. v Romney is another case where the court instructed HUD to vigorously enforce Title VI. In this particular case, Gautreaux et al., a group of blacks charged that George Romney, the Secretary of Housing and Urban Development had violated Title VI when he approved of funding for the construction of Chicago's racially segregated public housing projects. Romney did not contest the charge brought against him; in fact, he sought to justify his decision to fund the construction of Chicago's racially segregated public housing system. Specifically, Romney contended that HUD had funded low-income housing projects in predominantly black areas because 1) there was a desperate need for more low-rent public housing in Chicago, and 2) efforts to locate low-income housing in racially mixed neighborhoods had run into stiff community opposition. Romney maintained that given the desperate need for low-rent housing in Chicago and given community opposition to this type of housing in racially mixed areas, he felt it was better to fund a segregated system than to deny housing altogether.

The court ruled that HUD (or Romney's) approval of funding of segregated housing sites in Chicago was a violation of Title VI and "could not be excused as an attempted accommodation of an admittedly urgent need for housing with the reality of community opposition."[97]

Clearly, the court in Gautreaux v Romney was requiring HUD to adhere to Title VI. The Supreme Court's ruling in the case of The Regents of the University of California v Bakke also seemingly has had a positive impact on HUD's Title VI enforcement operations. In this case, a fragmented Supreme Court ruled 5-4 that a university special admission (or affirmative action) program for minorities discriminated against nonminorities on the basis of race and thus violated Title VI. But the court also ruled, by a 5-4 vote that race was among the factors that could be considered in a university's admission policies.

Civil rights officials at HUD contended that by "endorsing affirmative action for the first time in the Bakke case, the Court had indirectly supported their affirmative action guidelines and regulations which had been increasingly coming under attack as being illegal."[98]

Similarly, the Court's ruling in Kaiser Aluminum Chemical Corporation v Weber may also be viewed as generally supporting HUD's civil rights enforcement effort. In this particular case the Court ruled that "employers and unions could establish voluntary [affirmative action] programs, including the use of quotas, to aid minorities and women in employment, even where there was no evidence of previous discrimination by employers."[99]

Civil rights officers at HUD contended that by upholding Kaiser's affirmative action program, the Court had indirectly given legal support to various affirmative action programs, including HUD's.

In addition, the Supreme Court ruling in Fullilove v Klutznick was perceived as generally supporting HUD's civil rights enforcement effort. In this particular instance, the Court upheld "Congress's authority to make some limited use of racial quotas to remedy past discrimination against black businessmen."[100] HUD officials asserted that the Supreme Court ruling in Fullilove generally created a milieu favorable for enforcing Title VI and Title VIII (The Open Housing Act of 1968).

Thus, some court rulings have been viewed as encouraging HUD to vigorously implement Title VI.

On the other hand, however, the court has rendered decisions which have seemingly discouraged HUD from enforcing Title VI. The City of Cheyenne v Lynn is one such case where the court ruling seemingly discouraged HUD from vigorously implementing Title VI. In this particular case, the City of Cheyenne sought to overturn an administrative law judge ruling that it had operated its model cities programs in a racially discriminatory manner, and thus had violated Title VI. The City of Cheyenne contended that it had not violated Title VI and stressed that the evidence presented by HUD officials at the administrative hearing failed to show conclusively that the City of Cheyenne was guilty of violating the law (Title VI). Consequently, the City charged that the administrative law judge erred when he found the City of Cheyenne in noncompliance with Title VI.

The federal district court of Wyoming ruled that the finding of HUD officials that Cheyenne had violated Title VI was not supported by substantial evidence and that the administrative law judge ruling was clearly erroneous. As a result, the court ordered HUD to discontinue withholding Cheyenne's model cities

funds. Subsequently, HUD appealed to the Federal
Court of Appeals to overturn the district court ruling.
However, the appellate court upheld the ruling of the
federal district court. When this occurred, HUD did
not appeal this case to the U. S. Supreme Court.

Washington v Davis is another case which can
generally be viewed as discouraging HUD from vigorously
enforcing Title VI. Here the court ruled that in order
for minorities to prove that they are the victims of
racial discrimination, they must prove discriminatory
intent. In short, minorities who allege that they are
the victims of racial discrimination must show that
those discriminating against them advertently meant
to do so.

Civil rights officers at HUD believed that the
Court's ruling in Washington v Davis had definitely
made it more difficult for them to enforce Title VI.
They contended that by requiring discriminatory intent
be proven in supporting allegations of discrimination,
the Court had made it difficult for HUD officials to
document discrimination because "documenting purposeful
discrimination is a herculean task and is almost
impossible."[101]

Memphis v Greene is another case which was
perceived as not helping HUD's civil rights operations.
In the case of Memphis v Greene, the Supreme Court
ruled 6-3 that the "city of Memphis, Tennessee, could
block vehicular traffic between a white neighborhood
and a black neighborhood without violating the rights
of black residents."[102] Under controversy here was a
street that ran across both neighborhoods. An all
white community association constructed a physical
barrier to close the street at a certain point between
the neighborhoods. The association central contention
was that "closing the street would cut down traffic
congestion noise and would reduce air pollution."[103]
Nearby black residents, compelled to use other streets
through the white area, sued to halt the closing.
They contended that "the street closing was illegal
and unconstitutional, infringing on property rights
protected by the 1866 Civil Rights Act and constituting
a badge of slavery forbidden by the 13th Amendment,
which abolished slavery."[104]

Justice Stevens, who authored the 6-3 decision,
disagreed with blacks. He contended that "the injury
to blacks which resulted from the street closing was

too trivial to constitute a violation either of the 1866 act or of the 13th Amendment."[105] As far as Stevens was concerned, "the only proven impact on property rights was the need to use one street rather than another."[106] Without any evidence of racial motivation for the city action, he charged, "the street could not be considered a badge of slavery."[107]

The dissenting Justices--Marshall, Brennan and Blackman--asserted that "if one applied a dab of common sense to the evidence in the case it was clear that a group of white citizens had decided to keep Negro citizens from traveling through their urban utopia, and the city has placed its seal of approval on the enclaves."[108]

Civil rights officials at HUD felt that though the Supreme Court's ruling in Memphis v Greene did not pertain to their Title VI activities, "this decision, which seemed to condone subtle racial discrimination, did little to create an environment conducive for enforcing the nondiscriminatory requirements of Title VI."[109]

In general, most HUD officials felt that court decisions had facilitated HUD's enforcement of Title VI in some instances but had inhibited it in others. Let us now highlight how the activities of interest groups have influenced HUD's Title VI operations.

Interest Group Activities and
HUD's Title VI Enforcement Effort

This section examines how interest groups have sought to influence HUD's Title VI enforcement operations, and the political strategies or tactics they have employed to accomplish this objective. There are, to be sure, an array of groups which have endeavored to influence HUD's Title VI enforcement operations, but there have been three groups most active in seeking to achieve this goal. They are the National Association for the Advancement of Colored People, the Leadership Conference on Civil Rights, and the National Committee Against Discrimination in Housing.

The NAACP, for example, not only investigated HUD's enforcement of Title VI and Title VIII (Open Housing Act), but it has also sought to influence

HUD's implementation of these laws.* The NAACP has undertaken to affect HUD's implementation of Title VI by 1) testifying before congressional committees and urging Congressmen to compel HUD to meet its Title VI duties: 2) lobbying "agency officials urging them to use stronger Title VI sanctions;"[110] and 3) taking HUD to court when it believes HUD has been remissful in meeting its Title VI obligations. For example, it was the NAACP which aided Hicks et al. to bring the suit against HUD in Bogalusa. Similarly, the Leadership Conference on Civil Rights not only lobbied Congress to pass the Civil Rights Act of 1964 and 1968, but it has also endeavored to ensure that these statutes are implemented. To be sure, the Leadership Conference has scrutinized HUD's implementation of Title VI of the Civil Rights Act of 1964 and Title VIII of the Civil Rights Act of 1968 and has pinpointed shortcomings in HUD's enforcement of these acts. As a result, the Leadership Conference "has made specific recommendations to HUD officials concerning how HUD can ameliorate its enforcement of Title VI and Title VIII."[111] And just at the NAACP, the Leadership Conference has likewise attempted to affect HUD's Title VI enforcement efforts by appearing before congressional committees, by commenting on HUD's proposed regulations, guidelines, and handbook, and by urging HUD officials to use the termination of funds sanction more frequently to secure compliance with Title VI.

The National Committee Against Discrimination in Housing (hereafter referred to as NCADH) has also taken an interest in HUD efforts to implement Title VI of the Civil Rights Act of 1964 and Title VIII of the Civil Rights Act of 1968. The NCADH has been especially active in seeking to influence how HUD implements Title VI. It has sought to do this by lobbying HUD officials, the courts, and Congress. Specifically, it has attempted to influence HUD's Title VI enforcement effort by sending Title VI memorandums to HUD's local, regional, and national Title VI offices, and "urging HUD officials to

---

*It was the NAACP, together with the Leadership Conference on Civil Rights and the National Committee Against Discrimination in Housing, who lobbied Congress to put teeth into the 1968 Open Housing Act.

withhold funds from recipients who the NCADH believes have violated Title VI."[112]

Besides lobbying HUD officials, the NCADH has also lobbied the courts in its efforts to influence HUD's Title VI enforcement effort. Indeed, on those occasions where HUD officials have rejected the NCADH recommendations that it (HUD) initiate Title VI enforcement proceedings against certain recipients for violating Title VI, the NCADH has gone to federal courts, urging the courts to compel HUD to take actions against HUD recipients guilty of not complying with Title VI.

The NCADH has also lobbied the Congress in seeking to affect HUD's Title VI enforcement effort. In 1972 and in 1976, the NCADH appeared before the House's Civil Rights Oversight Committee and requested that Congress put pressure on HUD to enforce Title VI, because HUD was not taking seriously its Title VI responsibilities.

When HUD's Title VI officials were asked whether interest group activities helped or hindered HUD's implementation of Title VI, most stressed that civil rights group activities have facilitated HUD's implementation of Title VI. More specifically, officials observed that civil rights groups had helped HUD to implement Title VI by pinpointing flaws in HUD's Title VI enforcement operations and recommending ways to rectify those flaws.

Conclusion

This chapter has examined how the Department of Housing and Urban Development has undertaken to implement Title VI of the Civil Rights Act of 1964. Specifically, it has examined the overall effectiveness of the HUD's Title VI operations by focusing on 1) the compliance instruments that HUD has employed in seeking to implement Title VI; 2) the attitudes and the competing and conflicting objectives of HUD officials who are responsible for enforcing Title VI; 3) the impact of executive, legislative, and judicial activities on HUD's Title VI enforcement effort; 4) the impact of clientele and interest group activities on HUD's implementation of Title VI, and 5) the resources HUD has at its disposal. In general, HUD has instituted an array of compliance instruments to

secure compliance with Title VI. But HUD has neglected
to use effectively these instruments, primarily because
of the competing and conflicting objectives of agencies
officials, political pressures, and inadequate staffing.
Moreover, HUD generally has used voluntary compliance
action more frequently than other Title VI sanctions
because of a number of factors. First, key HUD
officials--the Assistant Secretary for Fair Housing
and Equal Opportunity, the Deputy Assistant for Fair
Housing and Equal Opportunity, and the Director of
HUD's Program Compliance Office--believe that the
voluntary compliance sanction is the most effective
means to deter discrimination in federally assisted
programs.   Second, noncomplying recipients often
comply voluntarily with the law rather than risk losing
federal funds. Third, the voluntary compliance sanction does not get agency officials in trouble with
congressmen or mayors. Fourth, the procedures for
using this sanction are not lengthy, cumbersome, and
legalistic. Fifth, the voluntary sanction does not
run counter to HUD's major mission-housing production.
And finally, the sanction does not impact negatively
on intended program beneficiaries.

Overall, this analysis shows that the president
has facilitated HUD's implementation of Title VI in
some instances but has inhibited it in others.
Similarly, actions of the judiciary have helped in
some instances and hurt in others. But, in general,
we have found that activities of the legislative
branch have hampered HUD from vigorously enforcing
Title VI. On the other hand, however, activities of
civil rights interest groups have tended to facilitate
HUD's enforcement of Title VI.

FOOTNOTES

[1]U. S., Department of Housing and Urban Development, HUD on the Move (Washington: Government Printing Office, 1979), p. 7.

[2]Ibid.

[3]Harrell, R. Rodgers, Jr., and Charles S. Bullock, III, Law and Social Change: Civil Rights Laws and Their Consequences (New York: McGraw-Hill, 1972), Chapter 6. Also, see U. S. Commission on Civil Rights, Twenty Years After Brown (Washington: Government Printing Office, December, 1975), Chapter 4 and Gary Orfield, Must We Bus? (Washington: The Brookings Institute, 1977), Chapter 3.

[4]U. S. Commission on Civil Rights, The Status of Civil Rights--1979, (Washington, D. C.: Government Printing Office, 1980), p. 39.

[5]U. S., Department of Justice, The Department of Housing and Urban Development Title VI Enforcement Effort (Washington: The Department of Justice's Federal Program Section, January, 1976), p. 11.

[6]Ibid., p. 12.

[7]Ibid.

[8]Ibid., p. 13.

[9]Ibid.

[10]Statement by Lloyd Henderson, Director of HUD's Voluntary Compliance Office, in a personal interview, Washington, D. C.: August 28, 1978; Kenneth Holbert, Director of HUD's Title VIII Office, in a personal interview, Washington, D. C.: August 29, 1978; Mary Pinkard, Equal Opportunity Specialist, in a personal interview, Washington, D. C.: October 20, 1978.

[11]Ibid.

[12]Statement by Zina Greene, Equal Opportunity Specialist at the Department of Housing and Urban Development, in a personal interview, Washington, D. C.: August 15, 1978; Richard Mapp, Specialist Assistant to the Federal Housing Commissioner, in a

personal interview, Washington, D. C.:   August 29,
1978.

[13]Ibid.

[14]Ibid.

[15]Statement by Larry Pearl, Director of HUD's
Program Compliance (on Title VI) Office, in a personal
interview, (Washington, D. C.:   August 9, 1978; Mildred
Morse, Deputy Director of HUD's Program Compliance
Office, in a personal interview, Washington, D. C.:
August 23, 1978, and August 12, 1981.

[16]Ibid.

[17]Statement by Maxine Cunningham, Director of
the Equal Opportunity Divison--Baltimore Area Office,
in a personal interview, Washington, D. C.:
September 13, 1978; William Walker, Director of Equal
Opportunity Office, Washington, D. C. Area Office, in
a personal interview, Washington, D. C.:   September 11,
1978.

[18]Ibid.

[19]Ibid.

[20]U. S., Department of Justice, The Department of
Housing and Urban Development's Title VI Enforcement
Effort (Washington: The Department of Justice's
Federal Programs Section, August, 1975), p. 41.

[21]Ibid.

[22]Ibid.

[23]U. S., Department of Housing and Urban Develop-
ment, Compliance and Enforcement Procedures for
Title VI of the Civil Rights Act of 1964 (Washington:
Government Printing Office, 1976), p. 5.

[24]Ibid.

[25]Ibid.

[26]Statement by Larry Pearl and Mildred Morse,
op. cit.

[27]Ibid.

116

[28]Statement by Brenda Cleaver, Assistant Title VI Branch Chief in HUD's Regional Office in Philadelphia, PA., in a personal interview, Philadelphia, PA., October 3, 1978; Bob Myers, Title VI Branch Chief in HUD's Regional Office, in a personal interview, Philadelphia, PA., October 4, 1978; Chester McGuire, Assistant Secretary for Fair Housing and Equal Opportunity, in a personal interview, Washington, D. C., July 26, 1978; Tex Wilson, Deputy Assistant Secretary for Fair Housing and Equal Opportunity, in a personal interview, Washington, D. C., August 7, 1978.

[29]Ibid.

[30]Ibid.

[31]Ibid.

[32]Ibid.

[33]U. S., Department of Justice, The Department of Housing and Urban Development's Title VI Enforcement Effort, op. cit., p. 48.

[34]Statement by Tex Wilson and Zina Greene, op. cit.

[35]Ibid.

[36]Ibid.

[37]Ibid.

[38]Statement by Fannie Kizzie, Equal Opportunity Specialist in HUD's Regional Office in Philadelphia, in a personal interview, Philadelphia, PA., October 3, 1978. See also statement by Brenda Cleaver and Bob Myers, op. cit.

[39]Ibid.

[40]Statement by Larry Pearl, Mildred Morse, Brenda Cleaver, and Fannie Kizzie.

[41]Ibid.

[42]Ibid.

[43]U. S., Department of Housing and Urban Development, Compliance and Enforcement Procedures for

<u>Title VI of the Civil Rights Act of 1964</u>, op. cit.,
p. 13.

[44]Ibid.

[45]Ibid.

[46]Ibid.

[47]Ibid.

[48]Statement by Larry Pearl, Mildred Morse, Zina
Greene, Bob Myers, Chester McGuire, op. cit.

[49]Statement by Zina Greene, op. cit.

[50]Ibid.

[51]Statement by Bob Myers, op. cit.

[52]U. S. Commission on Civil Rights, <u>The Federal
Civil Rights Enforcement Effort--1974, Volume VI To
Extend Federal Financial Assistance</u> (Washington:
Government Printing Office, 1974), p. 13.

[53]Ibid.

[54]Statement by Chester McGuire, Tex Wilson, Larry
Pearl, op. cit.

[55]Ibid.

[56]Statement by Zina Greene, op. cit.

[57]Statement by Maxine Cunningham, op. cit.

[58]Statement by Zina Greene, Larry Pearl, and
Richard Mapp, op. cit.

[59]Statement by Zina Greene, op. cit.

[60]Statement by Larry Pearl, op. cit.

[61]Statement by Zina Greene, Richard Mapp, and
Mildred Morse, op. cit.

[62]Statement by Richard Mapp, op. cit.

[63]Statement by Zina Greene, op. cit.

[64]Statement by Chester McGuire, Tex Wilson, Larry Pearl, and William Walker, op. cit.

[65]Ibid.

[66]Statement by Mildred Morse, Brenda Cleaver, and Maxine Cunningham, op. cit.

[67]Statement by Samuel J. Simmons, Former Assistant Secretary for Fair Housing and Equal Opportunity, in a personal interview, Washington, D. C.: July 28, 1978. Also see statement by Mildred Morse, Larry Pearl, Zina Greene, Tex Wilson and Chester McGuire, op. cit.

[68]Statemetn by Zina Greene, op. cit.

[69]Ibid.

[70]Statement by Bob Myers, op. cit.

[71]Statement by Maxine Cunningham, op. cit.

[72]Statement by Mildred Morse, Bob Myers, and Brenda Cleaver, op. cit.

[73]Ibid.

[74]Statement by Brenda Cleaver, op. cit.

[75]Stephen Hess, Organizing the Presidency (Washington, D. C.: The Brookings Institute, 1973), p. 13.

[76]U. S., President, Public Papers of the Presidents: Lyndon Johnson 1965 (Washington: Government Printing Office, 1966), p. 36.

[77]Richard P. Nathan, The Plot that Failed: Nixon and the Administrative Presidency (New York: John Wiley and Sons, 975), pp. 36-37.

[78]U. S. Commission on Civil Rights, The Federal Civil Rights Enforcement Effort--1974, Volume VII: To Preserve, Protect, and Defend the Constitution (Washington: Government Printing Office, June, 1977), p. 29.

[79]Statement by Samuel Simmons, op. cit.

[80]Ibid.

[81] Ibid.

[82] Statement by Bob Myers, Mildred Morse, and Zina Greene, op. cit.

[83] Ibid.

[84] See Footnote 15.

[85] Statement by Samuel Simmons and Larry Pearl, op. cit.

[86] Ibid.

[87] Statement by Samuel Simmons, op. cit.

[88] Statement by Larry Pearl and Zina Greene, op. cit.

[89] Statement by Paul Newton, Office of Management and Budget-- Budget Examiner for the Department of Housing and Urban Development, in a personal interview, Washington, D. C.: September 20, 1978.

[90] Ibid.

[91] Statement by Larry Pearl, Mildred Morse, and Zina Greene, op. cit.

[92] Statement by Ralph Carter, Director of Fair Housing and Equal Opportunity Budget Office, in a personal interview, Washington, D. C.: October 2, 1978.

[93] Statement by Chester McGuire, Tex Wilson, and Samuel Simmons, op. cit.

[94] U. S. Congress, House Commiteee on Appropriations, Subcommittee on Appropriations, _Hearings_, 1979.

[95] Aaron Wildasky, _The Politics of the Budgetary Process_ (New York: Little, Brown, and Co., 1974), p. 48.

[96] _Hicks et al._ v _Weaver_ 302 F Supp. 619 (1969).

[97] _Gautreaux_ v _Romney_ 326 F Supp. 480 (1970).

[98] Statement by Mildred Morse, Brenda Cleaver and Bob Myers, op. cit.

[99]*United Steelworkers of America* v *Weber* 99 S. Ct. 2721 (1979).

[100]*Fullilove* v *Klutznick* 65 L. Ed. 2d 902 (1980), p. 902.

[101]Statement by Brenda Cleaver and Mildred Morse, op. cit.

[102]"City Streets and Civil Rights," *Congressional Quarterly Weekly Report*, April 25, 1981, p. 734.

[103]Ibid.

[104]Ibid.

[105]Ibid.

[106]Ibid.

[107]Ibid.

[108]Ibid.

[109]See Footnote 15.

[110]Statement by William Morris, Attorney for the National Association for the Advancement of Colored People, in a personal interview, Washington, D. C.: October 16, 1978.

[111]Statement by Glendora Sloane, Chairperson of The Leadership Conference for Civil Rights, in a personal interview, Washington, D. C.: October 13, 1978.

[112]Statement by Martin Sloane, General Counsel for the National Committee Against Discrimination in Housing, in a personal interview, Washington, D. C.: August 18, 1978.

CHAPTER V

HEW'S ENFORCEMENT EFFORT:
"PRACTICALLY RUINED FOR DOING ITS JOB"

Our analysis in Chapter IV described how the
Department of Housing and Urban Development had undertaken to implement Title VI. This chapter focuses on
the Department of Health, Education and Welfare's
efforts to enforce this law. As we shall see, HEW,
in contrast to HUD, has been more inclined to apply
stringent sanctions upon discovering non-compliance
with Title VI. Because of this, its (HEW's) enforcement machinery has basically been destroyed. More will
be said about this later. Here we consider: 1) the
resources (e.g., staff and compliance instruments) HEW
has at its disposal; 2) the attitudes and objectives
of HEW officials who are responsible for enforcing
Title VI; 3) the impact of executive, legislative,
and judicial activities on HEW's Title VI enforcement
effort; and 4) the influence on clientele and interest
group activities on HEW's Title VI enforcement
operations.

Established in 1953, the major purpose of the
Department of Health, Education and Welfare is to
assist the President in improving and coordinating
federal activities regarding the education, health,
and welfare status of all Americans. In an attempt
to fulfill its missions, HEW employs 160,000 workers
who administer some 350 programs. These programs
cover the gamut of health, education, and welfare
activities. They provide 1) funds to state and
municipalities to construct hospitals (Hill-Burton);
2) financial assistance to college students (BEOG);
3) grants to states "to develop new methods or techniques for providing state vocational rehabilitation
services for handicapped individuals;"[1] 4) health
insurance coverage for those unable to afford any
other kind of insurance or health care (Medicaid);"[2]
5) low-cost health insurance to the aged and disabled,
social security, and railroad retirement beneficiaries
(Medicare);[3] 6) aid to culturally deprived youngsters
either before they reach public shcools, or in their
first few years in the classroom (Project Head Start
and Follow Through);[4] and 7) welfare assistance to the
aged, disabled, and impoverished (SSIP).

HEW also has numerous civil rights responsibilities. These responsibilities are included in various
federal laws and executive orders that prohibit
discrimination in federally assisted and federally
funded programs against persons on account of race,
age, sex, or against the physically or mentally
handicapped. For example, the Public Health Service
Act of 1973 forbids discrimination on the basis of sex
in admission to health-related training programs.
Executive Order 11245, prohibits employment discrimination on the basis of race, color, sex, religion, and
national origin and requires affirmative action on the
part of government contractors and subcontractors.

Of course, these various programs and the governmental actions which gave rise to them, have been in
response to the pervasive racism and invidious
discrimination suffered by minorities and others in
the health, education, and welfare areas. Let us take
a brief look at the racism and discriminatory practices
in these fields.

Discrimination in Health, Education, and Welfare: A Brief Overview of the Problem

Education: "With all deliberate speed." A brief
look at the history of racial discrimination in
education reveals that, for most of this nation's
history, blacks were blatantly denied the kind of
educational opportunities afforded whites. Moreover,
this denial was accomplished by policies (e.g.,
separate but "equal") adopted by national, state, and
local governments. It was also accomplished by
threatened or actual physical intimidation and
violence. As a result, racial segregation and discrimination in education, just as in other areas, was
quite complete, very rigid, and altogether repressive.
Accounts of these activities are voluminous[5] and need
not be repeated here except to say that it took the
direct action of the Civil Rights Movement, in combina-
tion with vigorous action on the part of the Warren
Court, and on the part of two presidents (Kennedy and
especially Johnson) in order to turn the tide. This
activity resulted in the enactment of measures, such
as Title VI of the 1964 Civil Rights Act designed to
overcome such discriminatory practices.

To be sure, the federal government has made
considerable progress in both the North and South in

furthering equal education opportunities for blacks and other minorities. Still, more needs to be done. The Civil Rights Commission reported in 1980 that racial discrimination in education still continues despite laws outlawing racial segregation in education. Yet, it should be noted that the federal courts have and are taking action to extirpate racial discrimination in education. In fact, the Supreme Court and a number of other federal courts, as far back as 1970, began ordering the busing of school children to dismantle racially segregated school districts. However, there has been intense political and public opposition to busing. The public (for the most part white parents) have expressed their opposition to busing by voting out of office school board members who have endorsed busing, by picketing, and by conducting mass meetings. These are precisely the types of things that white parents did in Los Angeles in 1980 when they objected to and successfully stopped an on-going desegregation plan that resulted in their children being bused to racially integrated schools.*

In some instances busing has led to racial violence. In Boston, for example, black and white students and parents clashed after a federal district judge ordered the Boston school board to bus school children to end the city's dual school systems. And when a court ordered busing to dismantle a racially segregated school system in Lamar, South Carolina, "thirty-five black (elementary) children were mobbed by two hundred white men and women."[6]

Responding to pressure from anti-busing forces, Presidents Nixon, Ford, and Reagan, and a number of congressmen (whose districts were affected by court-order busing) proposed or endorsed legislation to limit busing. However, despite the widespread opposition to busing, some courts, particularly the Supreme Court, continue to order using as a means of dismantling unconstitutional segregated schools. In July 1979 the court ordered school officials in Columbus and Dayton, Ohio, to bus over thirty thousand black and white pupils to bring about school desegregation

---

*The United States Supreme Court is expected to consider a case concerning the busing controversy in Los Angeles in 1981.

in these cities.[7] Similarly, in March 1980, the
Supreme Court ordered school officers in Cleveland,
Ohio to bus thousands of school children in order to
dismantle that city's racially segregated school
system.[8] Still, in spite of such court efforts to
eliminate racially segregated school systems, racial
discrimination in education persists. The Civil Rights
Commission reported in February 1979 that "46% of all
students in the United States still attend racially
segregated schools."[9]

Health. A brief analysis of racial discrimination
in the health field reveals that like education,
policies adopted by the local, state, and national
governments fostered racial segregation in American
health facilities. As late as 1940, many local and
state hospitals refused to grant black physicians
staff privileges and did not admit black patients
because of racially discriminatory policies. The cycle
of discrimination haunted black doctors in particular.
First, many black physicians could not attend predominantly white medical schools because of the racially
exclusionary policies in these institutions. As a
result, most doctors had to attend one of two black
medical schools--Howard University or Meharry Medical
College. After completing their medical studies,
many black physicians were denied privileges at
predominantly white hospitals because they simply
refused to afford black doctors staff privileges or
they required that in order to acquire staff privileges,
the doctor in question had to be a member of and in
good standing with a local American Medical Association.
Interestingly enough, most local medical societies in
the forties and fifties did not accept black members.
Consequently, black doctors were often compelled to
work at predominantly black hospitals. However,
getting staff privileges at predominantly black hospitals was no guarantee for black physicians, especially
when their directors (who by and large were white)
refused to grant them staff privileges. One black
physician, who had grown up in New Orleans and had
returned to practice medicine, explained why he had
to leave the city after being denied staff privileges
at the predominantly black Charity Hospital. He noted:

I had spent. . .over twenty years
preparing myself to be a qualified
pediatriciam, and I returned to New
Orleans with high hopes. Approximately
95% of Negro infants born in New Orleans
are delivered at Charity Hospital, a tax

126

supported institution. Yet no Negro
physician had been admitted through its
doors, much less on its staff. The
Department Chairman working on my
behalf. . .met opposition on every front.
The final request, that I be permitted
to make ward rounds--in the Negro wards
only--and stand quietly at the foot of
the bed and listen to the discussions, was
also flatly refused. . . .there were few
medical meetings, few discussions, few
forums, in the city that a Negro physician
might attend.[10]

Clearly, in the 40's and 50's things were not good
for black physicians.

Conditions in the health field in the 40's and
50's were also not good for blacks who needed medical
assistance. Many hospitals, as noted earlier, did not
admit blacks, "A 1949 health survey of Chicago
pointed out that a serious problem faced by the Blue
Cross Plan for hospital care in this area is its
inability to fulfill its obligation to the 50,000
Negro subscribers, since they are not accepted by all
member hospitals."[11] Far more common, however, was
the practice of hospitals to maintain racially segregated facilities--wings, rooms, and beds. Commenting
on segregated hospital facilities in Chicago, a black
physician observed:

Many hospitals do admit blacks but do
so on a segregated and discriminating basis.
Some hospitals which do admit Negroes place
them in the oldest rooms, in basements, in
all Negro wings and often there is a quota
system limiting the number of Negro patients
they will admit. . .[12]

This physician's observations were partially substan-
tiated by the United States Public Health Service
Report in 1946, which estimated that "approximately
15,000 out of a total of 1,500,000 hospital beds in
the country were available to black patients."[13]
These national statistics indicate that hospitals
discriminatory policies were widespread. Even more
striking, the statistics seem to indicate that "once
the quota of so called "black beds" were occupied,
blacks were turned away, despite the fact that other
hospital beds were available."[14]

Though blacks had to contend with discriminatory practices in hospitals all over the country, the situation in the South was by far the worse. For example, "though blacks constituted almost half of the population in Virginia, Mississippi, North Carolina, and Virginia, they had access to fewer than one third of the available hospital beds."[15] In Mississippi, "black fathers could not see their newborn because they were not allowed on the floor where the babies were located."[16]

Like local and state governments, the federal government also endorsed hospitals discriminatory policies. Congress, for example, expressed its approval of hospitals' discriminatory practices when it enacted the Hill-Burton Construction Act of 1946. This particular act "provided for the building of hospitals with federal funds, but provided also for separate but equal facilities, resulting in the exclusion of blacks from hospitals for whites."[17] One study of the Hill-Burton Construction Program from 1946 to 1962 found that "federal grants had aided in the construction or remodeling of 89 medical facilities intended for exclusive use of either white or negro persons."[18]

The Department of Health, Education and Welfare also approved of hospitals racially discriminatory policies. Delegated the responsibility to implement the Hill-Burton Construction Act, HEW developed regulations and policies permitting state and federally assisted hospitals "to separate patients within a facility, deny staff privileges to professionally qualified people, and deny training opportunities to residents and interns on the basis of race."[19]

Surely, the policies adopted by the federal government indicated federal support for hospitals discriminatory policies.

It should be stressed that from 1946 to 1962 that blacks (physicians, dentists, patients, the NAACP) did not casually accept hospitals discriminatory policies. Rather, they protested. For example, black physicians, together with the NAACP, picketed medical societies which refused to grant black doctors membership and held sit-ins at hospitals which denied black doctors staff privileges or which did not serve black patients. In addition, black physicians, along with the NAACP, repeatedly urged the federal government to withhold money from state agencies hiding behind the separate but equal clause of the Hill-Burton Act. And they filed suits in Illinois and North Carolina "charging that these states hospitals separate but equal policies violated their rights to equal protection of the laws under the 5th and 14th Amendments of the Constitution."[20]

However, the protests and legal challenges accomplished very little. Admittedly, Kentucky granted black physicians staff privileges after the NAACP picketed many of its hospitals. Still, for the most part, little had changed. After intense lobbying by the NAACP, Congress had refused to drop the separate but equal clause from the Hill-Burton Construction Act, most hospital administrators continued their racially discriminatory policies, and the courts, both state and federal, upheld the legality of the separate but equal doctrine in the field of health.

Despite major setbacks, the NAACP and black physicians continued to challenge the legality of hospitals separate but equal policies. Finally, in 1968, the Fourth Circuit Court of Appeals in Simkins v Moses ruled that the separate but equal doctrine was unconstitutional in the field of health.

In 1964, the United States Congress expressed its support for the Simkins decision when it enacted Title VI of the Civil Rights Act of 1964. In enacting Title VI, Congress mandated that programs which receive federal assistance could not discriminate on the basis of race, color, or national origin, and authorized agencies to cut off funds to projects which did not comply with the provisions of this statute. The adoption of Title VI meant that hospitals could not receive federal funds and discriminate on the basis of race, color, and national origin.

The Department of Health, Education and Welfare, the agency responsible for administering health programs and Title VI, changed its health regulations to ensure that hospitals would abide by Title VI. For example, under HEW's revised regulations, before hospitals can receive federal assistance they must first sign Title VI assurance forms, promising that 1) "patients would not be segregated within their facilities and that qualified professionals would be admitted as staff and with hospital privileges without

129

respect to race, color, or national origin."[21]

Title VI has had a tremendous effect on altering
many hospitals discriminatory practices. For example,
"over 3,000 hospitals changed discriminatory practices
in order to comply with the nondiscrimination requirements of Title VI."[22] No doubt, considerable progress
has been made in eliminating discrimination in the
health field. However, it is important to note that
evidence abounds which shows that despite the federal
government's efforts to end discrimination in the
health care area, it still exists. For example, the
Comptroller General of the United States, after conducting an extensive study of health care in the
United States in 1972, reported:

> . . .this country has essentially a
> dual health care system for minorities and
> nonminorities. . .minority group patients
> often received their health care from public
> hospitals and were sometimes unaware that
> their Medicare and Medicaid entitled them to
> use private hospitals, and. . .many hospitals
> and nursing homes were treating patients of
> only one race.[23]

And in 1977, a Civil Rights Commission concluded that
in the United States "racial discrimination operates
subtly and overtly, inhibiting access to adequate
health care services."[24]

Welfare. Racial discrimination in welfare
discloses that like education and health, policies
endorsed by both the state and federal government
promoted racial discrimination in the welfare area.
As late as 1960, many Southern states were still
blatantly discriminating against blacks in the field
of welfare. For example, "Alabama, Louisiana, and
Mississippi's welfare offices had separate waiting
rooms and restrooms for blacks and whites,"[25] and
these states nursing homes and mental institutions
assigned patients to rooms on the basis of race.
Even more striking, black community leaders were
systematically excluded from local and state welfare
boards and "black welfare applicants were often
treated discourteously and sometimes were denied
public assistance because of states racially discriminatory welfare practices and policies."[26]

130

Though blacks, particularly the NAACP, protested against states racially discriminatory welfare policies, these protests were largely ignored by both state and federal policy makers. In fact, federal policy makers--Congress and the President--tacitly approved of the discriminatory welfare policies of Southern states by taking no action against states which received federal welfare funds but distributed them on a racially discriminatory basis.

However, in 1964, the federal government did take action to end discrimination in the welfare area when Congress enacted Title VI of the Civil Rights Act of 1964. This particular act banned discrimination in federally assisted programs and authorized agencies to terminate funds to projects which did not comply with the provisions of this statute. Since the enactment of Title VI, both the federal and state governments have moved to eliminate discrimination in federally assisted welfare programs. For example, HEW, the federal agency responsible for administering welfare programs and also responsible for ensuring enforcement of Title VI, has formulated and published guidelines banning discrimination in federally funded welfare projects. Even more important, where states have shown no inclination to abide by Title VI, HEW has shown its determination to enforce Title VI. For example, in 1965 when the state of Alabama welfare office refused to honor the anti-discriminatory provision of Title VI, HEW initiated action to terminate the state's federal funds. However, it should be noted that most states have responded positively to the anti-discriminatory provision of Title VI by including blacks on welfare boards and by abolishing separate waiting and restrooms.

Still, it seems appropriate to emphasize that despite efforts to end racial discrimination in welfare programs, this type of discrimination continues. A Civil Rights Commission study in 1974 reported that "many states which receive federal welfare funds continue to discriminate against blacks and other minorities--Spanish speaking Americans and Orientals."[27]

In general then, though this overall review of discrimination in the education, health, and welfare areas indicate that much progress has been made, it also indicates that many problems of discrimination remain. Hence let us consider how HEW has used

Title VI as a weapon against discrimination based on such factors as race and sex.

HEW's Title VI Organizational Structure

The Secretary of Health, Education, and Welfare is charged with the overall enforcement of the nondiscriminatory provisions of Title VI in all HEW-funded programs. However, in 1964, the bulk of this responsibility was delegated by the Secretary to the Director of the Office for Civil Rights (OCR). Consequently, since this time, the Director of the OCR has been the chief departmental official responsible for enforcing Title VI. As such, the Director "sets the overall direction and priorities for the Office for Civil Rights,"[28] and determines policies and standards for HEW's compliance programs. Additionally, he decides when the OCR can initiate the termination of funds proceedings against noncomplying recipients. However, it should be kept in mind that though the Director of OCR plays a major part in HEW's implementation of Title VI, the Secretary retains the authority to veto any decision made by the Director.

Within the OCR, there are four other offices which are responsible for compliance activities under Title VI. HEW's Compliance and Enforcement Office, which is under the direction of the Deputy Director of OCR, is one such office. It provides policy guidance to regional offices which are responsible for conducting Title VI complaint investigations and compliance reviews. It should be emphasized here that the Compliance and Enforcement Office does not conduct complaint investigations or compliance reviews; rather, it formulates and clarifies guidelines for regional officials who conduct the investigations and compliance reviews. Yet, it is important to note that the Compliance and Enforcement Office does screen the recommendations of its divisions--Elementary and Secondary, Higher Education, and Health and Human Development--and makes final recommendations to the Director regarding cases where noncomplying recipients' funds should be terminated.

Inside the Compliance and Enforcement Office, as noted above, are three divisions--Elementary and

132

Secondary, Higher Education, and Health and Human Development.* Each of these divisions has a director and each has a corresponding office on the regional level. The major missions of the divisions are to monitor and assist their regional counterparts as they (the regional divisions) conduct Title VI investigations and compliance reviews. The divisions seek to accomplish this task by preparing Title VI manuals and memorandums, by periodically reviewing their regional counterparts Title VI operations, and by responding to their corresponding offices' policy inquiries. In addition, the national divisions--Elementary and Secondary, Higher Education, and Health and Human Development--advise their regional counterparts on the strategies and techniques they (the regional staff) can utilize to induce noncomplying recipients to adhere to Title VI, and the national divisions also make recommendations to the Director of the Office of Civil Rights concerning recipients whose funds should be cut off for disobeying Title VI. It seems appropriate to emphasize here that before the national divisions can send out Title VI policy instructions or recommendations to their regional counterparts, they must first obtain the consent of the Director of the Compliance and Enforcement Office and the Director of the OCR. Further, it should be noted that the national divisions seldom if ever actually conduct investigations or reviews. Rather, they merely provide policy guidance to their regional counterparts.

The Office of Standards Policy and Research is another sector of the OCR which assists in the implementation of Title VI. This particular office develops and disseminates compliance policies, assists other units (national divisions) in interpreting policy guidelines and regulations, and designs, collects, and analyzes the results of civil rights surveys conducted by the OCR.

Another division of the Office for Civil Rights which helps with the enforcement of Title VI is the

---

*When HEW was reorganized in 1979, its Office for Civil Rights' elementary, secondary, and higher educations divisions were transferred to the Department of Education. However, that office's human development section was delegated to the Department of Health and Human Services. Despite these changes, these divisions Title VI organizational structures have remained virtually the same.

Management and Administration Office. This office
assists in the preparation of the OCR's budget,
directs and develops Title VI training programs for
the civil rights staff at both the national and
regional levels, and hires new civil rights personnel.
In addition, the Management and Administration Office
maintains records on those recipients who have and
have not filed Title VI assurances (pledges to comply
with the nondiscriminatory provisions of Title VI),
keeps the Office of Compliance and Enforcement informed
about those recipients who refuse to file Title VI
assurances, and often recommends that these recipients'
funds be cut off.

The Program Review and Assistance Office also
helps the Office for Civil Rights with the implementation of Title VI. The major function of this office
is to make sure that program officials (those persons
who disburse federal grants but who do not work in the
OCR) incorporate civil rights requirements into their
programmatic regulations and daily operations. In an
effort to accomplish this goal, the Program Review and
Assistance Office monitors program officials' operations by requiring them to submit quarterly reports,
and to outline actions they have taken to incorporate
civil rights into their regulations and daily
operations.

The Office for Civil Rights has ten regional
offices whose primary responsibility is to investigate
complaints and conduct compliance reviews. Each of
the regional offices has a director for civil rights
who reports directly to the Director of the Compliance
and Enforcement Office in Washington and is the chief
civil rights official on the regional level. It is
the regional director who recommends to the national
office cases for enforcement; i.e., noncomplying
recipients whose funds should be deferred or cut off.

Also, each of the regional offices, as pointed
out earlier, has three major divisions--Elementary
and Secondary, Higher Education, and Health and Human
Development. Each of these divisions conducts complaint investigations and compliance reviews in their
areas of specialization. For example, if the parents
of a fourth grader file a Title VI complaint because
they believe their child has been discriminated
against on the basis of race, this complaint would be
handled by the Elementary and Secondary division. On
the other hand, a complaint filed against a university

would be investigated by the Higher Education division.
Similarly, a Title VI complaint lodged against a
hospital or welfare agency would be examined by the
Health and Human Development division. Besides
carrying out complaint investigations and compliance
reviews, the divisions of Elementary and Secondary
and Higher Education, as well as the Health and Human
Development division conduct negotiations with noncomplying recipients in an attempt to induce them to
voluntarily comply with Title VI. They also determine
when voluntary compliance cannot be achieved, and
recommend to regional director for civil rights those
cases which should be forwarded to the OCR for
enforcement.

To get a better feel of the nature and operations
of an HEW regional office, I visited the regional
office in Philadelphia. Established in 1970, this
office is responsible for supervising Title VI enforcement in the District of Columbia, and in four states--
Maryland, Virginia, Pennsylvania, and West Virginia.

Overall, HEW's Title VI organizational structure
may be graphically illustrated as follows:

(1) Secretary of HEW

(2) HEW's Reviewing Authority

(3) Director of the Office for
    Civil Rights

(4) Deputy Director of the Office
    for Civil Rights

(5) National Office Civil Rights
    Directors (Elementary
    Education, Higher Education
    and Health and Social
    Welfare

(6) Regional Director for
    Civil Rights

(7) Regional Office Civil
    Rights Divisions Chiefs
    (Elementary Education
    and Health and Human
    Development

1. The handbook situation. Basically, HEW has
used an array of instruments in its efforts to implement Title VI. First, since 1965 it has developed a
variety of guidelines, manuals, and memorandums for
the guidance of officials charged with Title VI.[29]
Specifically, these materials outline 1) the procedures
and techniques for conducting Title VI complaint
investigations and compliance reviews, 2) the types
of documentation which are needed for proving a recipient has violated Title VI, and 3) the conditions
under which HEW officials should employ Title VI
sanctions. In addition, this collection of materials
indicates the steps HEW has taken to ensure the
enforcement of Title VI. However, it is important to
note that though HEW has issued these various guidelines, manuals, and memorandums for implementing
Title VI, it has failed to develop these materials
into a single document--i.e., a Title VI handbook--
which would outline a uniform set of guidelines and
procedures for enforcing Title VI. Among other things,
this would provide an opportunity to clarify conflicts
or confusion that might exist in the various rules,
procedures and guidelines. Why has HEW failed to
undertake such a project? This question was actually
put to HEW officials who gave varying responses. One
group of officials pointed out that a handbook had not
been developed because there had been "little time"[30]
to devote to such a project. These officials reasoned
that "over the years HEW's civil rights office had
operated and still does operate on a crisis basis and
thus has had little or no time to devote to developing
and publishing a Title VI handbook."[31]

However, another group of officials suggested
that HEW had not developed a Title VI handbook because
of "politics."[32] These officials suggested that "in
the past when HEW had formulated and published Title
VI guidelines, such as in 1966, Congress had applied
intense political pressure, compelling the agency
(HEW) to weaken its guidelines."[33] Consequently, these
officials explained, "HEW is bent on avoiding political
pressure and has opted not to develop a Title VI handbook [for fear] that the development and publication
of [such a document] would attract political
pressure."[34]

While it may be debatable whether "lack of time" or "politics" or both had prevented HEW from developing a Title VI handbook, one thing does seem certain and that is that "HEW's failure to develop a handbook has not helped its Title VI enforcement effort."[35] This point was emphasized again and again by civil rights officials in HEW's regional office in Philadelphia. These officials stressed that "a Title VI handbook is needed because current guidelines, manuals and memorandums for enforcing Title VI are conflicting and confusing and do not facilitate vigorous enforcement of Title VI."[36] One veteran civil rights official in HEW's regional office in Philadelphia commented in some detail on why HEW's current procedures for enforcing Title VI are inadequate and why there is a definite need for a Title VI handbook. He commented:

> The guidelines, manuals and memorandums that have been sent to us from the national office have been conflicting and confusing. The reasons for this are that there has been a lack of leadership in the national office, and this national office has failed to develop a Title VI handbook. There have been. . .at least seven Directors of the Office of Civil Rights since the enactment of Title VI. Each director has had his (or her) own policies and procedures for enforcing Title VI. Consequently, Title VI guidelines, manuals and memorandums have been subject to varied interpretations. . . . Different standards have been developed for enforcing this statute. For example, some directors told us that in order to prove discrimination, we needed to prove intent; . . .others have told us that we did not have to prove intent; rather we need only prove disparate effect to document discrimination. . . .Title VI policy is in a continuous state of flux. . . .It is often unclear what policies or procedures we should follow; . . .sometimes memorandums are lost or misplaced; . . .the lack of clarity in regard to Title VI policy often delays Title VI investigations and compliance reviews. . . .If we had a Title VI handbook many problems could be solved. With a handbook we could go to court to block constant changes in Title VI policies and procedures. . . .Federal courts have looked

with disfavor on efforts to change agencies'
published handbooks and procedures. . . .
With a Title VI handbook, we would not have
to wait weeks or months to hear from the
national office concerning a particular
Title VI policy procedure. Instead, we
would have the answer at our fingertips. . . .
Further, a Title VI handbook would allow us
to give better directions to [HEW] recipients
and would give us some defense when they
[recipients] charge that we have not published
our guidelines or they are arbitrary and
capricious. . . .Under current arrangements,
our recipients do not have a good notion of
what is expected of them, primarily because
we have not sent them any specific guidelines
outlining what they must do to comply with
Title VI. . . .The sad thing about it all is
that we have guidelines but they have not
been published or distributed. . . .Yes, we
have various internal office memorandums,
outlining specifically what a recipient must
do to comply to Title VI. . . .Where we have
accused recipients of violating Title VI,
they have taken us to court, charging we have
not published any guidelines or they are
arbitrary and capricious. . . .In some cases
they [recipients] have been right. . .and
they have won. . . .A Title VI handbook would
help us to prevent noncomplying recipients
from using unpublished and arbitrary guidelines as a defense for their discriminatory
policies.[37]

This official's observations and views were widely
shared by civil rights officials in HEW's regional
office in Philadelphia.

It should be noted that the Civil Rights Commission, which has investigated HEW's Title VI enforcement
operations, has taken the position that "HEW should
develop a Title VI handbook, because its current
guidelines are of little assistance to victims of
discrimination and to HEW recipients and officials who
are responsible for enforcing Title VI."[38] Specifically, the Commission has taken the position that
HEW's failure to adopt a Title VI handbook has meant
that victims of discrimination, in many instances, do
not know how to file Title VI complaints; that recipients have no idea of what their Title VI obligations

are; and that many HEW officials responsible for enforcing Title VI have no clear comprehension of how to conduct complaint investigations and compliance reviews.

2. <u>The Survey Technique</u>. Surveys represent another compliance instrument used by HEW. These surveys are designed to ascertain whether recipients are abiding by the provisions of Title VI. Every two years HEW sends out civil rights survey forms to various recipients such as educational institutions and hospitals to determine whether they are administering their programs on a nondiscriminatory basis. For example, in its bi-annual civil rights survey of elementary and secondary schools, HEW requires school districts to report by race and ethnicity the following: "pupil membership for the individual school, the number of pupils retained in the same grade they attended the previous years, the number of students suspended and the total number of days suspended, the number of students placed in special classes--educable mentally retarded, trainable mentally retarded, expulsion statistics for the system, and full- and part-time professional and instructional staff."[39] Similarly, in its bi-annual survey of colleges and universities, HEW requires college and university officials to submit racial and ethnic data on the composition of their faculty and their student enrollment. In addition, the survey examines the recruitment practices of colleges and universities in order to determine whether attempts are made to attract minorities. And in its civil rights survey of hospitals, HEW collects racial and ethnic data on patients, staff, and population served. The hospital survey seeks to assess whether patients are assigned to rooms or wards on the basis of race. According to HEW officials, "the civil rights surveys are important because they can provide adequate basis for identifying actual or possible discrimination, thereby pinpointing programs, facilities, and services which require more intensive scrutiny and/or enforcement."[40]

Two points need to be stressed about HEW's civil rights survey. First, though HEW is supposed to conduct all civil rights surveys--elementary and secondary, higher education and health and human development--on a bi-annual basis, it has, by and large, conducted only the elementary and secondary survey according to schedule. Put another way, HEW has conducted more surveys of elementary and secondary school districts than of colleges and universities and health and welfare institutions. Indeed, the evidence reveals that of the civil rights surveys conducted by HEW from 1966 to 1978, ten were aimed at elementary and secondary school districts, four related to institutions of higher education and two pertained to health and human development facilities.[41] HEW has clearly conducted more civil rights surveys of elementary and secondary school districts than of colleges and universities and health and welfare institutions. The question arises: why has HEW conducted more civil rights surveys of elementary and secondary school districts than of colleges and universities and health and welfare institutions? When asked this question, HEW officials generally agreed that this situation prevailed "because HEW's Office of Management and Administration, which is responsible for conducting civil rights surveys was (and is) understaffed, and had given top priority to conducting the elementary and secondary survey."[42]

It is worth noting that civil rights officials in the Health and Human Development Division stressed that "the fact that HEW had done so few surveys of health and welfare facilities was generally in keeping with the Office for Civil Rights' general neglect of the Health and Human Development Division."[43] These officials explained that historically HEW has stressed civil rights enforcement with respect to education, not health. "The exceedingly small number of civil rights surveys conducted of health and welfare institutions," these officials stated, "is further proof that health takes a back seat to education."[44] Yet, it seems fitting to note here that Title VI officers emphasized that the reorganization of HEW's Office for Civil Rights will change this situation. Indeed, these officers explained that the fact that the Department of Health and Human Services has a civil rights unit specifically dedicated to enforcing Title VI in health and social welfare agencies means that health will now surely get top priority.

A second point that should be mentioned about surveys as compliance mechanisms is that HEW has significantly modified, and in one instance cancelled, its elementary and secondary school civil rights survey because of congressional pressure. Prior to 1977, HEW conducted an annual civil rights survey of 16,000 elementary and secondary school districts. However, for the school year 1977-1978, HEW cancelled

140

its survey of elementary and secondary school districts and for the school year 1978-1979 reduced the number of districts to be surveyed from 16,000 to 3,000. According to Arthur Besner, congressional liaison specialist for HEW's Office for Civil Rights, HEW's decision to modify and in one instance cancel its elementary and secondary civil rights survey "was due to Congressional pressure."[45] To back up his contention, Besner pointed out that "only after HEW gave assurances to the House-Senate conference committee that it would cancel its elementary and secondary survey for the 1977-1978 school year and would reduce the number of districts surveyed for the following school year did the members of the conference committee decide not to adopt a Senate Amendment to HEW appropriation bill which prohibited the use of funds by HEW to conduct an elementary and secondary school survey in 1977-1978."[46]

3. _Assurance pledges_. HEW's policy requiring its recipients--elementary and secondary school districts, colleges and universities, hospitals and welfare agencies--annually to submit Title VI assurance forms (pledges to adhere to Title VI) is another instrument that it employs to enforce Title VI. Under this policy, if an HEW recipient refuses to sign a Title VI assurance form or is found guilty of discriminating, HEW can initiate action to discontinue funding that particular recipient's activities. The effect of HEW's policy that all recipients must file Title VI assurance forms is to put recipients on notice that one of their chief responsibilities is to enforce Title VI and to alert them (recipients) to the fact that failure to comply with Title VI can result in the loss of federal assistance. However, it should be emphasized that while most of HEW's recipients annually file Title VI compliance forms, pledging to adhere to Title VI, "HEW generally has not monitored the bulk of its recipients' activities to determine whether they are complying with the law as promised."[47] In sum, HEW has inordinately relied on paper or verbal assurances as opposed to demonstrated results in evaluating its recipients' Title VI performance.

When asked why they had generally neglected to monitor their recipients' activities, most HEW officials offered two explanations. First, officials explained that they had failed to monitor their recipients' activities "because of their effort to comply with the Adams court order, which directed HEW

to give top priority to eliminating 3,000 (Title VI)
backlog complaints."[48] These officials asserted that
their "efforts to comply with the Adams order had
meant that they had virtually no time to monitor their
recipients' Title VI performance."[49]

HEW officials also emphasized that they had
neglected to monitor their recipients' Title VI activities because "the size of their staff had not kept
pace with their increased civil rights responsibilities."[50] These officials explained that since the
enactment of Title VI, they had become responsible for
enforcing a number of other civil rights statutes:
Title IX of the Education Amendments of 1972, which
prohibits discrimination on the basis of sex in
federally assisted education programs and activities;
Section 504 of the Rehabilitation Act of 1973, which
prohibits discrimination against handicapped persons
in federally assisted programs and acitivities, and
the Age Discrimination Act of 1975, which prohibits
discrimination on the basis of an individual's age in
all federally funded programs. However, these officials stressed that while their civil rights
responsibilities had increased, the size of their
staff had remained either fairly constant or had not
increased in proportion to their new responsibilities.
Consequently, these officials stressed that they have
had less and less time to devote to checking their
recipients' activities.[51]

4. Complaint Investigations. HEW officials
also employ complaint investigations to determine if
its recipients are adhering to the anti-discriminatory
provisions of Title VI. These investigations are
triggered by persons who complain that their rights
under Title VI have been violated. Essentially, a
complaint investigation is an agency inquiry into one
or more of its recipients' activities to determine if
those activities violate Title VI. At this point, it
seems appropriate to raise the following questions:
How many complaints has HEW received and investigated
since the enactment of Title VI? How many times has
HEW found that its recipients were not complying with
the law? What is the extent of HEW's backlog or
carryover complaints? Most of these questions can be
answered by studying Table 5.1 (p. 142).*

---

*Figures are not presented for calendar years
1964 through 1973 because Title VI records for those

Table 5.1. HEW Complaints and Compliance (1974-1980)

Calendar years	Complaints received	Complaints investigated	Backlog complaints	Non-jurisdic- tional complaints	Incomplete complaints	Compliance findings	Noncompliance findings
1974							
ES	152	99	53	4	37	6	52
HE	164	96	68	21	46	23	6
HHD	49	25	24	6	1	2	16
	365	220	145	31	84	31	74
1975							
ES	527	317	210	15	203	11	88
HE	175	120	55	21	66	24	9
HHD	134	80	54	28	16	1	35
	836	517	319	64	285	36	132
1976							
ES	580	342	238	26	191	33	92
HE	211	141	70	30	61	41	9
HHD	180	121	59	48	39	5	29
	971	604	367	104	291	79	130
1977							
ES	699	486	213	38	218	151	79
HE	297	164	92	31	66	49	18
HHD	180	163	58	49	69	26	19
	1,176	813	363	118	353	226	116

143

Table 5.1. HEW Complaints and Compliance (1974-1980)

Calendar years	Complaints received	Complaints investigated	Backlog complaints	Non-jurisdictional complaints	Incomplete complaints	Compliance findings	Noncompliance Findings
1978							
ES	828	437	392	70	193	96	76
HE	374	191	184	40	96	33	20
HHD	462	284	179	112	103	41	26
	1,666	912	755	224	394	170	122
1979							
ES	832	410	320	80	160	111	84
HE	323	205	150	90	84	28	20
HHD	621	300	170	110	100	45	36
	1,776	915	640	280	244	184	**140**
1980							
ES	800	400	350	75	151	123	86
HE	400	200	175	80	68	68	42
HHD	700	350	280	115	88	71	51
	1,900	950	805	270	307	252	179
N	8,690	4,931	3,394	1,091	1,958	978	893

Data were obtained from Clark Lemming, Chief Data Clerk for HEW's Office for Civil Rights. The complaints investigated column was computed by adding the non-jurisdictional complaints, incomplete complaints, compliance findings, and noncompliance findings columns. The data for 1978, 1979, and 1980 are estimates.

ES=Elementary and Secondary Division; HE=Higher Education Division; HHD=Health and Human Development Division; N=Grand total.

Overall, Table 5.1 indicates that the complaints received by HEW's Office for Civil Rights increased substantially from 365 in calendar year 1974 to 1,900 in calendar year 1980. With respect to these increases several questions come to mind: 1) what accounts for the large increase in complaints received by HEW from 1974 to 1975; and 2) what accounts for the substantial increase in complaints received by HEW from 1974-1980. Most HEW officials stated that they did not know what accounted for the large increase in complaints received by HEW from 1974 to 1075. However, they did speculate. These officials suggested that "the increase in complaints from 1974 to 1975 was due to the 1973 Adams Court Order, which directed HEW to eliminate its Title VI backlog, and investigate new complaints in a prompt fashion."[52] They theorized that "because the Adams order received so much media attention, many victims of discrimination became aware of the order and subsequently filed Title VI complaints believing their complaints would be acted on in an expeditious manner."[53]

When HEW officials were asked what accounted for the substantial increase in the complaints HEW received from 1974 to 1980, most stressed that the increase was probably due to the fact that "minorities were becoming more and more aware of their rights under Title VI and thus were increasingly filing complaints when they felt their rights were being violated."[54]

Further, it should be noted that Table 5.1 indicates that the Elementary and Secondary Division of HEW's Office for Civil Rights received more Title VI complaints than that office's Higher Education and Health and Human Development Divisions. According to officials in HEW's Office for Civil Rights, "the Elementary and Secondary Division received more complaints than the other divisions--Higher Education and Health and Human Development--because HEW had placed greater emphasis on combatting discrimination in elementary and secondary school districts than it had in colleges and universities and health and

---

years were not kept or were incomplete. Clark Lemming, Chief Data Analyst for HEW's Office for Civil Rights, observed that prior to 1974, HEW officials did not keep Title VI records and stressed that those which were kept were inadequate.

welfare facilities."[55] Consequently, the Elementary and Secondary Division had received more complaints than both the Higher Education and Higher Education Divisions.

Who filed Title VI complaints? What are the racial and ethnic characteristics of such persons? Table 5.2 (p. 147) gives a breakdown on the number of blacks and national origin minorities--Spanish speaking Americans and Orientals--who filed Title VI complaints with HEW's Office for Civil Rights from 1974 to 1980.* These data show, for example, that HEW received 365 Title VI complaints in 1974. Of the 365 complaints, 314 were filed by blacks and 51 were filed by national origin minorities--Spanish speaking Americans and Orientals. And of the 1,900 complaints filed with HEW in 1980, twenty-eight were filed by national origin minorities--and 1,872 were filed by blacks.

Overall, Table 5.2 shows that the vast majority of Title VI complaints filed with HEW's Office for Civil Rights came from blacks. Next to blacks in terms of Title VI complaints filed were national origin minorities. And the fact that HEW did not and does not keep a data file on the number of whites who filed Title VI complaints suggest that whites, for the most part, filed fewer Title VI complaints than blacks or national origin minorities.

A comparison of the number of complaints OCR received with the number it investigated indicates that OCR did not investigate all of the complaints it received for calendar years 1974 through 1980 (see Table 5.1). OCR officials asserted that "a shortage of staff prevented them from investigating all of the complaints they had received."[57] And evidence indicates that OCR's backlog complaints has generally increased. Indeed, 38% of the complaints received by OCR are backlog complaints. Why does HEW have such a large number of backlog complaints? When this question was put to officials in HEW's Office for Civil Rights, they cited two reasons. First, OCR officials stressed that "they had such a large number of backlog complaints because they were

---

*It is important to note that HEW does not maintain data files on the number of whites who filed Title VI complaints because "whites seldom file complaints."[56]

146

Table 5.2.* HEW Complaints Filed By Race and National Origin (1974-1980)

Calendar years	Complaints received	Blacks	National origin minorities
1974			
ES	152	131	21
HE	164	141	23
HHD	49	42	7
	365	314	51
1975			
ES	527	453	74
HE	175	151	24
HHD	134	115	19
	836	719	117
1976			
ES	580	499	81
HE	211	182	29
HHD	180	155	25
	971	836	135
1977			
ES	699	701	98
HE	256	220	36
HHD	221	190	31
	1,176	1,011	165
1978			
ES	828	713	115
HE	374	322	52
HHD	462	393	63
	1,666	1,428	230

Table 5.2.* HEW Complaints Filed By Race and National
             Origin (1974-1980)
                   (continued)

Calendar years	Complaints received	Blacks	National origin minorities
1979			
ES	832	810	22
HE	323	317	6
HHD	621	617	4
	1,776	1,734	42
1980			
ES	800	789	11
HE	400	389	11
HHD	700	694	6
	1,900	1,872	28

*Data were obtained from Clark Lemming, Chief
Data Clerk for HEW's Office for Civil Rights.

ES =Elementary and Secondary Division
HE =Higher Education Division
HHD=Health and Human Development Division

understaffed."[58] In effect, officials maintained that they lacked the staff to investigate all complaints and consequently their carryover complaints (or backlog complaints) had increased.

Also, officials emphasized that the _Adams_ court order had contributed to their large Title VI backlog. They asserted that "in their efforts to comply with _Adams_ they had virtually stopped all compliance activities--complaint investigations and compliance reviews."[59] As a result, officials noted, their complaint backlog had increased.

Table 5.1 also lists the number of nonjurisdictional complaints received by OCR for calendar years 1974 through 1980. A nonjurisdictional complaint is a complaint over which OCR lacks jurisdiction. For example, an airline stewardess files a complaint with OCR charging that she lost her job because of racial discrimination. Clearly, in this matter, HEW's Office for Civil Rights has no jurisdiction, for its jurisdiction extends primarily to elementary and secondary school districts, colleges and universities, and hospitals and welfare agencies.

The evidence shows that the number of nonjurisdictional complaints received by OCR have increased. Even more interesting, almost 11% of the complaints received by OCR are nonjurisdictional. Immediately the question arises why OCR has received so many nonjurisdictional complaints. This question was put to OCR officials and they gave two responses. First, officials explained that OCR has received many nonjurisdictional complaints because it is the most visible of the federal government's civil rights agencies. These officials explained that "of all the federal agencies with civil rights responsibilities, OCR had been the most active and most visible,"[60] Consequently, when a person believes that he (or she) has been a victim of any form of discrimination, he (or she) is much more likely to file a complaint with OCR than with any other federal office responsible for enforcing Title VI.

OCR officials also stressed that OCR had received a large number of nonjurisdictional complaints "because OCR and other federal offices and agencies with Title VI responsibilities had neglected to launch an aggressive campaign to inform the general public how and where to file a Title VI complaint."[61]

Also, Table 5.1 indicates the number of incomplete complaints received by HEW's Office for Civil Rights for calendar years 1974 through 1980. An incomplete complaint is one which fails to give OCR the information needed to initiate an investigation. Put another way, "an incomplete complaint is one which does not identify the affected institution or individual alleged to have discriminated in sufficient detail to inform OCR what discrimination occurred and when it occurred to permit HEW to commence an investigation."[62] For example, a student charges that he was the victim of discrimination but neglects to identify how or when he was discriminated against. In this matter, OCR would not have adequate data to process this particular complaint. As a result, this complaint would be categorized as incomplete.

An examination of Table 5.1 suggests that the number of incomplete complaints received by OCR have increased over the years. Even more interesting, the data show that 28% of the complaints received by OCR were incomplete. When OCR officials were asked why OCR had received so many incomplete complaints, most stated that "the public simply did not (and does not) know how to file Title VI complaints."[63] Also, these officials emphasized that OCR had received a large number of incomplete complaints because OCR had not adopted an aggressive campaign of informing the public how to file Title VI complaints.

Furthermore, Table 5.1 shows OCR's findings of compliance and noncompliance for calendar years 1974 through 1980. Perhaps the most striking aspect about OCR's findings for the years 1974 through 1980 is that while OCR's findings of noncompliance exceeded its findings of compliance for 1974 through 1976, for 1977 through 1980, OCR's findings of compliance surpassed its findings of noncompliance. Why have OCR's findings of compliance exceeded its findings of noncompliance for calendar years 1977 through 1980? When asked this question, OCR officials mostly stressed that OCR findings of compliance had surpassed its findings of noncompliance for the last four years "because discrimination has become more subtle and more difficult to prove."[64] One veteran civil rights official in the Elementary and Secondary Division described the situation as follows:

> We are no longer dealing with blatant acts of discrimination. Rather we are

presently contending with more subtle forms
of discrimination which are more difficult
to prove. For example, we have evidence
that minority students are being kept out
of school as a disciplinary measure more
frequently and for longer periods of time
than nonminority students. . . .We have also
evidence that the frequency of expulsions
and suspensions of black, Spanish-surnamed,
Asian Americans, and Native American students is nearly twice that of white
students. . .

The evidence suggests discrimination
but the problem is how do we prove that
minorities are intentionally being kept
out of schools because of racial and
ethnic discrimination. . . .This is a
serious problem that we have yet to
overcome. . . .In many instances, we have
been unable to present hard-core proof that
minority students are being kept out of
schools because of discrimination. As a
result, recipients accused of discriminating
have been found in compliance with the law.[65]

Similarly, a civil rights official at the Health and
Human Development Division pointed out the difficulty
of proving discrimination in hospitals. This official
stated:

The major problem now is not whether
minorities will be admitted to hospitals,
but whether once admitted minorities will
be afforded the same services accorded non-
minorities. Our evidence shows that minorities to a greater degree than nonminorities
are much more likely to be treated by surgeons
in training (residents) as opposed to staff
surgeons. Does this constitute discrimination? We think so because it happens all
over the country. However, our problem is
proving that minorities are being discriminated against. . . .We simply have serious
difficulty proving that hospitals are still
discriminating against minorities.[66]

The observations of the official cited above lend
support to the contention that OCR's findings of
compliance have surpassed its findings of noncompliance

because discrimination has become more difficult to prove.

It should be noted here that civil rights officials in HEW's regional office in Philadelphia repeatedly complained about HEW's stringent evidentiary requirements for proving discrimination. These officials pointed out that "under HEW's evidentiary requirements, they must come up with 'smoking gun' evidence to prove discrimination, which is often very difficult to do."[67] To back up their contention, OCR officials noted how arduous it was under HEW's Title VI requirements to prove that a recipient had discriminatory employment policies. They stressed that in order to prove that a recipient used discriminatory employment policies under HEW's requirements, they would have to demonstrate 1) that the recipient purposely discriminated against the person alleging employment discrimination and 2) would have to show that the dismissal or firing of the person alleging discrimination adversely affected program beneficiaries. A concrete example best illustrates the difficulty of proving employment discrimination under HEW's Title VI requirements. A professor lodges a complaint with OCR contending she lost her job because of racial discrimination. To demonstrate that this professor was a victim of racial discrimination under HEW's requirements, civil rights investigators would have to prove 1) that the university purposely dismissed the professor in question because of race; and 2) that the firing of the professor would adversely affect students. OCR officials pointed out that proving that the professor was intentionally dismissed because of race would be very difficult and that proving that the firing of the professor would adversely affect students would be almost impossible.

Overall, the data presented in Table 5.1 reveal that OCR investigates most but not all of the complaints it receives; that many of the complaints investigated by OCR have been nonjurisdictional and incomplete, and that only a few of the complaints investigated by OCR have resulted in findings of noncompliance.

5. Compliance Reviews. Another technique used by HEW officials to determine if HEW-funded recipients are abiding by Title VI is the compliance review. Basically, a compliance review is a comprehensive, on-site examination of an HEW recipient's policies

and practices to determine whether that recipient is
complying with the nondiscrimination requirements of
Title VI. According to David Tatel, the Director of
the Office of Civil Rights (from 1976-1979) "the
comprehensive compliance review is the most effective
means of enforcing the civil rights statutes and will
often, by comparison with a complaint investigation,
yield the most impact in terms of the number of beneficiaries affected."[68] Given the Director's contention
that the compliance review is the most effective means
of enforcing civil rights laws, it seems fitting here
to examine the number of Title VI compliance reviews
conducted by HEW's Office for Civil Rights. Table 5.3
(below) lists for calendar years 1977, 1978, 1979,
and 1980 the number of compliance reviews conducted
by HEW's Office for Civil Rights. Figures are not
presented for calendar years prior to 1977 because HEW
did not maintain any records on the number of compliance for that time period. HEW conducted 1,299
compliance reviews in calendar year 1977 and 2,029
reviews in 1980.

Table 5.3.* Compliance Reviews Conducted 1977-1980

Calendar years	Compliance reviews
1977	1,299
1978	2,020
1979	1,981
1980	2,029

*Data were obtained from Clark Lemming, Chief
Data Analyst for the Office for Civil Rights.

According to HEW officials, "the major reason for the
increase in the number of reviews conducted by the
Office for Civil Rights was that this office (the
Office for Civil Rights) became more determined to do
more reviews."[69]

It needs to be emphasized here that the available
evidence indicates the HEW has never conducted more

than 2,029 compliance reviews. When this is placed in the broader context that HEW funds 31,000 recipients, it becomes apparent that HEW has conducted a small number of compliance reviews and may have no notion of whether the vast majority of its recipients are abiding by the nondiscrimination requirements of Title VI. But according to HEW officials, the small number of compliance reviews were done for two basic reasons. First, officials stressed that they had conducted a small number of compliance reviews because they lacked the staff to do more reviews. Also, civil rights officials pointed out that the Adams decision, which directed HEW to eliminate 3,000 Title VI backlog complaints in the elementary and secondary divisions of the Office for Civil Rights, had prevented them from doing more compliance reviews. Specifically, these officials reasoned that complying with Adams had meant that they had little time to devote to conducting compliance reviews.

Enforcement Mechanisms

1. Voluntary Compliance. Thus far, the primary focus of this study has been the compliance tools that HEW utilizes in its efforts to detect discrimination. Let us now turn attention to the enforcement instruments or sanctions that HEW uses when it determines that a recipient has violated Title VI. As noted in Chapter I, the Civil Rights Act of 1964 grants agencies four sanctions to induce noncomplying recipients to adhere to the law. These sanctions are voluntary compliance, referring a case to the Justice Department, deferring funds, and terminating funds. Voluntary compliance refers to the efforts of an agency to negotiate with or persuade a noncomplying recipient to obey Title VI before the agency resorts to ther sanctions. If voluntary compliance proves unsuccessful, for example, an agency may opt to refer a case to the Justice Department. Referring a case to the Justice Department usually indicates an agency's decision to file a legal suit against a noncomplying recipient.

When an agency decides not to refer a case to the Justice Department, it may defer a noncomplying recipient's funds; that is, it might delay or postpone a recipient's funds until the recipient takes steps to rectify discriminatory actions.

Finally, an agency might opt to terminate the funds of a noncomplying recipient. Basically, this means withdrawing the funds of a program which violates Title VI.

Obviously, of the fund sanctions that an agency has at its disposal, the least stringent is voluntary compliance and the most stringent is fund termination. The Civil Rights Commission has observced that "fund termination is not only the most austere sanction an agency can utilize, but it is also the most effective means of compelling a noncomplying recipient to abide by Title VI."[70]

A study of HEW's Title VI enforcement record over the last sixteen years reveals that it has inordinately relied on voluntary compliance as the major enforcement technique for gaining compliance with Title VI. Indeed, analysis of how HEW has utilized Title VI sanctions indicates that it has terminated funds 225 times, deferred funds 70 times, referred 13 cases to the Justice Department, and has used voluntary compliance 700 times. Clearly, the evidence shows that HEW has essentially used the voluntary compliance sanction as the key instrument for gaining compliance with Title VI. The question that should be addressed here is why has HEW utilized the voluntary compliance sanction more frequently than any of the other sanctions? OCR officials cited various explanations for this situation. First, officials pointed out that they had used voluntary compliance more frequently than other Title VI sanctions "because of a lack of policy direction from the national Office for Civil Rights."[71] "Prior to 1977," they explained, the national Office for Civil Rights had not provided any policy guidance regarding when and under what conditions they should or should not use voluntary compliance and other Title VI sanctions."[72] Thus, with virtually no policy direction, officials contended that they decided to rely primarily on voluntary compliance as the major sanction for gaining compliance with Title VI.

It should be noted here that Title VI of the Civil Rights Act of 1964 states that agencies with Title VI duties must first use voluntary compliance when they uncover Title VI infractions, and can use other Title VI sanctions only when they have determined that voluntary compliance has proven ineffective in securing compliance with the nondiscriminatory requirements of the law. Clearly, Title VI does not set any specific time frames regarding how long agencies should negotiate with noncomplying recipients before they opt to use other Title VI sanctions. Interestingly enough, HEW did not adopt any specific guidelines regarding the use of Title VI sanctions until 1977, when a federal district court ordered it to develop these guidelines. Prior to this time, civil rights officials had generally relied on voluntary compliance as sole instrument for implementing Title VI because the OCR had neglected to adopt specific guidelines detailing how long compliance officers should negotiate with noncomplying recipients before they concluded that other Title VI sanctions should be utilized.

Politics is another reason why HEW has utilized the voluntary compliance sanction more frequently than other sanctions. OCR officials emphasized over and over again that HEW had employed the voluntary compliance sanction more often than other sanctions because of political considerations. These officials explained that "as long as they used voluntary compliance, they did not have to contend with political pressure from Congress and the White House."[73] However, they stressed that "when they attempted to defer or terminate the funds of a Congressman's constituents, they had to cope with intense political pressure from both Congress and White House."[74]

Indeed, there is evidence that when HEW officials have used or have sought to use the deferral of funds and the termination of funds sanctions, Congress and the White House have applied political pressure. Consider, for example, the case of Chicago, Illinois in 1965. Here HEW officials had determined that Chicago schools were violating Title VI. As a result, they attempted to convince Chicago's school officials to voluntarily comply with Title VI. When school officials refused to do so, agency officials deferred Chicago's schools funds. When HEW took this action, the Mayor of Chicago, Richard Daley, and a number of Congressmen from Chicago demanded that President Johnson order HEW to release Chicago's funds. The president did just that. In short, President Johnson ordered HEW to fund Chicago's schools, even though civil rights officials at HEW had concluded that Chicago's schools were blatantly violating Title VI.[75]

The case of Jackson, Mississippi in 1969 is another example where Congress and the White House have applied political pressure when civil rights officials have attempted to enforce Title VI. In this particular case, civil rights officials at HEW had determined that Jackson's public schools were violating Title VI. As a result, they attempted to persuade Jackson school officials to voluntarily comply with Title VI. When school officials refused to do so, HEW initiated action to terminate the city's school funds. When HEW took this action, the Mayor of Jackson and the Congressmen from the state called on President Nixon to prevent HEW from terminating Jackson's school funds. The President responded favorably to this request. In effect, President Nixon ordered HEW not to terminate Jackson's school funds, in spite of the fact that civil rights officials had found that Jackson's schools were not complying with the anti-discriminatory provisions of Title VI.[76]

The cases in Chicago and Jackson clearly illustrate that the White House and Congress have exerted political pressure when HEW has endeavored to vigorously implement Title VI. Also, these cases show that Presidents Johnson and Nixon directed HEW to violate the law by ordering it to fund segregated school systems.

It seems appropriate to emphasize here that political pressures concerning civil rights enforcement do not only come from the White House or Congress, but they may also emanate from an agency's director office. Consider what occurred in July, 1979, when Pat Harris (a black) replaced Joe Califano as Secretary of Health, Education and Welfare. Upon becoming the director of this huge agency, Mrs. Harris, in a meeting with civil rights officials at HEW, remarked that "political sensitivity should be considered in pursuing civil rights cases. Her remarks* deeply

---

"Remark by Mrs. Harris Stirs Rift on Politics in Civil Rights Cases," New York Times, August 3, 1979, p. 10.

*Mrs. Harris' comments seemed to be in response to OCR's activities under Califano's leadership. Indeed, under Califano, HEW's civil rights office had alleged that universities in southern states, particularly in North Carolina and Louisiana, were not complying with Title VI. Responding to HEW

upset civil rights officials who construed them as
meaning that the politics should take precedence over
civil rights enforcement. Indeed, David Tatel, the
Director of HEW's Office for Civil Rights was report-
edly so dismayed by Mrs. Harris' comments that this
one factor that supposedly prompted his resignation
several months after the meeting with the new Secretary
of HEW. Similarly, Thomas Atkins, special counsel for
the NAACP, expressed outrage about Mrs. Harris observations. Said he: "we view with alarm, approaching
outrage, any efforts by anyone, including Pat Harris,
to sidetrack, undermine, slow down, or in any way
impede the efforts under way in school desegregation
systems."[78]

In general, it seems clear that the fear of
political pressures influences the type of sanction
that officials utilize in securing compliance with
Title VI. Take, for example, the case of Chicago.
HEW officials pointed out that Chicago schools had
been in noncompliance with Title VI since 1965.
However, officials noted that despite repeated attempts
to convince Chicago to comply with Title VI, as of
September 1981, school officials had refused to honor
the nondiscriminatory requirements of Title VI. When
HEW officials were asked why they had not terminated
Chicago's school funds, most replied that "that cannot
be done."[79] One official summed up the situation this
way:

> People around here are acutely aware of
> the fact that Chicago's schools have been
> violating the law for years. But nobody here
> is going to take any steps to force those
> schools to obey the law, because everybody is
> afraid. . . .People are afraid because they

---

allegations, southern politicians in these states
called on the White House to halt HEW's desegregation
efforts in southern schools, because this could jeopardize President Carter's re-election chances in
these states in 1980. President Carter heeded these
politicians warning because he put pressure on HEW to
cease its desegregation efforts in southern educational
institutions and he fired Joe Califano, the Secretary
of HEW for political reasons.

158

remember what happened in 1965. . . .They
are afraid because Chicago's Congessional
delegation is still very powerful and
carries enormous influence over there at
1600 Pennsylvania Avenue [The White House]
. . .you see, officials here realize that
the minute they seek to commence proceedings to cut off Chicago's schools funds,
Chicago's Congressional delegation would
go over to 1600 Pennsylvania Avenue and
would urge the President to block HEW's
Title VI proceedings. . .There is no doubt
in anybody's mind here that once that
happens, the President, without hesitation
would order the Secretary [of HEW] to stop
Title VI proceedings against Chicago.[80]

Basically, the evidence indicates that the fear
of political pressure influences the type of sanction
OCR officials are subject to employ.

Deferring funds and terminating funds. Sanctions
such as the deferral of funds and the termination of
funds are rarely used because they run counter to HEW's
major missions--disbursing funds to elementary and
secondary school districts, colleges and universities,
hospitals and welfare agencies. OCR officials emphasized that when they recommended the funds of
noncomplying recipients be deferred or terminated,
their recommendations were disregarded. This occurred,
they felt, because "HEW's Secretary, Joe Califano and
program officials are primarily concerned about funding
elementary and secondary schools, colleges and universities, hospitals and welfare agencies [and are not
concerned with] civil rights enforcement."[81] One civil
rights official summed up the situation this way:

Keep the money flowing is the dominant
philosophy here at HEW. Needless to say,
this philosophy has been adopted and strongly
supported by the Secretary and program officials. As a result, our efforts [civil
rights officials] to postpose or terminate
the funds of recipients who have broken the
law have caused conflicts with program
officials. . . .Unfortunately, when these
conflicts have arisen, they have been solved
by the Secretary, and most times he has not
supported our position. . . .He has not

159

supported us because like program officials,
he is opposed to efforts that will disrupt
the flow of funds to HEW recipients.[82]

This view that HEW was and is primarily concerned about
funding elementary and secondary school districts,
colleges and universities, and hospitals and welfare
agencies, and not civil rights enforcement was generally shared by civil rights officials in HEW's Office
for Civil Rights.

Termination of Funds. The fact that various
Secretaries of HEW--Richardson, Weinberger, Matthews,
Califano, Harris, Bell, and Schweiker--have taken the
position that the termination of funds was (and is)
not an effective means to deter discrimination in
federally assisted programs may explain why HEW has
not frequently used the termination of funds sanction.
HEW secretaries generally have taken the position that
"the termination of funds sanction was (and is) not an
effective means to deter funds in federally assisted
programs because it adversely affects intended program
beneficiaries--black and white minorities."[83] Essentially, HEW secretaries have emphasized that the
termination of funds sanction was (and is) ineffective
because it merely ends a federal program and the
intended beneficiaries of that program are hurt.

That various secretaries of HEW have adopted this
view is significant since these officials, by virtue
of their position, have had (and have) the authority
and opportunity to veto attempts to apply the termination of funds sanction.

It is worth noting here that this general view--
that the termination of funds sanction was (and is) an
ineffective means for implementing Title VI--seemingly
has had an impact on HEW's usage of this sanction.
For example, "HEW has not utilized the termination of
funds since 1973."[84] According to OCR officials, HEW
had not used the termination of funds sanction since
1973 because the "Secretaries of HEW generally have
not given their approval to recommendations to cut off
the funds of noncomplying recipients."[85] These officials explained that when they had recommended that
noncomplying recipients' funds be terminated, "the
secretaries had either ignored their recommendations
or had vetoed them"[86]

160

There is some evidence to support OCR's officials' contention. The Civil Rights Commission, which over the years has investigated HEW's Title VI operations, has consistently found that since 1968, HEW's secretaries have generally been reluctant or have simply refused to terminate the funds of recipients found in noncompliance with Title VI. For example, in its 1974 study of HEW's Title VI program, the Civil Rights Commission criticized HEW's Secretary Casper Weinberger for refusing to use the termination of funds sanction against HEW recipients which had been found in noncompliance with Title VI for over three years. And in its 1979 study of HEW's Title VI machinery, the Commission sharply criticized HEW's Secretary, Joseph Califano, for virtually ignoring for twenty-one months the recommendations of OCR officials that certain noncomplying recipients' funds be terminated.

It seems appropriate to note here that though the secretaries of HEW generally have taken the stance that terminating funds was (and is) not an effective means to deter discrimination in federally assisted programs, OCR officials, including the director, and deputy director of the OCR, and the regional director for civil rights at HEW's regional office in Philadelphia have taken the opposing position. In short, OCR officials unanimously concurred that the termination of funds sanction was the most effective method for combatting discrimination in federally financed programs. These officials reasoned that "only when noncomplying recipients feel threatened that they will lose federal monies or actually lose funds, do they take action to comply with Title VI."[87] Otherwise, officials explained, "noncomplying recipients will halfheartedly comply with Title VI or simply will disregard HEW directives ordering them to rectify acts of discrimination."[88]

Given OCR officials' belief that terminating funds was an effective means of securing compliance with Title VI, the question arises as to whether using the termination of funds sanction might adversely affect intended program beneficiaries--blacks, Spanish speaking American, Orientals, and impoverished whites. Most officials replied that cutting off a noncomplying recipients' funds would most definitely hurt minorities. However, OCR officials quickly pointed out that "while minorities would be hurt by the usage termination of funds sanction, they would be hurt even more

if they [OCR officials] would take no action to
correct acts of discrimination."[89]

Further, OCR officials explained that even though
minorities would be hurt by the usage of termination of
funds sanction, they would not be adversely affected
for any long period of time because noncomplying recipients quickly abide by the law once their funds are
cut off.

The fact that the procedures for terminating
funds are very cumbersome and lengthy is another reason
why HEW has rarely utilized the termination of funds
sanction. Many OCR officials emphasized that they
"had used the termination of funds sanction so infre-
quently because the processes for using this sanction
are burdensome and time consuming."[90] Certainly, the
evidence corroborates these officials contention that
the procedures for implementing Title VI are cumbersome
and protracted. Before OCR officials (or civil rights
officials) can terminate funds, they must first negotiate with a noncomplying recipient for 115 days. If
after 115 days OCR regional officials have failed to
convince a noncomplying recipient to abide by Title VI,
they must then notify the recipient that the matter is
being referred to the national OCR for formal enforcement proceedings. Once the case reaches the national
office, it examines the case to assess whether there
has been a violation of Title VI. If the national
office determines that there has been a Title VI violation, this office may attempt once more to convince
the noncomplying recipient to voluntarily comply with
Title VI. If these efforts at negotiation fail, the
national office can request that a hearing be held.
However, before a hearing can be held, HEW's general
counsel office must be consulted and the lawyers in
this office usually decide whether there is sufficient
evidence to take the case in question to a hearing.
Assuming the general counsel's office agrees that a
hearing should be held, the consent of the Secretary
of HEW must be obtained. If the Secretary agrees that
there is sufficient evidence to go to a hearing, the
recipient involved is notified and is given 28 days
to prepare its case. The hearing is then held before
an administrative judge. If the judge determines that
the recipient accused of violating Title VI is guilty,
OCR officials still cannot terminate that recipient's
funds. Indeed, the recipient found in noncompliance
with Title VI can then appeal to HEW's Reviewing
Authority, a committee of six lawyers appointed by the

162

Secretary of HEW from outside of the agency. If the Reviewing Authority rejects his appeal, the recipient can then appeal to the Secretary. If the Secretary turns down the noncomplying recipient appeal, the funds of that recipient still cannot be terminated because OCR must then submit the findings of the administrative judge to committees of Congress which have legislative jurisdiction over HEW. Thirty days after submitting its report to Congress, OCR officials may still be prevented from terminating the noncomplying recipient's funds, for if Congress agrees with OCR that the recipient funds should be terminated, the recipient can then appeal to a federal district court to enjoin HEW from terminating its funds. If a federal district judge turns down the recipient appeal, the recipient could then take its case as high as the Supreme Court.

When viewed in the overall context, it becomes quite apparent that the procedures for terminating funds are burdensome and protracted. Indeed, one study has found that "it takes HEW almost three years to terminate a noncomplying recipient's funds."[91]

In general, HEW has used the termination of funds sanction more frequently in the South than in the North. The evidence shows that of the 225 times that HEW has utilized the termination of funds sanction, it has applied this sanction 224 times in the South, but only one time in the North and that was in Ferndale, Michigan in 1973. OCR officials explained that "they had utilized the termination of funds sanction more frequently in the South than in the North because discrimination in the South was more blatant and thus easier to prove."[92] These officials stressed that racial segregation in schools and hospitals in the South was the direct result of laws adopted by Southern legislatures, but emphasized that racial segregation in Northern schools and hospitals was the result of residential segregation. Clearly, officials contended, it was much easier to prove discrimination in the South where state legislatures adopted laws requiring separation of the races.

Further, OCR officials stressed that they had employed the termination of funds more often in the South than in the North because political opposition to HEW's usage of this sanction had been more intense in the North than in the South. These officials stated that "while there had been political opposition

163

to HEW usage of the termination of funds sanction in the South, that opposition was not nearly as intense as it was in the North."[93] Given this intense political opposition to HEW's usage of the termination of funds sanction in the North, officials explained, HEW had been extremely reluctant to use this sanction in that region of the country.

OCR officials surmised that they had encountered more political opposition to their usage of the termination of funds sanction in the North because "Northern Congressmen had deluded themselves that discrimination exists only in the South."[94]

4. Referral of a case to Justice. HEW, as mentioned earlier, has referred only thirteen Title VI cases to the Justice Department. Most OCR officials emphasized that HEW had referred a small number of cases to the Justice Department because the "Civil Rights Division of the Justice Department, which handles Title VI cases, is understaffed and takes an enormous amount of time to take legal action against recipients which have violated Title VI."[95]

There is evidence that the Justice Department is understaffed and takes a considerable amount of time to process Title VI cases. The Center for National Policy Review, which has studied how the Justice Department handles cases referred by HEW, has concluded that the Justice Department lacks the staff to process Title VI cases in an expeditious manner and often take years to take legal action against HEW-funded programs found in noncompliance with Title VI.

The Impact of Executive Activity
  on HEW's Title VI Enforcement Operations

Just as in other areas, it seems that the attitude and posture of the president has some influence on Title VI enforcement operations. Let us take a closer look with respect to the impact of such activity on HEW's enforcement effort.

Johnson, HEW and the bureaucracy. Generally, Lyndon Johnson's very strong and favorable posture toward civil rights was well known. However, as mentioned earlier, Johnson thought highly of some bureaucracies, but lowly of others."[96] Johnson thought highly of HEW. This was made quite manifest by the fact that HEW's budget increased substantially under Johnson. For example, during the Johnson Administration, HEW's budget rose from eight billion dollars in 1965 to sixteen billion dollars in 1968.

That Johnson lobbied for the enactment of various pieces of legislation which increased HEW's responsibilities was another indication of his high regard for HEW. In 1965, for example, Johnson convinced Congress to enact the Elementary and Secondary Education Act, which provided aid to low-income students; the Higher Education Act, which provided aid to colleges and universities; and the Social Security Amendments (which contained the Medicare and Medicaid programs) which provided medical assistance to the aged, disabled and the needy. These pieces of legislation increased HEW responsibilities and its growth.

Johnson also displayed his high regard for HEW in 1966 by endorsing its Title VI guidelines when they came under heavy attack from Congress. In 1966, when HEW issued its Title VI guidelines requiring desegregation of schools and hospitals, Congress criticized the guidelines as being illegal and called on President Johnson to revoke them. However, the President refused to do so, contending HEW's guidelines were legal and that he supported them. HEW officials unanimously agreed that "Johnson's statements and actions had helped HEW's Title VI machinery."[97] In fact, these officials emphasized that Johnson's forceful assertions and actions regarding civil rights in general and Title VI in particular had created an environment conducive to enforcing civil rights laws.

Nixon, HEW, and Title VI. Given Nixon's generally hostile stance toward civil rights as well as his distrust of bureaucracy, it was altogether predictable that he would project a negative attitude toward HEW and its Title VI enforcement efforts. In 1973, for example, the President stated that "domestic agencies like HUD, HEW, and Transportation were too big, too bloated, and too expensive."[98] Further, he pointed out that many of the programs of these agencies could be trimmed down because they had failed. Indeed, Nixon set out to trim many of HEW's programs. Specifically, Nixon asked Congress for reduced funding for higher education facilities, land grant colleges, Hill Burton Hospital Construction programs, regional medical programs, and medical schools. His rationale for seeking to trim many of these programs was that many of them had outlived their usefulness and most were inflationary.

Understandably, then, HEW officials were unanimous in their view that Nixon's posture had severely hindered their Title VI operations. As one veteran official in HEW's Office for Civil Rights observed:

> Nixon practially destroyed our Title VI machinery. He appointed officials to head our civil rights operations who were not genuinely committed to civil rights. . . . He rejected our recommendations to vigorously enforce Title VI. He ordered us not to cut off funds to school districts even though the law required us to do so. He fired Panetta for enforcing the law. . . . He threatened to fire any HEW official who ordered busing. . . .And Nixon's Office of Management and Budget consistently rejected our requests for more staff and money. . . . There is no doubt about it. . . .Nixon's policies had a disastrous effect on civil rights enforcement. He simply made it extremely difficult for us to fulfill our civil rights duties.[99]

This official's observations were widely shared by civil rights officials at HEW's national office in Washington and at its regional office in Philadelphia.

Ford, HEW, and Title VI. In general, Gerald Ford, just like Nixon, adopted a hostile attitude toward civil rights enforcement.

Ford, too, disliked the bureaucracy because he felt it was "too big and too costly and because it interfered unnecessarily in the lives of American citizens."[100] Consequently, that Ford projected an unfriendly attitude toward HEW and its Title VI enforcement efforts came as no surprise. In 1975 and 1976, for example, Ford proposed that Congress cut HEW's budget, contending that "cuts in federal spending were essential to control inflation."[101] Moreover, civil rights officials at HEW had to go to court to induce the Ford Administration to grant them an increase in staff. And after Ford's Office of Management and Budget in 1975 and 1976 rejected their

166

requests for more staff, officials in HEW's Office for Civil Rights filed an affidavit in a federal district court in Washington, D. C., alleging that "the Ford Administration would not provide HEW's Office for Civil Rights with the manpower needed to fulfill its legal obligation to investigate and correct discrimination."[102] Shortly after civil rights officials filed the affidavit, the Office for Management and Budget granted them [HEW officials] part of the staff increase they were seeking.

Most HEW officials believed that Ford as president had inhibited their Title VI enforcement effort. Specifically, officials stressed that "Ford anti-busing statements and his consistent refusal to grant the Office for Civil Rights adequate manpower to meet its civil rights obligations made it extremely difficult for them to implement Title VI."[103]

Carter, HEW, and Title VI. As President, Carter generally helped HEW's Title VI enforcement efforts. For example, Carter's strong endorsement of Title VI, together with his directive to the Justice Department to improve the federal government's overall Title VI operations, indicated strong support for civil rights enforcement.

On the other hand, however, Carter at times vacillated in his support of HEW's Title VI enforcement efforts. For example, Carter's decision to block HEW's efforts to cut off federal funds to the North Carolina University System, despite the system's blatant violations of Title VI, was one indication of his vacillation in civil rights enforcement.[104]

Moreover, though Carter in fiscal year 1979 generally increased funding for HEW's programs, for fiscal years 1980 and 1981, he proposed that Congress reduce funding for many of these programs.

Furthermore, it is interesting to note that while Carter in fiscal year 1979 increased the budget of HEW's Office for Civil Rights, for fiscal years 1980 and 1981, he proposed that Congress reduce that office's budget.

But despite these negative actions, HEW officials thought that President Carter helped their Title VI operations.[105] Specifically, officials pointed out that Carter's generally strong endorsement of Title VI, plus his doubling the size of the Office for Civil Rights' staff, had enabled them to move forcefully in implementing Title VI. At the same time, however, many OCR officials stressed that Carter's budget for 1980, which called for reducing the Office for Civil Rights, certainly did not facilitate vigorous enforcement of Title VI.[106]

Reagan, HEW, and Title VI. Basically, Ronald Reagan, just like his Republican predecessors Ford and Nixon, adopted a hostile attitude toward civil rights enforcement.

Reagan, too, disliked the bureaucracy because he felt it was too large, too costly, unmanageable and interfered unnecessarily in the lives of the American people. As a result, that Reagan has projected a hostile attitude toward HEW comes as no surprise. In fiscal year 1982, Reagan convinced Congress to reduce funds for many HEW programs including Basic Opportunity Grants, Aid to Families of Dependent Children, Medicaid, and the Office for Civil Rights. His rationale for these cuts was that they would ameliorate the economy and help him to balance the federal budget in 1984.

In general, civil rights officials at HEW felt that Reagan had directly and indirectly hindered their Title VI enforcement efforts. These officials explained that "Reagan had directly hurt their Title VI machinery by trimming their civil rights budget."[107] The Reagan budget cuts, civil rights officials asserted, mean that they will not be able to aggressively implement the nondiscriminatory requirements of Title VI.

Furthermore, officials at HEW contended that Reagan had indirectly hampered their Title VI operations by appointing Terrell Bell to head the Department of Education. According to these officials, Secretary Bell had severely crippled their civil rights enforcement operations by ignoring or simply refusing to sign Title VI letters of findings. One veteran Title VI official, who has been at HEW for eighteen years, summed up the situation this way:

Each time we receive an allegation that a recipient has violated Title VI, we go out and investigate that recipient's program

168

> to determine whether it is being operated
> in compliance with the law. After making
> this determination, we send out a letter
> of findings to that recipient informing
> him if his program complies with the law.
> However, before we do this, we need to get
> the signature or consent of the Secretary
> [Bell]. Repeatedly, the Secretary has
> refused to give his consent to or sign
> such letters, even though in many instances
> we have uncovered blatant violations of
> Title VI.[108]

This particular official went on to observe that by
ignoring or refusing to sign these letters of findings,
Secretary Bell seemed to be saying that we can investigate and document discrimination, but we can do nothing
to check it, not even inform the recipient guilty of
violating this law. When asked had he and other Title
VI officers inquired why the Secretary had not acted
on these letters of findings, this officer responded
that they had done so and had discovered "the Secretary was playing games and was not seriously interested
in Title VI enforcement."[109] This Title VI officer
explained the situation as follows:

> When we asked why our letters of findings had
> not been signed, the Secretary's office told
> us they were not signed because they were
> obsolete. As a result, they instructed us
> to redo our investigation. We did so, but
> once again the Secretary refused to sign our
> letters of findings because they were obso-
> lete. . . .In fact, this seems to be the
> game of the Reagan Administration. They will
> not overtly seek to repeal Title VI and
> other civil rights statutes, but they will
> accomplish this desired end by making it
> extremely difficult to enforce these laws.[110]

This civil rights officer's observations were widely
shared by other equal opportunity officers at HEW.

It seems appropriate to note here that Secretary
Bell's office, when contacted about the letters of
findings situation, had no comment.

The Impact of Legislative-Bureaucratic Interactions on Agency Behavior

This section attempts to describe how HEW's interactions with Congress may have helped or hindered its Title VI enforcement efforts. Contact points which foster bureaucratic-legislative interaction include Congressional control over agencies' budgets, legislation, and oversight.

First, let us see how and to what extent funding of HEW's budget requests might have facilitated or inhibited HEW from meeting its Title VI responsibilities. To assess this impact of Congressional funding on HEW's Title VI enforcement effort, I studied HEW's OCR budget requests and Congressional appropriations for fiscal years 1970 through 1980 to determine if Congress had generally allotted, substantially decreased, or pointedly denied the OCR funding requests. In addition, I conducted interviews with OCR staff members to gain their views in this regard.

Table 5.4 (p. 171) lists the Office for Civil Rights budget requests and Congressional appropriations for fiscal years 1970 through 1980. An examination of Table 5.4 indicates that for the most part, Congress has honored OCR's budget requests. Put another way, Congress has generally given HEW the funds it has requested.

HEW officials, it should be noted, pointed out that generally they had no problem getting funds from Congress. Their real difficulty, these officials emphasized, came in obtaining funds from HEW's Budget Office and the Office of Management and Budget, particularly during the Nixon-Ford years. As one veteran civil rights official put it,

> Our problem has not been Congress as far as money is concerned, but the Department's Budget Office and the Office of Management and Budget, especially during the Nixon-Ford years. During the Nixon and Ford Administrations, the Department's budget office and OMB repeatedly refused to give us the staff and money essential for fulfilling our civil rights responsibilities . . . .Both OMB and the Department were consistently slashing our budget requests

Table 5.4.*   Office for Civil Rights' Budget Requests
and Congressional Appropriations (1970-
1980).

Fiscal years	OCR's budget request	Congressional Appropriation
1970	$ 5,259,000	$ 5,259,000
1971	8,581,000	8,581,000
1972	10,830,000	10,830,000
1973	13,587,000	13,587,000
1974	18,747,000	18,747,000
1975	22,861,000	22,207,000
1976	25,147,000	25,339,000
1977	31,304,000	31,304,000
1978	33,307,000	33,307,000
1979	39,612,000	29,612,000
1980	41,986,000	41,986,000

*Data were obtained from Roy McKinney, Budget
Officer for HEW's Office for Civil Rights.

and both seemed bent on crippling our civil
rights operations.[111]

Officials in HEW's Budget Office and the Office of
Management and Budget--Budget Examiner for the OCR
confirmed the contention that the OCR budget was "hit
hard during the Nixon-Ford years."[112]

By contrast, HEW officials noted that under the
Carter Administration both OMB and the Department's
budget office had been more receptive to their budget
requests. These officials observed that under Carter
not only had their budget increased substantially but
the size of their staff had also doubled. While it is
true that the OCR's budget and staff increased

significantly under the Carter Administration, it is
important to emphasize that these increases were due
largely to the 1977 Adams court decree, which directed
HEW to eliminate 3,000 backlog complaints and to
acquire more staff to meet its civil rights responsibilities. But as mentioned earlier, although Carter
increased OCR's budget in fiscal 1977, 1978, and 1979,
for fiscal years 1980 and 1981, he proposed that Congress reduce the Office for Civil Rights' budget.
The decreases for fiscal years 1980 and 1981 were
explained by an OMB official on the basis that popular
support for civil rights had declined and the president
was "generally concerned about reducing governmental
spending."[113]

In any event, when civil rights officials were
asked whether the proposed decrease in their 1980
and 1981 budgets signified that the Carter Administration was becoming less receptive to their budget
requests most replied they "did not know."[114] But one
thing these officials did know was that "the proposed
decrease in their 1980 and 1981 budgets certainly did
not facilitate civil rights enforcement."[115]

Furthermore, it seems important to note here that
OCR officers charged that President Reagan had
decreased their Title VI budget in fiscal year 1981,
and they contended this had crippled their efforts
to implement the nondiscrimination requirements of
Title VI.

Two points should be emphasized here. First, it
is important to note the process (and strategy) by
which HEW has presented its civil rights budget to
Congress, particularly in the last six years. Indeed,
in their budget presentations to Congress, directors
of the OCR have constantly emphasized the impact of
various court decisions on their operations.* These
decisions directed HEW to 1) eliminate 3,000 backlog
complaints; 2) seek more staff and funds from Congress
to meet its civil rights obligations; 3) vigorously
enforce Title VI in Northern and Southern school

---

*Adams v. Richardson 351 F. Supp. 636 (1972).
Adams v. Richardson 356 F. Supp. 92 (1973).
Adams v. Richardson 480 F. 2d. 1159 (1973).
Brown v. Weinberger 417 F. Supp. 1215 (1976).
Brown v. Califano 455 F. Supp. 832 (1977).

districts, and 4) develop a reporting system regarding HEW's compliance activities. Thus, the OCR budget strategy was obvious: stress various court decisions before the House and Senate Appropriatons Committees as the chief justification for acquiring more staff and money. Put another way, OCR directors have used court rulings regarding OCR's enforcement operations to pressure Congress into giving them more resources to fulfill their civil rights duties.

Also, it seems important to point out that during the last six years, the OCR budget presentations to Congress have placed greater emphasis on Section 504 (which bans discrimination against the handicapped) and Title IX (which prohibits sex discrimination) enforcement activities, and have placed less emphasis on Title VI (which prohibits discrimination on the basis of race and national origin) activities. Indeed, a study of OCR's budget presentations over the last six years reveals that increasingly they have devoted time and attention to describing the steps the OCR has taken to enforce Section 504 and Title IX and have devoted less time to outlining that office's efforts to implement Title VI. OCR officials pointed out that more emphasis has been placed on Section 504 and Title IX and less emphasis on Title VI "because OCR had come under considerable pressure to devote more attention to Section 504 and Title IX."[116] These officials explained that in the last six years the handicapped and women groups had gone to court to compel OCR to devote more resources to implementing Section 504 and Title IX.[117] These suits, civil rights officials explained, had resulted in their devoting more and more attention to Section 504 and Title IX compliance activities and less and less attention to Title VI activities. As a result, when OCR officials appeared before Congress in recent years, they emphasized their enforcement activities with respect to Section 504 and Title IX as opposed to Title VI activities.

Other officials suggested that OCR's budget presentations to Congress had placed more emphasis on compliance activities with respect to Section 504 and Title IX than Title VI because they realized that those provisions were not as controversial as Title VI. These officials were aware that Congress was somewhat more supportive of efforts to end handicap and sex discrimination than attempts to eliminate racial discrimination.

While appropriations hearings are used as forums by executive agencies to defend, explain and justify their budget request, they may also be utilized by members of appropriation committes to exert pressure on agencies or to determine whether agencies' action will adversely affect their constituents. Consider, for example, the exchange between Congressmen Robert Michel (Republican of Illinois) a member of the Subcommittee on Appropriation for HEW and David Tatel, Director of the Office for Civil Rights, during HEW's OCR appropriation hearings for fiscal year 1979:

Mr. Michel: My Superintendent of Schools in Peoria tells me that you people are planning on a compliance review of the Peoria school system and they were allotted over 350 man-days for the review. Why in the world would it take that much time to do a review?

Mr. Tatel: The Region V Office for Civil Rights has scheduled a compliance investigation of the Peoria school district. . .starting in April and to be completed before the end of the current fiscal year.

Considering the implications of the complaints against the district and the size of the district, the allotment of 350 person-days is not extravagant.

Mr. Michel: I'd like you to tell me the exact steps you people go through in a review such as this, from beginning to end.

Mr. Tatel: The following are the major steps in the conduct of a compliance review: 1) well in advance of the compliance review, the OCR regional director notifies the super-intendent of the school district that his district has been selected for a review and indicates the authority under which the office is conducting the review. A mutually agreeable on-site date is arranged. 2) The officer assigned to lead the review prepares a detailed proce-dural plan describing the precise issues to be investigated. 3) Members of the on-site team establish a schedule of interviews with school administrators,

174

staff, compliants and interested community groups to discuss the relevant issues. 4) In the course of the review, team members inspect facilities, schools records dealing with such items as employment, assignment, achievement, program policy. 5) In a close-out interview with the superintendent the team reviews the activities they have engaged in, and indicates areas of compliance concern that may have arisen during the course of the review. 6) The letter of findings is sent to the superintendent. If there is a disagreement between the agency and school district about compliance findings, informal negotiations take place, in an attempt to reach an agreement.

Mr. Michel: Why the review of Peoria? I can tell you that we do not have discrimination in Peoria. We may not have the exact balances you people like, but we do not have discrimination. So why the waste of tax dollars to conduct such a review.

Mr. Tatel: The Office for Civil Rights has responsibility to make a prompt investigation whenever a compliance review, report, complaint or any other information indicates a possible failure to comply with the regulation implementing the legislation that the office is authorized to enforce. . .

Since 1973 the Department has received complaints that the Peoria School District. . .has failed to desegregate its school. To this date, the Office for Civil Rights has never made an investigation.[118]

The exchange between Congressmen Michel and Director Tatel is fascinating in that it illustrates that the Congressmen was using HEW's appropriation hearings basically to discourage the Director of the Office for Civil Rights from investigating members of his constituency. Obviously, the Congressman sought to discourage HEW from investigating his constituents because he realized that if HEW uncovered discrimination

in his constituents' school programs, they stood to
lose federal assistance.

However, it should be noted here that despite
Congressman Michel's assurance that there was no
discrimination in Peoria, the Office for Civil Rights
still conducted the investigation of the school system
in the Congressman's district. However, as of
September 1981, the Office for Civil Rights still had
not determined if the Congressman's constituents were
in compliance or noncompliance with Title VI.

Legislation. Legislation is another factor which
fosters bureaucratic-legislative contact. Over the
years, Congress, by enacting various pieces of legislation, has continued to show interest in HEW's Title
VI operations.[119] More specifically, since the enactment of Title VI, Congress has adopted various pieces
of legislation which have had an impact on HEW's Title
VI enforcement effort. For example, in 1966, Congress
adopted the Fountain Amendment, which prohibited the
Commissioner of Education from deferring the funds of
HEW recipients found in noncompliance with Title VI
until a hearing was held. This particular Amendment
had the effect of delaying HEW from taking immediate
action to correct acts of discrimination. Specifically, prior to the adoption of the Fountain Amendment,
when HEW would uncover discrimination in one of its
recipient's programs, it would instantly withhold that
recipient's funds without holding a hearing. However,
under the Fountain Amendment, before HEW can defer a
noncomplying recipient's funds, a hearing has to be
held. In order to hold a hearing, it should be noted,
civil rights officials must get the consent of the
Secretary, HEW's General Counsel Office, and the
Director of the Office for Civil Rights. Getting
these officials' approval usually takes about six or
seven months. Surely the evidence suggests that when
Congress enacted the Fountain Amendment, it precluded
HEW from taking prompt enforcement action against
noncomplying recipients.

Congress has also adopted a number of anti-busing
amendments which have significantly affected HEW's
Title VI operations. In 1974, Congress adopted the
Esch Amendment "which prohibited any federal agency
from ordering the implementation of a desegregation
plan requiring the transportation of students beyond
the schools closest or next closest to their homes
that provide the appropriate grade level and type of

176

education for those students."[120]   In 1975 and 1976,
Congress adopted the Byrd Amendment, which went beyond
the Esch Amendment by forbidding "the use of appropriated funds, directly or indirectly, to require the
transportation of any student to a school other than
one that is nearest the students' homes and offers the
courses of study pursued by the student."[121]   And in
1977, 1978, 1979, and 1980 Congress adopted the
Eagleton-Biden Amendment, which "forbids HEW to require
directly or indirectly, the transportation of any
students to any paired or clustered schools."[122]

     Viewed collectively, these busing amendments
restricted the desegregation techniques that HEW could
utilize in its efforts to dismantle racially segregated
school systems. Specifically, the Congressional anti-
busing amendments banned HEW from ordering the busing
of school children past their neighborhood schools and
banned it from transporting students to paired or
clustered schools for desegregation purposes. The
effect of these anti-busing amendments on HEW's Title
VI operations is striking. For example, before Congressional adoption of the anti-busing amendments,
when HEW would discover that school systems were
unconstitutionally segregated and were receiving
federal assistance, it would take action to dismantle
these school systems. HEW generally would require
racially segregated schools to bus children past their
neighborhood schools or would require them to transport
students to paired or clustered schools to eliminate
racially segregated school systems. If segregated
schools systems refused to abide by HEW's requirement
(i.e., to transport students past their neighborhood
schools or bus them to paired or clustered schools),
HEW would then initiate action to cut off their federal
assistance. However, under the anti-busing amendments,
if HEW finds that federal funds are going to segregated
schools and determines that the only way to end racial
segregation in these schools is to order them to bus
students past their neighborhood schools or transport
them to paired or clustered schools, it could not issue
such an order. Even more striking, under the anti-
busing amendments, HEW is being forced to fund unconstitutional segregated schools. At least, this is the
position taken by the United States Civil Rights Commission, which has observed that "the anti-busing
amendments impair the effectiveness of Title VI by
denying to the Federal Government the important remedy
of cutting off federal funds to unconstitutionally
segregated schools."[123]

In general, civil rights officials emphasized that "anti-busing amendments practically ruined their Title VI operations."[124] As one civil rights official in the Elementary and Secondary Division put it:

> . . .Because illegally segregated school systems are most times the products of illegally segregated housing patterns, the only way that we can dismantle such schools is to transport students from their immediate neighborhoods. . . . Under Title VI we had done this. However, by adopting the anti-busing amendments, Congress has now stopped us from busing students. Congress has told us that we can find out whether schools are illegally segregated, but we can do nothing about them. . . .Surely, by adopting the anti-busing amendments, Congress has ruined our Title VI shop.[125]

Furthermore, these officials underscored the fact that "Congress did not enact anti-busing amendments until HEW started requiring busing in the North."[126] They explained that as long as they were requiring busing only in the South, they had the support of Northern Congressmen; consequently, these officials noted, anti-busing measures proposed by Southern Congressmen were defeated. However, these officials emphasized that when they started ordering busing in the North, a number of Northern Congressmen who had previously supported busing opposed it and sided with the Southern anti-busing forces in Congress. This coalition resulted in the enactment of various anti-busing amendments.

Oversight. That Congress has conducted various oversight hearings pertaining to Title VI is further evidence of its interest in HEW's implementation of this statute. In 1966, 1970, 1971, 1973, 1974, 1975, and 1976 Congress held hearings to assess how HEW had undertaken to enforce Title VI. Of all the Congressional hearings regarding HEW's enforcement of Title VI, the most fascinating was the one held in 1975 by the Senate Education and Labor Committee, which has legislative jurisdiction over the Department of Health, Education and Welfare. This particular hearing was called by Senator Beall of Maryland, a member of the Education and Labor Committee. The striking thing about the hearing was that the only persons present were Senator Beall (of Maryland), a group of public school officials from Maryland who were accused of violating Title VI, and officials from HEW's Office for Civil Rights. Throughout the course of the hearing, the Senator berated HEW officials for alleging that his constituents were not complying with Title VI. The Senator contended that "HEW was wasting the taxpayers' money investigating Maryland schools officials"[126] since these officials were adhering to the law.

Overall, this particular hearing illustrates the extent to which a Congressman will go to discourage HEW from investigating his constituents. Civil rights officials stressed that "in the course of conducting Title VI investigations, they had to contend constantly with congressmen who attempted to delay or prevent them from investigating their constituents."[127] One civil rights official in the Health and Human Development Division pointed out that "a Title VI investigation of eight Louisiana hospitals had lasted approximately eight years because Louisiana's Congressional delegation. . .sought to block the investigation every step of the way."[128]

In general, then, civil rights officials emphasized "the Congress had severely hindered their Title VI enforcement effort by enacting the anti-busing amendments and by taking steps to impede their Title VI investigations."[129]

The Impact of Judicial Activity on HEW's Title VI Enforcement Program

For the most part, there have been a number of cases concerning HEW's Title VI enforcement operations, and the court rulings have been mixed. Indeed, some court rulings have encouraged HEW to vigorously implement Title VI while other court rulings have tended to impede enforcement. First, let us look at cases that have called for vigorous Title VI enforcement. Consider, for example, the case of United States v Jefferson County Board of Education. In Jefferson, several Southern school districts challenged the legality of HEW's Title VI guidelines on two grounds. First, the school districts charged that HEW's Title VI guidelines ran counter to the Supreme Court's Brown v Board of Education in that the HEW guidelines required integration, but Brown v Board of Education

179

did not. Also, the school districts alleged that HEW's desegregation guidelines contravene the Congressional objective of the Civil Rights Act of 1964 in that HEW guidelines mandated assignment of students to public schools in order to overcome racial imbalance.

The school district's challenges were upheld by federal district courts in the South. However, in Jefferson, the United States Justice Department, which had contended in federal district courts that HEW guidelines were legal, asked the Fifth Circuit Court of Appeals to overturn the rulings of federal district courts. And the Court of Appeals responded favorably to the Justice Department request. The Appeals Court held that the lower court had erred in ruling HEW guidelines were not within the rationale of Brown ruling and the Congressional objective of the Civil Rights Act of 1964. Specifically, the Court held that it construed Brown v Board of Education to require integration, a policy endorsed by HEW's guidelines. Further, the Court noted that its reading of legislative debate surrounding the enactment of the 1964 Civil Rights Act compelled it to infer that Congress permitted the assignment of students to public schools in order to overcome racial imbalance, a policy supported by HEW's guidelines.130

Clearly, in Jefferson, the Fifth Circuit Court of Appeals expressed its support for HEW's guidelines by ruling that they were legal, thereby rejecting the arguments of Southern school districts and Congressmen that the guidelines were illegal. The effect of Jefferson was to encourage HEW to vigorously implement Title VI.

Adams et al. v Richardson is another case where the court directed HEW to forcefully implement Title VI. In this particular case, Adams et al., a group of blacks, alleged that HEW had not met its Title VI responsibilities by failure to initiate enforcement proceedings against 200 Southern elementary and secondary school districts and 10 colleges and universities which were not complying with Title VI. Specifically, Adams charged that though HEW was aware that these recipients had already been found in noncompliance with Title VI, "HEW for over three years had either failed to take action against them or had relied solely on voluntary compliance as the chief sanction for inducing these recipients to abide by the law, even though this sanction basically had proved to be ineffective."[131]

HEW responded to the charges by observing that under Title VI, it had unlimited discretion to negotiate with a noncomplying recipient as long as it desired.

The court, however, rejected HEW's contention and sided with Adams. Specifically, the court ruled that HEW had been derelict in meeting its Title VI responsibilities and had limited discretion under Title VI. Indeed, the court took the position that "after HEW had negotiated with a noncomplying recipient for a reasonable time period and that recipient exhibited no attempt to come into compliance with Title VI, HEW should initiate action to cut off that recipient's federal assistance."[132] Thus the Court ordered HEW to use more stringent sanctions where voluntary compliance had been shown to be ineffective.

But, in 1973, Adams went back to court alleging that HEW was disregarding the court's order. More specifically, the plaintiffs charged that HEW was ignoring this decree by continuing to rely solely on voluntary compliance. In their petition, the plaintiffs asked the court "to set up specific timetables instructing HEW when and under what conditions it should discontinue using voluntary compliance"[133] and begin to employ more stringent sanctions--the deferral of funds, the termination of funds--to gain compliance with Title VI.

The court upheld the plaintiffs' contention and ruled that HEW had relied on voluntary compliance long enough. Consequently, the court ordered HEW to commence cut-off-funds proceedings against noncomplying recipients who had shown no desire to voluntarily comply with Title VI. The court also established specific time limits for HEW to achieve voluntary compliance. Specifically, the court ruled that if HEW was unable to attain voluntary compliance after ninety days of uncovering a Title VI violation, it should commence Title VI enforcement proceedings, i.e., begin action which could lead to a noncomplying recipient's funds being terminated.

Besides establishing a time frame for HEW to achieve voluntary compliance, the court also required

HEW to develop a time limit for conducting complaint investigations and ordered it to develop a Title VI reporting system. Specifically, the district court held that "within 120 days of receiving a complaint, that complaint should be investigated and a record should be kept of the investigation."[134]

HEW reacted to the 1973 _Adams_ decree by calling on the Court of Appeals to overturn the ruling of the federal district court. But the appellate court, by a unanimous vote, upheld the decree of the federal district court.

Certainly the rulings of the district and appellate courts can be viewed as strengthening HEW's Title VI operations. These courts directed HEW to develop a Title VI reporting system and mandated that it set time limits for utilizing Title VI sanctions and for conducting complaint investigations. These actions would certainly lend stimulus to vigorous HEW enforcement of Title VI.

The court further urged HEW to vigorously implement Title VI in _Brown_ v _Weinberger_. In this particular case, _Brown_ et al., a group of students who attended a school which received federal assistance, contended that "HEW had disregarded its affirmative duty under Title VI by funding public schools in thirty-three northern and western states which discriminated on the basis of race and national origin."[135] Specifically, _Brown et al._ alleged that HEW defaulted in its duty to enforce Title VI by "failing to initiate investigations of possible acts of discrimination, by unlawfully delaying investigations which had been commenced, and by refusing to prosecute fund cut-off proceedings against schools which had been determined in violation of Title VI."[136]

HEW responded to the charges brought against it by pointing out that the data presented by the plaintiffs were obsolete and inaccurate.

The court acknowledged that in some instances the evidence presented by the plaintiffs was outdated. However, the courts held that by and large, the evidence was current and solid and that HEW had failed to enforce Title VI in 33 Northern school districts. Indeed, the court directed HEW to promptly investigate all complaints and ordered it to initiate action to

182

cut off the funds of Northern school districts which
has been found in noncompliance with Title VI.

Lau v Nicholls is another case where the court
endorsed HEW efforts to vigorously enforce Title VI.
In this particular case, Lau et al., a group of non-
English Speaking Chinese students, charged that the
San Francisco's school district, in failing to provide
them with English instruction, denied them a meaningful
opportunity to gain a public school education and thus
violated Title VI. A federal district court and a
federal court of appeals rejected the plaintiffs'
contention and held that their Title VI rights had not
been violated. However, the Supreme Court ruled in
favor of Lau et al., contending that San Francisco's
school district had violated plaintiffs' Title VI
rights and HEW's Title VI regulations pertaining to
bilingual education. The Court reasoned that "as a
recipient of federal funds, the San Francisco school
district had contractually agreed to comply with
Title VI and all regulations imposed by or pursuant
to the regulations of HEW which were issued pursuant
to the enactment of Title VI."[137] Specifically, the
Court noted that though San Francisco's school district
had promised to abide by HEW regulations which mandated
that school districts take affirmative steps to rectify
the language deficiencies of non-English speaking
minorities, it had taken no affirmative steps to
correct the language deficiency of non-English speaking
Chinese students and thus violated Title VI and HEW's
Title VI regulations. By its decision in Lau, the
Supreme Court became the first court to give legal
backing to HEW's Title VI regulations pertaining to
bilingual education.

In another action in 1977, a federal district
court in Washington, D. C., approved of agreements
HEW had reached with civil rights, women and handicapped groups to take more effective steps to combat
discrimination based on race, color, sex, or
handicap.[138] The Court directed HEW's Office for
Civil Rights to eliminate 3,000 backlog complaints,
to seek more staff from OMB and Congress, to investigate complaints in a prompt fashion, to conduct more
compliance reviews, and to employ stronger enforcement
sanctions to secure compliance with Title VI, Title IX,
and Section 504 once voluntary compliance proved
ineffective. Further, HEW was directed to report to

the court every six months regarding the progress it
(the Office for Civil Rights) was making toward meeting
its pledges under the consent agreement.

So far, the discussion has centered on court
rulings which seemingly have encouraged HEW to vigorously implement Title VI. However, there were court
rulings which seemingly have discouraged HEW from
forcefully implementing Title VI. For example, in the
Board of Public Instruction of Taylor County Florida v
Finch, the Court ruled that HEW could not cut off all
federal assistance to a school district when it had
only uncovered discrimination in one of the programs
administered by that district. In this case, HEW had
found that the Board of Public Instruction, which
received three federal grants (one for public schools
students, another for adults who had not received a
college education, and another for supplementary
education centers), had violated Title VI by operating
racially segregated public schools. As a result of
this finding, HEW discontinued all federal aid to the
Board of Public Instruction. When HEW took this
action, the Board of Public Instruction objected and
took HEW to court on the grounds that it violated
Title VI by cutting off all of its federal assistance
when it should have limited the fund cutoff to the
program where it uncovered discrimination. To back up
its contention, the Board cited the pinpoint provision
of Title VI, which states that "the termination of
funds shall be limited in its effect to particular
program, or part thereof, in which such noncompliance
is found."[139] The Board stressed that HEW had violated
the pinpoint proviso of Title VI by terminating all of
its federal aid for education as opposed to limiting
the cutoff of assistance to the education program where
it found noncompliance with Title VI.

As expected, HEW took the position that it could
terminate all of the Board's education funds. It
maintained that the term "program" in the pinpoint
provision of Title VI referred to the general education
program administered by the school district authorities and did not refer to individual federal grant
statute programs."[140] Further, HEW contended that
"Title VI. . .did not place an affirmative obligation
on federal agencies to make "pinpoint fact findings of
discrimination but merely created an affirmative
defense for school districts and other recipients,
under which they could try to exclude parts of their

184

operations from the sweep of a termination order by showing that those parts were untainted by discrimination."[141]

The court was not swayed by HEW's contentions, and held the term "program" in the pinpoint provision referred to the federal grant programs and that HEW must make specific findings of noncompliance with Title VI under each program for which it proposed to terminate funds.

Undoubtedly, this ruling had a negative impact on HEW's Title VI operations, and made it more difficult for HEW to cut off funds of noncomplying recipients. Further, as a result of the court's ruling, HEW was prohibited from terminating the funds of forty school districts which had been determined to be in noncompliance with Title VI."[142]

Lee v Macon County Board of Education is another case where the Court seemed to discourage HEW from forcefully implementing Title VI. In this particular case, a group of school officials sought to block HEW from terminating their school financial assistance on the grounds that "HEW acting independently and without court approval,"[143] did not have the authority to terminate their school financial assistance because the school was under a court order to desegregate and had given assurances to HEW of being in compliance with Title VI.

As expected, HEW responded to the school officials' argument by pointing out that it could terminate their school's financial assistance because they (school officials) were not complying with the court order and were not obeying Title VI.

The court rejected HEW's contention and sided with the school officials. It reasoned that the mere fact that the Macon County school officials had filed desegregation plans with the court indicated that they were complying with those plans. Also, the court noted that the fact that school officials had filed Title VI assurances with HEW suggested that they were complying with Title VI. Then the court pointed out that HEW could not cut off funds to any school system which was under a court order and which had filed an assurance with it to abide by Title VI, unless it had judicial approval to do so. In the case at hand, the court noted, HEW had not obtained the consent of the court to terminate the funds of Macon County school system, and thus could not terminate that county's school funds.

Even though it does not pertain directly to HEW's Title VI enforcement operations, Washington v Davis is another case which generally can be viewed as discouraging HEW from forcefully implementing Title VI. Indeed, civil rights officials at HEW emphasized that the Supreme Court's ruling in Davis had adversely affected their Title VI operations. These officials alleged that after the Court's ruling, HEW changed its evidentiary requirements for proving discrimination. Prior to Washington v Davis, officials stressed, the Depratment required only that they (civil rights officials) show that a recipient's action had a disparate effect on minorities to prove discrimination. However, they emphasized that after the Davis case the Department (HEW) not only required that civil rights officials demonstrate that a recipient's actions had a disparate effect on minorities, but it also required them to show that a recipient intentionally discriminated against minorities. Proving discriminatory intent, officials maintained, "was [and is] not only difficult but nearly impossible."[144]

Overall, the effect of the Supreme Court's ruling in Davis was to make it more difficult for HEW officials to prove discrimination, thus weakening the Title VI enforcement.

Unlike Davis, the 1978 Supreme Court ruling in the celebrated case of the University of California v Bakke, which did involve Title VI, has apparently had no bearing on HEW's Title VI operations. Indeed, HEW, which requires its recipients to adopt measures to correct acts of past discrimination, reacted to the Bakke decision by stressing that the "Bakke ruling would have no effect on its Title VI operation or its guidelines policies and regulations regarding affirmative action."[145] Similarly, HEW officials contended that the Supreme Court's ruling in the Weber case that private employers could adopt affirmative action plans and racial quotas, even though they had no previous history of discrimination, would have little or no effect on HEW's civil rights operations.

Furthermore, civil rights officials at HEW claimed that the Supreme Court's ruling in Fullilove v Klutznick, which upheld the power of Congress to make some limited use of racial quotas to remedy past discrimination against black businessmen, had not significantly helped or hindered their Title VI operations.

In general, most HEW officials stressed that court decisions, particularly the Adams decisions, had helped HEW's Title VI program. These officials explained that the Adams' decisions had helped HEW's enforcement operations "by mandating that it [HEW] develop a reporting system for Title VI compliance activities, by setting specific time frames for using Title VI sanctions and conducting complaint investigations and compliance reviews, and by ordering HEW to eliminate 3,000 backlog complaints."[146] As one official explained "the Adams decisions compelled HEW to do what it should have been doing all along--to take steps to insure vigorous enforcement of Title VI."[147]

Interest Group Activities and HEW's Title VI Enforcement Effort

This section examines how interest groups have sought to influence HEW's Title VI enforcement operations, and the political strategies or tactics they have employed to accomplish this objective. There are, to be sure, an array of groups which have endeavored to influence HEW's Title VI enforcement operation, but there have been four groups most active in seeking to accomplish this task. They are the National Association for the Advancement of Colored People, the Leadership Conference on Civil Rights, and the Council of Chief State School Officers, and the National School Board Association. Let us take a closer look at the activity of these groups.

The National Association for the Advancement of Colored People. The NAACP has not only examined how HEW has endeavored to implement Title VI, but it has also sought to affect HEW's enforcement of this statute. Indeed, the NAACP has used various means to influence HEW's implementation of Title VI. First, it has sought to affect HEW's Title VI enforcement operations by testifying before Congressional committees, urging Congressmen to compel with HEW to meet its Title VI duties. For example, in its testimony before the Senate Select Committee on Equal Education Opportunity, the organization charged that HEW was not meeting its Title VI obligations, and called on Congress to pressure HEW to fulfill its Title VI duties.

The NAACP has also undertaken to influence HEW's enforcement of Title VI by taking HEW to court when it believes that HEW has been derelict in meeting its Title VI responsibilities. For example, in both Adams v Richardson and Brown v Weinberg, the NAACP aided plaintiffs in filing suit against HEW for failing to enforce Title VI in both Southern and Northern cities.[148]

Furthermore, the NAACP has attempted to influence HEW's enforcement of Title VI by lobbying HEW officials. For example, the NAACP urged HEW officials to cut off Chicago's schools funds because the city's schools have been violating Title VI for years. And the NAACP has also alerted HEW officials to HEW-funded recipients which are in noncompliance with Title VI.

Leadership Conference on Civil Rights. In its efforts to achieve equal opportunity and advance civil rights, the Leadership Conference lobbied Congress to pass the Civil Rights Act of 1964 and subsequently has sought to influence the implementation of this statute. For example, the Leadership Conference has undertaken through various means to influence HEW's implementation of Title VI. First, the Leadership Conference has sought to influence HEW's enforcement of Title VI by appearing before Congressional committees and urging Congressmen to induce HEW to vigorously implement Title VI. For example, in its testimony before the House's Civil Rights Oversight Committee in 1973, the Health Task Force of the Leadership Conference on Civil Rights pointed out that HEW had neglected to take effective steps to ensure that hospitals were complying with Title VI, and urged Congressmen on that committee to pressure HEW to develop effective mechanisms for determining whether hospitals were abiding by the nondiscriminatory requirements of Title VI.

The Leadership Conference has also endeavored to affect HEW's implementation of Title VI by lobbying HEW officials. For example, the Leadership Conference has called on HEW officials to terminate the North Carolina University system's funds because "the university has blatantly disregarded the provisions of

Title VI"[149] and has exhibited no sign of voluntarily complying with Title VI.

Also, the Conference has sought to influence HEW officials by sending them memoranda and reports suggesting ways in which they (HEW officials) might improve their Title VI operations. For example, in one of its reports in July 1978, the Leadership Conference pointed out that minority students are much more likely to be disciplined than nonminority students in public schools around the country and urged HEW officials to develop guidelines to ensure that schools were not utilizing disciplinary measures on a racially discriminatory basis.

Council of Chief State School Officers. The major objectives of the Council are 1) "to resist the development of guidelines, rules and regulations deleterious to state education agencies; 2) to work for the establishment of a cabinet level Department of Education; 3) to establish and maintain a working relationship with members of Congress; and 4) to keep the United States Office of Education informed regarding the positions of the chiefs."[150] To fulfill it objectives, the Council of Chief State School Officers (hereafter referred to as the CCSO) has called for more federal aid for education, has continually emphasized the need for less federal paperwork, procedures and regulations regarding education and has lobbied for the creation of a cabinet level Department of Education.

With respect to civil rights, it is interesting to note that the CCSO opposed Congressional adoption of the Civil Rights Act of 1964. However, after Congress passed the Civil Rights Act, CCSO promised to abide by the provisions of this statute. Despite its promise, it should be noted, the CCSO has vigorously opposed HEW's efforts to conduct civil rights surveys of elementary and secondary school districts because these surveys place excessive demands on school administrators. Specifically, the CCSO has charged that in order to complete HEW's civil rights survey, school administrators must devote an enormous amount of time collecting data regarding the racial and ethnic characteristics of students who have been suspended, disciplined, or dismissed. Collecting this data, a CCSO official asserted, "has placed excessive demands on the time of school administrators and in

189

many instances has meant that other administrative chores have been neglected."[150] As a result of this, CCSO officials have generally opposed HEW's civil rights surveys and have lobbied Congress to prevent HEW from carrying on this activity.

The National School Boards Association. The only major education organization representing school board members is the National School Board Association (NSBA). To achieve its objectives, NSBA among other things has lobbied for less federal paperwork, guidelines, and regulations that affect the authority of its member boards. In this regard the NSBA opposed Congressional enactment of the Civil Rights Act of 1964 on the basis that it would mean more federal control over education. However, after Congress enacted the Civil Rights Act, the NSBA pledged to abide by nondiscrimination requirements of this statute. Still, despite the pledge, the NSBA has vigorously opposed HEW's efforts to conduct biannual civil rights surveys of elementary and secondary schools because it contends these surveys distract school officials from carrying out their educational duties and are unnecessary and burdensome federal paperwork. Indeed, the NSBA has exhibited its nonsupport for HEW's civil rights survey by urging Congressional committees to prevent HEW from conducting its biannual civil rights surveys of elementary and secondary schools. For example, in testimony before the House Education and Labor Committee in 1973, the NSBA criticized HEW's civil rights surveys as being "unnecessary and burdensome federal paperwork which distract school officials from meeting their daily educational chores."[151] Consequently, the NSBA called on Congress to take steps to preclude HEW from conducting these surveys.

In general, and not unexpectedly, HEW officials thought that "some interest groups activities had helped their Title VI enforcement operation while others had not."[152] Some officials pointed out that "civil rights groups had generally helped their Title VI enforcement operations by alerting them to recipients in noncompliance with Title VI"[153] and by suggesting ways in which they might improve their Title VI enforcement effort. But other officials maintained that groups such as "the National Association of School Boards and The Council of Chief State School Officers had hindered their Title VI operations

190

by lobbying Congress to put pressure on HEW not to conduct its civil rights surveys."[154] Specifically, these officials asserted that "as a result of the intense lobbying efforts of the Council of Chief State School Officers and the National Association of School Boards, Congess had put pressure on them not to conduct their civil rights surveys."[155]

Conclusion

This chapter has examined how the Department of Health, Education and Welfare has undertaken to implement Title VI of the Civil Rights Act of 1964. The study shows that HEW has developed a number of compliance instruments to gain compliance with Title VI, but has generally neglected to use these instruments effectively because of 1) the competing and conflicting objectives of agency officials; 2) a lack of standardized procedures for implementing Title VI; 3) pressures from Congress and private interest groups; 4) staff limitations; and 5) other civil rights obligations. Specifically, we have found that HEW generally has employed the voluntary compliance sanction more frequently than other Title VI sanctions. This sanction has been used because 1) HEW's Secretaries have generally believed that voluntary compliance is the most effective means to deter discrimination in federally assisted programs; 2) it does not clash with HEW's major missions--disbursing grants to elementary and secondary school districts, colleges and universities, and health and welfare agencies; 3) its procedures are not protracted and cumbersome; 4) it does not get agency officials in trouble with the White House or Congress; and 5) it does not adversely affect intended program beneficiaries.

Further, we found that in some instances the actions of the President have facilitated HEW's implementation of Title VI, but in other instances the actions of the President have inhibited Title VI implementation. Similarly, the actions of the courts as well as civil rights groups have helped HEW's implementation of Title VI in some instances, but have hurt in others. By contrast, actions of the Congress seem to have been in one direction, and have tended to severely hinder HEW from forcefully implementing Title VI.

FOOTNOTES

[1]U. S., Department of Health, Education, and Welfare, _This Is HEW_ (Washington: The Department of Health, Education and Welfare's Public Affairs Office, 1979), p. 1.

[2]Ibid.

[3]Ibid, p. 2.

[4]Ibid.

[5]Harold R. Rodgers, Jr., and Charles S. Bullock, III, _Law and Social Change: Civil Rights Laws and Their Consequences_ (New York: McGraw-Hill and Co., 1972), Chapter 4; Gary Orfield, _Must We Bus_ (Washington: The Brookings Institute, 1977), Chapter 2; Meyer Weinberg, _A Chance To Learn: A History of Race and Education in the United States_ (Cambridge and New York: Cambridge University Press, 1977), Chapters 1 and 2. Also, see U. S. Commission on Civil Rights, _Twenty Years After Brown_ (Washington: Government Printing Office, Dec. 1975), Chapter 2.

[6]James Bolner, _Busing: The Political and Judicial Process_ (New York: Praeger, 1974), p. 131.

[7]_Dayton Board of Education et al. v Brinkman et al._, 99S Ct. 2971 (1979); _Columbus Board of Education et al._ v _Penick_, 99S Ct. 2941 (1979).

[8]Ibid.

[9]U. S. Commission on Civil Rights, _Desegregation of the Nation's Public Schools: A Status Report_ (Washington: Government Printing Office, February, 1979), p. 42.

[10]Dorothy Newman et al., _Protest, Politics, and Prosperity: Black Americans and White Institutions, 1940-1975_ (New York: McGraw-Hill, 1976), p. 138.

[11]Talcott Parsons and Kenneth B. Clark, _The Negro American_ (Boston: The Riverside Press, 1965), p. 28.

[12]Ibid., p. 27.

[13]Dorothy Newman et al., Protest, Politics, and Prosperity: Black Americans and White Institutions, 1945-1975, op. cit., p. 139.

[14]Ibid.

[15]Ibid.

[16]Max Schaw, Blacks and American Medical Care (Minneapolis: University of Minnesota Free Press, 1973, p. 14.

[17]U. S., Commission on Civil Rights, Civil Rights 1963 (Washington: Government Printing Office, 1963), p. 52.

[18]Ibid.

[19]Dorothy Newman et al., Protest, Politics, and Prosperity: Black Americans and White Institutions, 1945-1975, op. cit,. p. 140.

[20]U. S., Commission on Civil Rights, Civil Rights 1963, op. cit., p. 53.

[21]Dorothy Newman et al., Protest, Politics, and Prosperity: Black Americans and White Institutions, 1945-1975, op. cit., p. 142.

[22]Ibid.

[23]Ibid.

[24]U. S., Commission on Civil Rights, Civil Rights Digest/Health Care (Washington: Government Printing Office, Fall 1977), p. 7.

[25]Comment, "Title VI of the Civil Rights Act of 1964--Implementation and Impact," 36 George Washington Law Review 952 (1968).

[26]Ibid.

[27]U. S., Commission on Civil Rights, The Federal Civil Rights Enforcement Effort--1974, Volume VI: To Extend Federal Financial Assistance (Washington: Government Printing Office, November 1975), p. 767.

[28]U. S. Code of Federal Regulations, 45 Public Welfare (Washington: Government Printing Office, October 1979), pp. 311-46. It seems important to point out here that the universe of institutions subject to the provisions of Title VI is far-reaching and includes 16,000 school systems; 2,000 institutions of higher education; 7,000 hospitals; 6,700 nursing homes and home health agencies; hundreds of libraries, day care centers, educational broadcasting facilities, medical laboratories, and various state and local governmental agencies. Also, it seems appropriate here to note that HEW's Office for Civil Rights has 1,906 employees. However, under Carter's proposed budget for 1980, the number of OCR employees is subject to decrease from 1,906 to 1,772.

[29]Ibid.

[30]Statement of Marie Cromer, Special Assistant to the Deputy Director of the Office for Civil Rights, in a personal interview, Washington, D. C.: December 20, 1978; Cynthia Brown, Deputy Director of the Office for Civil Rights, in a personal interview, Washington, D. C.: January 9, 1979; Lloyd Henderson, Director of Compliance and Enforcement, in a personal interview, Washington, D. C.: January 17, 1979.

[31]Ibid.

[32]Statement by Theodore Nixon, Director of the Office for Civil Rights' Elementary and Secondary Division in Philadelphia, in a personal interview, Philadelphia, Pa., February 25, 1979; Robert Harvey, Director of the Office for Civil Rights' Higher Education Division in Philadelphia, in a personal interview, Philadelphia, Pa., February 25, 1979; Yvonne Brown, Director of the Office for Civil Rights' Health and Human Development Division in Philadelphia, Pa., February 25, 1979; Dewey Dodds, Regional Director of the Office for Civil Rights in Philadelphia, in a personal interview, Philadelphia, Pa., February 25, 1979; Ron Gilliam, Assistant Regional Director of the Office for Civil Rights in Philadelphia, in a personal interview, Philadelphia, Pa., February 25, 1979.

[33]Ibid.

[34]Ibid.

[35] Ibid.

[36] Ibid.

[37] Ibid., statement by Theodore Nixon.

[38] U. S. Commission on Civil Rights, The Federal
Civil Rights Enforcement Efforts--1974, Volume III:
To Ensure Equal Educational Opportunity (Washington:
Government Printing Office, January 1975), p. 378.
Further, it should be noted that the General Accounting
Office, which investigated HEW's Title VI operations,
found that HEW's failure to develop uniform procedures
for enforcing Title VI has hampered its Title VI operations. Specifically, the GAO discovered that the fact
that HEW has not instituted standardized procedures
for enforcing Title VI has meant that HEW's Title VI
officers are often unaware of the strategies and
tactics they can employ to secure compliance with
Title VI and has meant HEW-funded programs often do
not know what they must do to comply with the anti-
discriminatory requirements of Title VI. (Letter from
Senator Birch Bayh of Indiana to Joseph Califano,
Secretary of HEW, March 31, 1977, concerning the
General Accounting Office Report regarding HEW's civil
rights operations B-164031 1.

[39] Ibid., pp. 27-31.

[40] Statement by Marie Cromer and Lloyd Henderson,
op. cit.

[41] Statement by Peter Jacobson, Acting Director of
HEW's Health and Human Development Division in
Washington, D. C., in a personal interview, Washington,
D. C., January 20, 1979.

[42] Statement by Valida Sheppard, Compliance Officer
for the Office for Civil Rights' Health and Human
Development Division in Washington, D. C., in a
personal interview, Washington, D. C., March 12, 1979;
Peter Jacobson, op. cit. These officials backed up
their contention that HEW had neglected the Health and
Human Development Division by noting that "HEW had
neglected to develop models for detecting discrimination in health and welfare institutions."

[43] Ibid.

[44]Ibid.

[45]U. S. Commission of Civil Rights, Desegregation of the Nation's Public Schools: A Status Report, op. cit., pp. 17-18. Bisner's contention was confirmed by A. J. Howell, Compliance Officer for the Office for Civil Rights' Elementary and Secondary Division in Washington, D. C., in a personal interview, Washington, D. C., December 18, 1978; January 21, 1979; February 4, 1979; and February 8, 1979.

[46]Ibid. U. S. Commission on Civil Rights, Desegregation of the Nation's Public Schools: A Status Report, op. cit., p. 19.

[47]Statement by Theodore Nixon, Yvonne Brown, and Robert Harvey, op. cit.

[48]Ibid.

[49]Ibid.

[50]Ibid.

[51]Ibid.

[52]Statement by A. J. Howell, Dewey Dodds, Robert Harvey, and Theodore Nixon, op. cit.

[53]Ibid.

[54]Statement by Lloyd Henderson, Marie Cromer, Cindy Brown, and Valida Sheppard, op. cit.

[55]Ibid.

[56]Ibid. Statement by Clark Lemming, Chief Data Clerk for HEW's Office for Civil Rights, in a personal interview, Washington, D. C., January 31, 1979.

[57]Statement by Theodore Nixon, Cindy Brown, Robert Harvey, and Yvonne Brown, op. cit.

[58]Ibid. Statement by Robert Harvey and Theodore Nixon, op. cit.

[59]Statement by Valida Sheppard, Peter Jacobson, Cindy Brown, and Marie Cromer, op. cit.

[60]Ibid.

[61] Statement by Theodore Nixon, Yvonne Brown, and Robert Harvey, op. cit.

[62] Adams v Califano, 455 F. Supp. 837 (1977).

[63] Statement by Theodore Nixon, Yvonne Brown, and Robert Harvey, op. cit.

[64] Statement by Ben Saunders, Acting Supervisor of the Office for Civil Rights' Higher Education Division in Washington, D. C., in a personal interview, Washington, D. C., February 9, 1979; Waite Madison, Director of the Office for Civil Rights' Higher Education Division in Washington, D. C., in a personal interview, Washington, D. C., February 7, 1979.

[65] Statement by Theodore Nixon, op. cit.

[66] Statement by Valida Sheppard, op. cit.

[67] Statement by Timothy Burke, Branch Chief of the Office for Civil Rights' Higher Education Division in Philadelphia, in a personal interview, Philadelphia, Pa., February 25, 1979; Theodore Nixon, op. cit.

[68] U. S., Congress, House Committee on Appropriations, Subcommittee on Appropriations for HEW, Hearings, 95th Congress, 1st Session, March 13, 1979 (Washington: Government Printing Office, 1979), p. 1293.

[69] Ibid.

[70] U. S. Commission on Civil Rights, The Federal Civil Rights Enforcement Effort--1974, Volume VI: To Extend Federal Financial Assistance, op. cit.

[71] Statement of Theodore Nixon and Robert Harvey and Yvonne Brown, op. cit.

[72] Ibid.

[73] Statement by Lloyd Henderson and A. J. Howell, op. cit.

[74] Ibid.

[75] For a detailed discussion of the Chicago case, see Gary Orfield, The Reconstruction of Southern

Education: The Schools and the 1964 Civil Rights Act
(New York: Wiley-Interscience, 1969); Leon Panetta
and Peter Gall, Bring Us Together (Lippincot, 1971).
To get some notion of the impact of the Chicago case
on HEW's Title VI enforcement, see Center for National
Policy Review, Justice Delayed and Denied: HEW and
Northern School Desegregation (Washington Center for
Policy Review, 1974).

[76]For an intriguing discussion of the Jackson
case, see Frederick Wirt, Politics of Southern
Equality: Law and Social Change in a Mississippi
County (New York: Aldine, 1970), Chapter 3.

[77]"Remark by Mrs. Harris Stirs Rift on Politics
in Civil Rights Cases," New York Times, August 3,
1979, p. 10.

[78]Ibid.

[79]Statement by A. J. Howell, Theodore Nixon, and
Robert Harvey, op. cit.

[80]Ibid., statement by A. J. Howell.

[81]Statement by Theodore Nixon, Valida Sheppard,
and Peter Jacobson, op. cit.

[82]Ibid.

[83]U. S. Commission on Civil Rights, The Federal
Civil Rights Enforcement Effort--1974, Volume III: To
Ensure Equal Educational Opportunity, op. cit.,
p. 130. This view was widely supported by civil
rights officials at the Department of Health, Education and Welfare, Education, and Health and Human
Services.

[84]Statement by Fred Cioffi, Director of the
Office for Civil Rights' Elementary and Secondary
Division in Washington, in a telephone interview,
Washington, D. C., March 12, 1979. See also Center
for National Policy Review, Justice Delayed and
Justice Denied (Washington: Center for National
Policy Review, 1975), p. 38.

[85]Statement by Dewey Dodds, Theodore Nixon, and
A. J. Howell, op. cit.

[86]Ibid.

[87]Ibid.

[88]Ibid.

[89]Ibid.

[90]Statement by Lloyd Henderson and Marie Cromer, op. cit.

[91]Center for National Policy Review, Justice Delayed and Justice Denied, op. cit., p. 38. The case of Ferndale, Michigan, clearly illustrates that it takes HEW a long time to terminate a noncomplying recipient's funds. In 1968, HEW determined that Ferndale's schools were violating Title VI, but it took almost four years to terminate that school's financial assistance.

Ferndale

Oct. 1968	- initial compliance review
Nov. 1968	- report written
Dec. 1968	- letter of noncompliance sent to Ferndale school officials
(date unknown)	- district notified of hearing
July and Sept. 1969 and April 1970	- hearing examiner finds the Ferndale school district in noncompliance with Title VI
Dec. 1970	- Ferndale files a request for review
Sept. 1971	- on appeal, the Reviewing Authority affirms the administrative judge's finding
Nov. 1971	- Office for General Counsel recommends Secretary to decline Ferndale's review
April 1972	- Congress notified of cutoff to be effective in 30 days
May 1972	- Secretary of HEW delays termination for 30 days to allow the district to perfect a petition for judicial review to apply to Sixth Circuit Court of Appeals for a further stay of the HEW order

June 1972   - order of termination of funds
                               becomes effective, when the
                               Sixth Circuit Court denies
                               Ferndale's request for a stay
                               of HEW's order

[92]Statement by Theodore Nixon, A. J. Howell, and
Peter Jacobson, op. cit. It is worth noting here that
HEW officials constantly emphasized that the department (HEW) would take no action against big cities
because the bigger the city, the greater the political
pressure. One official, who asked not to be identified, pointed out that though there was evidence that
New York's schools and hospitals were not in compliance with Title VI, HEW was not going to take any
action against New York because the city's Congressional delegation is large, extremely influential, and
could exert pressure to block any move by HEW to
vigorously enforce Title VI. Also, this official
pointed out that HEW had not taken any strong enforcement action against New York because of narrow
political considerations. Specifically, this official
explained that because the Secretary of HEW, Joe
Califano, was and is contemplating running for the U.
S. Senate in 1980, he had blocked attempts to forcefully implement Title VI in New York, fearing that
strong enforcement of Title VI could antagonize powerful New York Democrats and thus jeopardize his chances
of winning a U. S. Senate seat.

[93]Statement by A. J. Howell, Theodore Nixon, and
Lloyd Henderson, op. cit.

[94]Ibid.

[95]Ibid.

[96]Stephen Hess, Organizing the Presidency (Washington: The Brookings Institute, 1973), p. 13.

[97]Statement by Lloyd Henderson, Ben Saunders, and
A. H. Howell, op. cit.

[98]Richard P. Nathan, The Plot that Failed: Nixon
and the Administrative Presidency (New York: John
Wiley and Sons, 1975), pp. 36-37.

[99]Statement by Dewey Dodds, op. cit.

[100] _Congressional Quarterly_, "Gerald Ford--1974 (Washington: Congressional Quarterly, 1975), p. 88.

[101] _New York Times_, February 4, 1975, Sec. I, p. 21, col. 5.

[102] Ibid., February 16, 1976, Sec. I, p. 22, col. 4.

[103] Statement by Lloyd Henderson, A. J. Howell, Theodore Nixon, and Dewey Dodds, op. cit.

[104] Statement by Joseph Rauh, Attorney for the NAACP and President of the Americans for Democratic Action, in a personal interview, Washington, D. C., April 7, 1979.

[105] Statement by Yvonne Brown, Cindy Brown, Robert Harvey, Ben Saunders, and Marie Cromer, op. cit.

[106] Statement by Theodore Nixon, Lloyd Henderson, Marie Cromer, Cindy Brown, and Robert Harvey, op. cit.

[107] Ibid.

[108] Ibid.

[109] Ibid.

[110] Ibid.

[111] Statement by A. J. Howell, op. cit.

[112] Statement by Roy McKinney, Budget Officer for HEW's Office for Civil Rights in Washington, in a personal interview, Washington, D. C., April 19, 1979; Art Ellis, Office of Management and Budget--Budget Examiner for the Office for Civil Rights, in a personal interview, Washington, D. C., April 20, 1979.

[113] Ibid., statement by Art Ellis.

[114] Statement by Marie Cromer, Cindy Brown, and Peter Jacobson, op. cit.

[115] Ibid.

[116] Statement by Theodore Nixon, Dewey Dodds, and Timothy Burke, op. cit.

[117]Ibid.

[118]Departments of Labor and Health, Education and Welfare Appropriations for 1979, Hearings before a Subcommittee of the House Committee on Appropriations, Part III (Washington: Government Printing Office, 1978), p. 1086.

[119]Congress restricted HEW's powers to desegregate hospitals in 1966 by adopting the Stennis Amendment, which banned HEW from terminating hospitals' funds simply because they assigned patients to rooms on a racially segregated basis. Specifically, the Stennis Amendment stated that if hospital administrators believed that integrating patients by rooms would adversely affect their (patients) mental or physical well-being, they (hospital administrators) could assign patients to rooms according to race and HEW could not terminate their federal assistance. This amendment has had a major impact on HEW's efforts to desegregate hospitals. Essentially, the Stennis Amendment makes it more difficult for HEW to cut off federal monies to hospitals which assign patients to rooms on the basis of race. Prior to the adoption of the Stennis Amendment, if HEW found that a hospital was assigning patients to rooms on a racially segregated basis, it would take action to terminate that hospital's federal funds. However, under the Stennis Amendment, if HEW discovers that a recipient (a hospital) assigns patients to rooms accoding to race, it cannot cut off funds if its (the hospital) administrators believe that integrating patients by room would impair their (patients) mental or physical well-being. Surely, under the Stennis Amendment, those hospital administrators who oppose the anti-discriminatory provisions of Title VI, can easily adopt discriminatory assignment policies under the guise of protecting their patients' physical well-being.

[120]U. S. Commission of Civil Rights, The State of Civil Rights: 1977 (Washington: Government Printing Office, February 1978), p. 11.

[121]Ibid.

[122]Ibid.

[123]Ibid.

[124]Statement by Lloyd Henderson, A. J. Howell, and Theodore Nixon, op. cit.

[125]Ibid., statement by Lloyd Henderson.

[126]U. S., Congress, Senate, Committee on Labor and Public Welfare, Oversight Hearing on HEW Enforcement of School Related Civil Rights Problem, 1975, 94th Congress, 1st Session. Examination of the Administration and Enforcement of the Civil Rights Act in the Elementary and Secondary Areas of Education (Washington: Government Printing Office, 1976), p. 381.

[127]Statement by Theodore Nixon, Timothy Burke, Yvonne Brown, and Valida Sheppard, op. cit.

[128]Ibid., statement by Valida Sheppard.

[129]Statement by A. J. Howell, Lloyd Henderson, and Cindy Brown, op. cit.

[130]United States v Jefferson County Board of Education 372 F. 2d. 836 (1966).

[131]Adams v Richardson 351 F. Supp. 636 (1972).

[132]Ibid.

[133]Adams v Richardson 356 F. Supp. 92 (1973).

[134]Ibid.

[135]Brown v Weinberger 417 F. Supp. 1215 (1976).

[136]Ibid.

[137]Lau v Nicholls 414 U. S. 563 (1974).

[138]Adams v Califano 430 F. Supp. 118 (D. D. C. 1977).

[139]Board of Public Instruction of Taylor County, Florida v Finch 414 F. 2d. 1068.

[140]Ibid.

[141]Ibid.

[142]U. S. Department of Health, Education and Welfare, 1970 Annual Report (Washington: Government Printing Office, 1970), p. 3.

[143]Lee v Macon County Board of Education 270 F. Supp. 859 (1967).

[144]Statement by A. J. Howell, Theodore Nickens, and Lloyd Henderson, op. cit.

[145]"HEW Programs Said Unaffected by Bakke Ruling," The Washington Post, April 22, 1979, sec. 1, p. 10, col. 5.

[146]Statement by Cindy Brown, Marie Cromer, A. J. Howell, and Yvonne Brown, op. cit.

[147]Ibid.

[148]Statement by William Morris, Attorney for NAACP, in a personal interview, Washington, D. C., October 13, 1978.

[149]Statement by Glendora Sloane, Chairperson of the Leadership Conference for Civil Rights, in a personal interview, Washington, D. C., Oct. 13, 1978.

[150]Council of Chief School Officers Pamphlet, The Role, Scope, and Function of the Council of Chief State School Officers (Washington: Council of Chief State School Officers, 1979), p. 1.

[151]Statement of Jim Polkinham, Assistant Public Affairs Officer for the Council of Chief State School Officers, in a telephone interview, Washington, D.C., April 6, 1979.

[152]Statement by Lloyd Henderson, A. J. Howell, and Theodore Nixon, op. cit.

[153]Ibid.

[154]Ibid.

[155]Ibid.

CHAPTER VI

THE LABOR RECORD:
"DEPENDING ONLY ON PROMISES"

In the last chapter we considered how the Department of Health, Education and Welfare had endeavored to enforce Title VI. The present chapter assesses how the Department of Labor has sought to implement this statute. As will become obvious in the following pages, Labor, unlike HEW, has not utilized rigorous sanctions in enforcing the nondiscriminatory provisions of Title VI. Indeed, in determining whether its recipients are adhering to the provisions of this law, Labor has generally relied on their promises as opposed to demonstrated results. This point will be addressed more fully later. Here we discuss: 1) the resources (e.g., staff and compliance instruments) Labor has at its disposal; 2) the attitudes and objectives of Labor officials who are responsible for enforcing Title VI; 3) the impact of executive, legislative and judicial activities on Labor's Title VI enforcement effort; and 4) the influence of clientele and interest group activities on Labor's Title VI enforcement operations.

The Department of Labor was created in 1913, and its major objective is to promote and develop the welfare of the wage earners of the United States. In its efforts to meet this objective, Labor employs 17,281 workers who administer more than 130 labor laws "guaranteeing workers' right to safe and healthful working conditions, a minimum hourly wage and overtime pay, . . .unemployment insurance, and workers compensation."[1] Furthermore, Labor employees are responsible for formulating and implementing guidelines to protect workers' pension rights and they are responsible for sponsoring a number of job training programs. The Comprehensive Employment Training Act Program (or CETA program), which seeks to train and employ the hard-core unemployed, is perhaps one of the best known training programs sponsored by the Department of Labor.

Labor also has numerous civil rights responsibilities. These responsibilities are included in various federal statutes and executive orders that ban discrimination in federally funded programs against persons on such basis as race, age, political affiliation, religion, sex, or against the physically or mentally handicapped. For example, the Comprehensive

Employment and Training Act of 1973 prohibits discrimination in federally aided employment training programs on the basis of race, creed, color, national origin, age, handicap, political affiliation, or beliefs, the Equal Pay Act of 1964 forbids an employer from discriminating on the basis of sex by paying employees difference wages for doing equal work on jobs requiring equal skill, effort, and responsibility; Executive Order 11246 prohibits discrimination on the basis of race, color, sex, religion, or national origin in any employment and training grant or contract (whether prime or subcontract) under which supplies or services are applied to the government, and Executive Order 11478 establishes and maintains an affirmative action program of equal employment opportunity in the federal government.

To be sure, these federal programs and statutes and the governmental action which gave rise to them came about in response to pervasive racism and discriminatory practices suffered by minorities in the employment field. Let us now briefly look at the racism and discriminatory practices in the employment field.

Discrimination in Employment:
  A Brief Overview of Employment:
    "The Last Hired and the First Fired"

A brief look at discrimination in employment reveals that for most of the nation's history, blacks were blatantly denied the kind of employment opportunities afforded whites. Moreover, this denial was accomplished by discriminatory practices and policies adopted and strongly endorsed by the local, state, and national governments. These governmental units racially biased employment policies resulted "in blacks being excluded from apprenticeship programs, craft unions, the construction industry,"[2] and essentially from white collar jobs. Such policies also contributed to black families median income being considerably lower than their white counterparts; to the black unemployment rate being twice that of whites; to blacks essentially receiving the least skilled and lowest paying jobs and to blacks being the last to be hired and the first to be fired.[3] Accounts of the governments' discriminatory practices and policies and their adverse impact on blacks and other minorities are well documented[4] and need not be reiterated here except to say that enormous pressure from civil rights interests helped to persuade major decision makers--mayors, governors, the president, Congress, and the court to take steps to strike down discriminatory employment policies. Indeed, over the years, the local, state, and federal governments have all adopted measures aimed at barring discrimination in the American workforce. Local and state governments have adopted ordinances requiring fair employment practices and policies, and on the national scene, the executive, legislative, and judicial branches have adopted measures to bring about equal employment opportunities for all. Presidents, including Kennedy, Johnson, Nixon and Carter, have issued executive orders requiring government contractors and governmental agencies to adopt affirmative action programs to overcome decades of racial discrimination in employment.* The Department of Labor and the Equal Employment Opportunity Commission, which are both responsible for ensuring the enforcement of executive orders and laws banning employment discrimination, have issued guidelines to make sure that persons are not denied jobs or admissions to job-training programs on the basis of race, color, sex, national origin, handicap, or religion.

Congress has also taken action to end discrimination, as for example, Title VI of the Civil Rights Act of 1964 which bars discrimination in federally assisted projects, and Title VII of this same Act, which forbids employers from discriminating against persons in the labor force on the basis of race, sex, religion, or national origin.

In addition, the Supreme Court's recent ruling in the Weber case illustrates how the judiciary may affect efforts to end discrimination in the American labor force. In this particular case, the Supreme Court ruled that "employers and unions could establish voluntary [or affirmative action] programs, including the use of quotas, to aid minorities and women, even

---

*It is worth noting that the Reagan Administration is currently endeavoring to revoke these executive orders, claiming the orders are not constitutionally or statutorily based.

where there was no evidence of past discrimination by employers."[5]

Labor's Title VI
Organizational Structure

Though the Secretary of Labor is primarily responsible for ensuring the enforcement of the non-discrimination requirements of Title VI in all Labor-funded programs, in 1965 the bulk of this responsibility was delegated by the Secretary to the Assistant Secretary for Employment Training. However, after being delegated this responsibility, the Assistant Secretary named the Director of the Office of Compliance and Investigation as the key departmental official responsible for enforcing Title VI. Consequently, since 1965, the Director of Compliance and Investigation has been the chief official at the Department of Labor responsible for implementing Title VI. As such, the Director sets the general policy direction of the Office of Compliance and Investigation and determines policies, regulations, and standards for Labor's Title VI compliance operations. However, it should be noted that though the Director of the Office of Compliance and Investigation plays a major role in Labor's implementation of Title VI, the Assistant Secretary for Employment and Training and the Secretary of Labor retain the authority to veto any decision made by the Director.

Within the office of Compliance and Investigation, there are two divisions: 1) Investigation and 2) Compliance. The Investigation division has no civil rights duties and its primary purpose is to eradicate all fraud and nepotism in Labor's employment training programs. By contrast, the Compliance (or Equal Opportunity) Section does have civil rights obligations and is primarily responsible for providing policy guidance to regional offices which conduct complaint investigations and compliance reviews. In meeting this overall objective, the Compliance Division holds training sessions for Title VI officers in Labor's ten regional offices and periodically visits these offices to oversee Title VI enforcement. Once again, however, we should point out that the Equal Opportunity or Compliance Division does not conduct complaint investigation or compliance reviews; rather it draws up and clarifies guidelines for regional equal opportunity officials who conduct complaint investigations and compliance reviews.

While the Equal Opportunity or Compliance Division provides policy direction to Labor's ten field or regional offices, it has "no direct link with its field components; it must channel all communication and policy direction through program staff in the Office of Field Operations."[6] The Equal Opportunity Division also has "no direct control over the actions or performance of regional civil rights staff."[7] Indeed, the "regions are semi-autonomous with regional staffs accountable for their performance to the Regional Administrator."[8] Hence, it is the Regional Administrator, a program official (that is, an official whose primary goal is to get federal funds to recipients as soon as possible) who determines whether Labor's Title VI officers can initiate Title VI enforcement proceedings against noncomplying recipients. Be that as it may, it should be stressed that the Assistant Secretary for Employment and Training and the Secretary for Labor retain the authority to overturn any decision made by the Regional Administrator.

To get a better feel for the nature and operations of one of Labor's regional offices, I visited the regional office in Philadelphia. Established in 1968, this office is responsible for supervising Title VI enforcement in the District of Columbia, and in four states--Maryland, Pennsylvania, Virginia, and West Virginia. Currently, the Philadelphia regional office for compliance has a staff of three.

Overall, Labor's Title VI organizational structure may be graphically illustrated on page 208. These then are the organizational units used by Labor to carry out its Title VI responsibilities. In the next section we describe the various compliance instruments used by the Department of Labor and their relative effectiveness in combatting discrimination in Labor-funded projects.

Labor's Compliance Instruments:
    Nature and Operations

1. The handbook situation. Basically, Labor has developed a number of instruments in seeking to

209

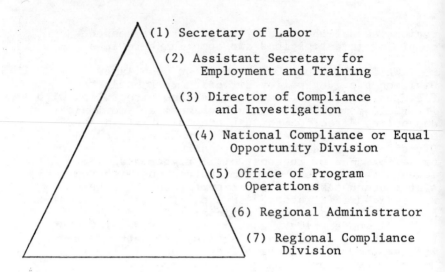

(1) Secretary of Labor

(2) Assistant Secretary for
Employment and Training

(3) Director of Compliance
and Investigation

(4) National Compliance or Equal
Opportunity Division

(5) Office of Program
Operations

(6) Regional Administrator

(7) Regional Compliance
Division

enforce Title VI. First, it has developed and
published a Title VI compliance manual which outlines
for Title VI compliance officers how to conduct complaint investigations and compliance reviews, and it
has stipulated the types of evidence they should
assemble to document discrimination. Certainly, the
fact that Labor has developed a Title VI manual or
handbook suggests that it has taken the important step
of making Title VI enforcement officers cognizant of
the action or actions they should take in assessing
whether Labor-funded programs are operating in compliance with Title VI.

Two points should be made concerning Labor's
Title VI handbook. First, Labor did not develop its
Title VI manual until 1972, almost a decade after
Congressional enactment of Title VI of the Civil Rights
Act of 1964. Surely, the question that arises is:
why did it take the Department of Labor almost a
decade to formulate and publish uniform guidelines
for implementing Title VI. When this question was
put to Labor officials they gave two responses.
First, one group of officials emphasized that Labor
had taken approximately ten years to develop a Title
VI handbook because top officials at the Department
of Labor generally were not and are not genuinely
committed to the vigorous enforcement of Title VI.
As one equal opportunity officer put it:

When the people at the top are not
concerned about civil rights enforcement,
this certainly delays the implementation
of guidelines or procedures for enforcing
Title VI. This has been our problem here
at Labor. The people at the top--the
Regional Administrator, the Assistant
Secretary for Employment and Training and
the Secretary of Labor--in the past and
even now have never been genuinely committed to civil rights enforcement and
this has hampered civil rights staffers'
efforts to implement Title VI.

Top officials have expressed this
lack of commitment by taking months and,
in some instances, years to approve guidelines and procedures essential for
strengthening Labor's Title VI program.
No doubt, these types of actions have
hindered our enforcement of Title VI.[9]

This official's viewpoint was shared by a number of
Title VI officials at the Department of Labor.

Another group of Labor officials stressed that
it had taken almost a decade to develop a Title VI
handbook because it takes an enormous amount of time
to formulate and publish uniform procedures for
enforcing Title VI. One equal opportunity official
summed up the situation this way:

Formulating and publishing guidelines
is no easy business. It requires a lot of
time and energy. It takes time to formulate
clear here-and-now language for conducting
Title VI investigations, and it takes months
and, in some cases, years to get the approval
of top officials to adopt and publish
Title VI guidelines.[10]

This observation was shared by various equal opportunity officials at the Department of Labor.

2. Assurance pledges. Labor's policy requiring
its recipients--employment training programs--to
annually submit Title VI assurance forms (pledges to
adhere to Title VI) is another compliance instrument
that it utilizes in implementing Title VI. Under this

policy, if a Labor recipient refuses to sign a Title VI assurance form or is found in noncompliance with the provisions of Title VI, equal opportunity officials can take action that could lead to that particular recipient's funds being terminated. Specifically, equal opportunity officers, upon discovering that a Labor-funded program has not submitted a Title VI assurance form or has disregarded the anti-discriminatory provisions of this law, can recommend that the regional administrator take immediate action to cut off this particular recipient's funds.

However, when equal opportunity officers at the Department of Labor have made such recommendations, they have been ignored or rejected by the regional administrator. In interview after interview, regional equal opportunity officers in Philadelphia stressed that when they recommended that the regional administrator take action to penalize recipients for violating Title VI, he had disregarded or rejected their recommendations. These officers contended that their recommendations were ignored or vetoed because the regional administrator's goals conflict with their objectives. Specifically, equal opportunity officers explained that the regional administrator's primary objective is to get the money to Labor-funded programs and keep it flowing, while the chief objective of the equal opportunity officer is to halt the flow of funds to recipients engaged in discriminatory practices. Consequencly, these officials stressed that when they recommended that the regional administrator take action to stop funding recipients guilty of violating Title VI, he had refused to do so because it was not in his interest.

The regional administrator, however, denied that he vetoed their recommendations because they ran counter to his interest. In fact, the regional administrator pointed out that he had vetoed suggestions of equal opportunity officers because they "failed to present convincing evidence that a particular recipient had violated the nondiscriminatory provisions of Title VI."[11] However, the evidence does not support such a contention. Studies conducted by the Department of Justice's Federal Program Section, which have thoroughly analyzed Labor's Title VI program, have repeatedly stressed that even when regional equal opportunity officers have presented cogent evidence that certain recipients have violated

Title VI and subsequently have recommended that
regional administrators penalize them, the regional
administrators have vetoed these recommendations.
According to the Justice Department's studies, the
regional administrators have behaved thus primarily
because "their major concern is distributing federal
employment grants, not civil rights enforcement."[12]

   3. Complaint investigations. Labor officials
also utilize complaint investigations to determine if
its recipients are abiding by the provisions of Title
VI. These investigations are triggered by persons who
complain that they are victims of discrimination.
Essentially, a complaint investigation is an agency
inquiry into one or more of its recipients' activities
to assess if those activities violate Title VI. At
this point, it seems appropriate to pose the following
queries: How many complaints has Labor received and
investigated since the enactment of Title VI? How
many times has Labor found that its recipients were
not complying with the law? What is the extent of
Labor's backlog or carryover complaints? Most of
these questions can be answered by studying Table 6.1
(p. 212). Overall Table 6.1 indicates that the
complaints received by Labor's Office of Compliance
and Investigation decreased substantially from 977 in
fiscal year 1975 to 400 in fiscal year 1980. With
respect to these decreases, the following question
comes to mind: Why did the number of Title VI complaints received by Labor decrease between fiscal
years 1975 and 1980. Most Labor officials candidly
stated they "did not know what accounted for the large
decrease in complaints received by Labor from fiscal
year 1975 to fiscal year 1980."[13] However, they did
speculate. One group of officials theorized that
Title VI complaints had decreased because the public
feels it is useless to file a complaint with the
Department of Labor. These officials reasoned that
"the public knows or has heard that Labor is unlikely
to take action against noncomplying recipients and
has calculated that it is senseless to file a complaint
with Labor because it [Labor] will not take action to
rectify acts of discrimination."[14]

   Other officials hypothesized that the decline in
Title VI complaints reflected poor record keeping on
the part of Labor's recipients. These officials
stressed that "in many instances where Labor had
delegated its recipients the responsibility to record

Table 6.1.*   Title VI complaints and the Labor
              Department

FY	CR	CI	BC	FNC
1975	977	367	610	220
1976	620	149	471	40
1977	428	147	271	30
1978	413	136	270	27
1979	470	171	259	23
1980	400	127	240	20

FY denotes fiscal year
CR denotes omplaints received
CI denotes complaints investigated
FNC denotes findings of noncompliance

---

*Data were taken from the Department of Justice
Title VI Forum Reports (Fiscal Years 1975, 1976, 1977,
1978, and 1979 and from the Office of Management and
Budget's A-11 Budget Submission regarding Title VI.

The table only presents figures for fiscal years
1975 through 1980 because data for fiscal years 1964-
1974 were incomplete or unavailable.   Interview with
Clifford Russell, Equal Opportunity Officer in Labor's
National Office in Washington, January 16, 1979.

---

the number of complaints lodged against them, these
recipients had failed to do so."[15] As a result,
these officials charged, Labor's recipients' failure
to institute an efficient Title VI reporting system
had meant that many complaints levied against Labor
have not been recorded.

There is some general evidence to support these
contentions.   The Department of Justice, which has
investigated Labor's Title VI program, found that
"many of Labor-funded programs, which have been
delegated the responsibility of recording and investigating Title VI complaints, have not kept records of
Title VI complaints."[16] Still other officials alleged

214

that Title VI complaints had declined "because people may fear the consequences of filing Title VI complaints."[17] These officials explained that in many cases where persons enrolled in Labor's employment training programs had filed Title VI complaints, those programs accused of discriminating had taken reprisals against complainants, such as dismissing them from these programs. Given the fact that victims of discrimination are subject to lose their jobs for filing complaints, equal opportunity officers emphasized, many have opted not to file Title VI complaints, fearing the consequences of doing so.

Two points need to be emphasized here. First, while Labor officials cited various reasons to explain why Title VI complaints had decreased, they unanimously agreed that "the fact that Title VI complaints had decreased certainly did not indicate that their [Labor] recipients in growing numbers were complying with this law."[18] Indeed, equal opportunity officials constantly emphasized that their own studies and those conducted by the Department of Justice regarding the operations of Labor-funded programs patently demonstrated that Labor's recipients in growing numbers were not complying with Title VI.

The second point that should be stressed is that though a majority of Labor's ten regional offices have reported a decrease in the number of Title VI complaints, Labor's regional office in Philadelphia reported an increase in Title VI complaints. Equal opportunity officials in Philadelphia reported that the number of complaints had increased from 30 in fiscal year 1975 to 70 in fiscal year 1977. These officials attributed the increase in Title VI complaints to a campaign they had been conducting to inform victims of discrimination about their rights under Title VI.

What are the racial and ethnic characteristics of persons filing Title VI complaints? Unfortunately, this question cannot be answered because Labor has not kept or published data regarding the racial and ethnic composition of complaints. Equal opportunity officials at the Department of Labor asserted that they did not know why the department (Labor) had not maintainted records regarding racial and ethnic data, but these officials stated "they did know that the bulk of Title VI complaints they received came from blacks."[19]

A comparison of the number of complaints Labor received with the number it investigated indicates that Labor did not investigate all of the complaints it received for fiscal years 1975 through 1980 (see Table 6.1). Labor officials contended that "a shortage of manpower had prevented them from investigating all complaints."[20]

The evidence also shows that Labor has a large number of backlog complaints but these complaints are declining (see Table 6.1). Equal opportunity officials contended that the number of backlog complaints were declining primarily because "the department [Labor], under pressure from the Department of Justice and civil rights groups to improve its civil rights enforcement program, had taken steps to clean up its Title VI backlog."[21]

Furthermore, the evidence shows that Labor's findings of noncompliance had generally declined since fiscal year 1975 (see Table 6.1). Equal opportunity officers at the Department of Labor did not know why Labor findings of noncompliance had decreased, but they did speculate. These officers hypothesized that findings of noncompliance had declined because Labor's new and inexperienced Title VI staff simply did not know how to document acts of discrimination.

Compliance reviews. Another instrument used by Labor to ensure enforcement of Title VI is the compliance review. Essentially, a compliance review is an on-site investigation of a recipient's program operation to assess whether it is complying with Title VI. In view of what a compliance review is, it seems appropriate here to examine the number of compliance reviews conducted by the Department of Labor. Table 6.2 (p. 215) lists the number of compliance reviews conducted by Labor for fiscal years 1975 through 1980. Data are not presented for fiscal years prior to 1975 because data for this time period were unavailable. An examination of Table 6.2 reveals that Labor conducted 407 compliance reviews in fiscal year 1975, 169 reviews in fiscal year 1976, 215 reviews in fiscal year 1977, 200 reviews in fiscal year 1978, 179 reviews in fiscal year 1979, and 150 reviews in 1980. Basically, the evidence shows that the number of compliance reviews conducted by Labor decreased between fiscal year 1975 and 1980. Why has the number of compliance reviews conducted by Labor decreased? When

216

Table 6.2.* Compliance Reviews Conducted by Labor's Compliance and Investigation (or Equal Opportunity) Office (1975-1980).

Fiscal years	Compliance reviews conducted
1975	407
1976	169
1977	215
1978	200
1979	179
1980	150

*Data were taken from the Department of Justice Title VI Forum Reports (Fiscal years 1975, 1976, 1977, 1978, 1979, 1980 and from the Office of Management and Budget's A-11 Budget Submissions regarding Title VI.

this question was put to Labor officials, most stressed they did not know; however, they did speculate. These officials hypothesized that the number of Title VI compliance reviews conducted by Labor had decreased "because Labor simply lacks the manpower to do more reviews."[22]

Further, it is worth noting that the number of compliance reviews conducted by Labor is extremely small. Indeed, the evidence shows that while Labor has 20,000 recipients, it has never conducted more than 407 reviews. Surely, the evidence suggests that Labor may not know whether most of its recipients are adhering to the anti-discriminatory requirements of Title VI. A question that immediately arises is: Why has Labor conducted such a small number of compliance reviews? When this question was put to Labor officials, they once again noted that "Labor had conducted a small number of compliance reviews because

217

of staff limitations."[23]

There is indeed evidence to back up these officials' contentions. The Justice Department, which has
investigated Labor's Title VI operations, found "that
Labor has conducted a small number of compliance
reviews because of a lack of manpower."[24]

But more than this, it should be noted that the
few compliance reviews conducted by the Department of
Labor have not been good. At least, this is the position taken by the Department of Justice, which has
carefully studied Labor's Title VI program. According
to Justice Department officials, Labor has not only
conducted a small number of on-site investigations
(or compliance reviews), but those done by the agency
have been extremely poor, primarily because Labor's
equal opportunity officials "lack experience, are
poorly trained, and simply do not know how to conduct
good investigations."[25]

Enforcement Mechanisms

1. <u>Voluntary Compliance</u>. Thus far, primary
attention has been given to the compliance instruments
that Labor employs to detect discrimination. However,
at this point the discussion revolves around what
Labor does upon discovering discrimination. In short,
what enforcement sanction or sanctions are Labor
officials likely to use when they find that their
recipients are violating Title VI? As noted in
Chapter IV, the Civil Rights Act of 1964 grants agencies four sanctions to induce recipients to adhere to
the law. These sanctions are voluntary compliance,
referring a case to the Justice Department, deferring
funds and terminating funds. Voluntary compliance
refers to the efforts of an agency to negotiate with
or persuade a noncomplying recipient to obey Title VI
before the agency resorts to other sanctions. If
voluntary compliance proves unsuccessful, for example,
an agency may opt to refer a case to the Justice
Department. Referring a case to the Justice Department usually indicates an agency's decision to file a
legal suit against a noncomplying recipient.

When an agency decides not to refer a case to the
Justice Department, it may defer a noncomplying recipient's funds; that is, it might delay or postpone a

recipient's funds until the recipient takes steps to rectify discriminatory actions.

Finally, an agency might opt to terminate the funds of noncomplying recipients. Basically, this means withdrawing the funds of a program which violates Title VI.

An analysis of Labor's Title VI enforcement record over the last thirteen years reveals that it has ordinarily relied on voluntary compliance as the major enforcement tool for gaining compliance with Title VI. Indeed, analysis of how Labor has utilized Title VI sanctions indicates that it has used voluntary compliance 300 times, but it has never terminated funds, deferred funds, or referred a case to the Department of Justice. Clearly, the evidence reveals that Labor has used voluntary compliance alone as the instrument for gaining compliance with Title VI. The question that should be addressed here is: Why has Labor only employed the voluntary compliance sanction as a means for enforcing Title VI? Equal opportunity officers cited various reasons for this situation. First, equal opportunity officers in Labor's regional office in Philadelphia contended that they had only used voluntary compliance because "the Department of Labor had never established any specific time limits regarding how long Title VI officers should negotiate with noncomplying recipients before they opt to use other Title VI sanctions--the termination of funds, deferral of funds, and referral of cases to the Justice Department."[26] Specifically, these officials' basic contention went something like this: Title VI of the Civil Rights Act of 1964 states that agencies with Title VI responsibilities must first use voluntary compliance when they uncover Title VI violations, and can use other Title VI sanctions only when they have determined that voluntary compliance has proven ineffective. Labor, equal opportunity officers charged, had not established any time limits for utilizing the voluntary compliance sanction, even though it was supposed to do so under the Department of Justice's Title VI regulations and even though on many occasions it was apparent that the use of voluntary compliance was not persuading noncomplying recipients to comply with Title VI.

There is indeed some evidence to support these officials' contention. The Department of Justice, which has probed Labor's Title VI operations, found

that "though Labor's equal opportunity officials had
discovered that many of Labor's recipients, for over
three years, were violating Title VI, they relied only
on voluntary compliance to induce these recipients to
comply with Title VI,"[27] in spite of the fact that they
realized that this particular sanction had proven
ineffective in bringing about adherence with the
nondiscriminatory provisions of Title VI. According
to the Justice Department, Labor officials had behaved
in this manner because "the Department of Labor had
never specifically outlined when equal opportunity
officers should cease using voluntary compliance and
begin using stronger enforcement sanctions"[28] such as
terminating of funds and the deferral of funds to
bring about compliance with Title VI.

2. Termination and deferral of funds. Sanctions
such as the termination of funds and the deferral of
funds have not been used because they clash with
Labor's major mission--distributing federal grants to
employment training programs. Equal opportunity officials stressed "that when the recommended that the
funds of noncomplying recipients be deferred or terminated, their recommendations were ignored."[29] They
felt that this occurred because the Secretaries of
Labor, Ray Donovan and Ray Marshall, the Assistant
Secretary for Employment and Training, Ernest Greene,
and the Regional Administrator, Dave Grant, were and
are chiefly concerned with funding employment and
training programs, not civil rights enforcement. One
equal opportunity officer summed up the situation this
way:

> The department's primary goal is to get the
> money flowing and to keep it flowing to
> employment training programs. Consequently,
> any attempts by the equal opportunity divi-
> sion to disrupt or stop the flow of funds to
> Labor's recipients found guilty of violating
> Title VI, foster conflicts between Labor's
> programmatic and civil rights objectives.
> . . . When these conflicts arise, the Secre-
> tary of Labor, the Assistant Secretary of
> Employment and Training and the Regional
> Director resolve them. Unfortunately, these
> officials have generally ignored civil
> rights units' recommendations to terminate
> the funds of noncomplying recipients and
> have sided with program officials who are

primarily interested in keeping the money
flowing to Labor-funded programs, despite
the fact that such programs are disregarding
the provisions of Title VI.[30]

This viewpoint that Labor was and is primarily
concerned about funding employment training programs
was generally shared by civil rights officials in
Labor's Title VI office.

The fact that key Labor officials believed the
voluntary compliance approach was and is the most
effective method for enforcing Title VI is another
reason why Labor has essentially relied on this
approach to secure compliance with Title VI. Some
suggest that top Labor officials such as the Secretary
of Labor, the Assistant Secretary for Employment and
Training, the Director of the Office of Compliance
and Investigation, and the Regional Administartor have
taken this stance because voluntary compliance frequently results in noncomplying recipients abiding by
the provisions of Title VI and does not impact negatively on intended program beneficiaries--blacks and
other minorities.[31] In short, using the voluntary
compliance method does not negatively affect minorities and generally results in noncomplying recipients
adhering to the provisions of Title VI.

That key Labor officials firmly believe that the
voluntary compliance approach is the most effective
means for securing compliance with the nondiscriminatory requirements of Title VI is significant since it
is these officials who have the authority to determine
when and how long this sanction is used.

It should be noted that many equal opportunity
officers at the Department of Labor disagreed with the
view that voluntary compliance was the most effective
tool for bringing about compliance with Title VI.
These officials emphasized that "Labor had tested and
tested voluntary compliance as the major instrument
for implementing Title VI and found this sanction
totally ineffective."[32] To back up their contention,
these officials noted that Labor had consistently
used voluntary compliance to persuade noncomplying
recipients to abide by the provisions of Title VI,
but these recipients, by their very actions, had
consistently made it clear that they were not going to
honor the provisions of Title VI. Clearly, these

221

officials contended "voluntary compliance had not worked."[33] Consequently, they argued, only when Labor decides to use more stringent sanctions--the deferral of funds or the termination of funds--would recipients take the department seriously and rectify their discriminatory behavior.

Politics is another reason why Labor officials have only used the voluntary compliance sanction in its efforts to implement Title VI. Equal opportunity officials at the Department of Labor emphasized repeatedly that "Labor's total reliance on the voluntary compliance approach to secure compliance with Title VI was largely based on political considerations."[34] One equal opportunity specialist summed up the situation this way:

> Politics is the major reason why Labor has strictly relied on voluntary compliance with the law. When the department has employed voluntary compliance as an instrument for enforcing Title VI, Mayors, Governors, and Congressmen generally have not interfered with out Title VI shop. However, when the department has threatened to use stronger enforcement sanctions such as the termination of funds or the deferral of funds, Mayors, Governors, and Congressmen have intervened and generally have stopped attempts to apply these sanctions. . . . Knowing that politicians will intervene when Labor undertakes to act or use strong enforcement sanctions, and aware of the fact that it is hard to beat city hall or capitol hill, many Labor officials have decided to use voluntary compliance, even though they know that this sanction will not produce compliance with Title VI. They do this because they do not want to antagonize Congres, and they [Labor] realize that politicians will make it difficult to use stringent Title VI sanctions.[35]

This view that Labor had largely relied on voluntary compliance because of political considerations was widely shared by equal opportunity officials in Labor's national office in Washington and in its regional office in Philadelphia.

3. Referral of a case to the Department of Justice. As noted earlier, Labor has never referred a case to the Department of Justice. Equal opportunity officials maintained that "they did not know why the Department had never referred a case to the Department of Justice"[36] and contended that it was striking that the Labor Department had never used this sanction, since it had found voluntary compliance to be ineffective and had been reluctant to deter funds or terminate funds for political reasons. These officials further observed that "Labor's failure to refer a case to the Department of Justice and its reluctance to use the termination of funds and the deferral of funds sanctions indicate that the Department [Labor] is not genuinely committed to implementing Title VI."[37]

Labor's Problems with Title VI Enforcement. What is the most pressing problem or problems Labor's Title VI officials have had to grapple with in fulfilling their civil rights obligations? When this questions was put to equal opportunity officers at the Department of Justice they gave various responses. Some equal opportunity officers contended that one of the most pressing problems that they had to grapple with was "the fact that they had no direct link or control over their regional operations."[38] These officials explained that before they can send Title VI policy instructions out to their regional counterparts, they must get the consent of five program offices. "Getting the approval of these offices," equal opportunity officials stated, "takes weeks and sometimes months, delays responses to Title VI policy inquiries of regional officials, and thus hinders the enforcement of Title VI."[39]

Other Labor officials stated that the most critical problem that they have had to contend with was "the low priority given civil rights by the Department of Labor."[40] These officials explained that "key officials at Labor, including the Secretary of Labor, the Assistant Secretary for Employment and Training and the Regional Administrators, had made it perfectly clear that their primary concern is distributing grants to Labor recipients, not civil rights enforcement."[41] "These key officials have made this clear," equal opportunity officials stated, by "rejecting recommendations to take enforcement action against noncomplying recipients, by using equal opportunity offices as a dumping ground for lazy, incompetent, and trouble-making bureaucrats, and by ignoring recommendations to strengthen Labor's Title VI operations."[42]

Still other Labor officials contended that the most pressing problem they must grapple with regarding Title VI enforcement was and is a shortage of staff. Equal opportunity officials in the national office contended that seventy-three staff persons were insufficient to assess whether 20,000 recipients were abiding by the provisions of Title VI.[43]

Equal opportunity officials in Philadelphia's Regional Office also asserted that the most pressing problem that they confronted regarding the enforcement of Title VI was a shortage of staff. These officials charged that "it was simply impossible for three people to determine whether fifty-six recipients are adhering to provisions of Title VI."[44]

The Impact of Executive Activity on Labor's Title VI Enforcement Operations

Just as in other areas, it seems clear that the attitude and posture of the president have some influence on Title VI enforcement operations. Let us take a closer look with respect to the impact of such activity of Labor's enforcement effort.

Johnson, Labor, and the Bureaucracy. Basically, equal opportunity officials in the Department of Labor believed that Lyndon Johnson's very strong and favorable posture toward civil rights has a positive influence on their work. Johnson proposed and vigorously supported many of Labor's employment training programs. For example, it was Johnson who proposed Job Opportunity Sector Programs, which seek to train the hard-core unemployed in order that they may find employment: the Work Incentive Program, which aims at assisting persons on welfare to acquire employment skills so that they may get off welfare rolls and join the national workforce; and the Neighborhood Youth Corps, which is aimed at training impoverished youth so that they can find jobs. Johnson not only proposed these programs but he actively supported them. In his budget message to Congress in 1965, 1966, 1967, and 1968, Johnson continually called on Congress to

increase federal spending for manpower or employment
training programs, and Congress granted him his
request. Indeed, the evidence shows that federal
spending for manpower increased from 265 million in
1964 to 2.2 billion in 1968. Overall, the evidence
suggests that Johnson supported and promoted civil
rights interests. It was in this general context
that equal opportunity officials at the Department
of Labor generally stressed that President Johnson's
statements and actions had a positive influence on
their Title VI enforcement operations.

   The Nixon-Ford Years: Labor and Title VI. Given
Nixon's general negative stand toward civil rights,
as well as his distrust of bureaucracy, it was
altogether predictable that he would project a hostile
attitude toward Labor. As president, Nixon constantly
sought to cut the growth of Labor's manpower programs.
In 1971, 1972, and 1973, Nixon proposed deep cuts in
federal spending for Labor's manpower program charging
these programs were too costly. However, Congress
rejected the president's proposals and enacted legislation to increase Labor's budget. When this occurred,
President Nixon vetoed this legislation. For the most
part, the evidence surely suggests that Nixon did not
think highly of Labor.

   Equal opportunity officials at the Department of
Labor unanimously agreed that Nixon's assertions and
actions had inhibited their implementation of Title
VI. One official summed up the situation this way:

> The theme song of the Nixon Administration
> was benign neglect. In effect the Nixon
> White House constantly disregarded our
> requests for staff and resources which were
> needed to ensure the enforcement of Title VI.
> By refusing to give us the resources essen-
> tial for vigorously implementing Title VI,
> the Nixon Administration impeded our civil
> rights operations.[45]

   In general, Gerald Ford, just like Nixon, adopted
a hostile attitude toward civil rights enforcement.
Labor's equal opportunity officers contended that
Ford's statements and actions had a negative influence
on their Title VI enforcement operations. Specifically, these officers pointed out that Ford's refusal

225

to grant them the staff increases necessary for implementing Title VI had inhibited them from vigorously enforcing Title VI.[46]

Carter, Labor, and Title VI. In general, equal opportunity officials at Labor thought that Carter's statements and actions did not assist their endeavors to enforce Title VI. To be sure, the climate for civil rights under Carter was much more favorable than it was under Nixon and Ford. However, equal opportunity officials at Labor contended that while Carter had made a number of positive statements urging vigorous enforcement of civil rights laws, he had neglected to take specific steps to ensure that these laws would be enforced. One official summed up the situation this way, "Carter called for forceful implementation of Title VI, but he failed to give Title VI agencies the money and staff needed to effectively enforce Title VI."[47]

Reagan, Labor, and Title VI. In light of Reagan's antagonistic attitude toward civil rights enforcement, as well as his intense dislike for the bureaucracy, it was surely altogether predictable that he would exhibit a hostile attitude toward Labor. For example, in fiscal year 1982, Reagan influenced Congress to vote cuts in Labor's programs including the Comprehensive Employment Training Act (CETA), Jobless compensation, and Equal Opportunity.

On the whole, equal opportunity officers at the Department of Labor felt that Reagan had not helped their Title VI operations. These officials contended that by trimming their budget, Reagan had made it extremely difficult for them to enforce Title VI. Before Reagan's budget cuts, these officials explained, their office was underfinanced and understaffed and it was not aggressively enforcing Title VI. The budget cut, these officials stressed, would make things worse. Furthermore, equal opportunity officers at Labor pointed out that Reagan's "anti-busing statements and his opposition to affirmative action in the area of employment created an environment that made it difficult to enforce anti-discrimination laws and signified that Reagan was adopting a benign neglect attitude toward civil rights."[48]

226

Legislative-Bureaucratic Interaction:
Impact on Agency Behavior

This section attempts to describe how Labor's
interactions with Congress may have helped or hindered
its Title VI enforcement effort. Contact points which
foster bureaucratic-legislative interaction include
Congressional control over agencies' budget, legislation, and oversight. First, let us see how and to what
extent funding of Labor's budget requests might have
facilitated or inhibited Labor from meeting its Title
VI responsibilities. To assess this impact on Congressional funding on Labor's Title VI enforcement effort,
I studied Labor's Equal Opportunity Office budget
requests and Congressional appropriations for fiscal
years 1970 to 1980 to assess whether Congress had
generally allotted, substantially reduced, or pointedly
denied the Equal Opportunity Division funding requests.
In addition, I conducted interviews with Equal Opportunity Officers to gain their views in this regard.

Table 6.3 (p. 226) lists the Equal Opportunity
Office budget requests and Congressional appropriations
for fiscal years 1970 to 1980. An examination of
Table 6.3 reveals that for the most part, Congress
honored Labor's Equal Opportunity Office budget
requests. Put another way, Congress has generally
given Labor the funds it has requested. Labor officials, it should be stressed, pointed out that while
Congress had generally given them the funds they had
requested, those funds had been inadequate. These
officials explained this seemingly paradoxical position
this way. Before we submit our budget to Congress,
we must first submit it to the Department's [Labor's]
budget office and then to the Office of Management and
Budget. By and large, Labor officials stated, Labor's
budget office and the Office of Management and Budget
had slashed their budget requests. Consequently, when
they submitted their budget request to Congress, it
had been cut twice and thus was insufficient to fulfill
their civil rights mission. Also, these equal opportunity officials emphasized that they had defended and
justified an inadequate budget before Congress' Appropriations Committees because it was customary for
agency officials to support the president's budget,
even though they may believe that that budget will
hinder their respective agency's performance. And
these officials pointed out that failure to support
the president's budget, however inadequate, could

Table 6.3.* Labor's Investigation and Compliance
(or Equal Opportunity) Office's Budget Requests and
Congressional Appropriations (1970-1980).

Fiscal Years	Investigation and Compliance's Budget Requests	Congressional Appropriations
1970	700,000	700,000
1971	725,000	723,000
1971	797,000	795,000
1973	816,000	814,000
1974	893,000	891,000
1975	1,810,000	1,810,000
1976	1,809,000	1,809,000
1977	1,890,000	1,890,000
1978	2,001,000	2,001,000
1979	2,410,000	2,410,000
1980	2,800,000	2,800,000

*Data were obtained from the Budget of the United
States Government Fiscal Years 1970, 1971, 1972, 1973,
1974, 1975, 1976, 1977, 1978, 1979, and from an inter-
view with Mary Braceral, Budget Officer for Labor's
Employment and Training Administration Office,
February 18, 1979.

result in officials losing their jobs. As William
Harris, Director of the Investigation and Compliance
Office, put it:

> In many cases we have known that the
> Administrations' [Nixon, Ford, and Carter]
> budget requests have been inadequate, but
> we have defended these requests because
> it is assumed that bureaucrats or agency
> heads will support the President's budget

and because we know that if we don't
support the administration's budget
request there is a good chance that we
could lose our jobs.[49]

Both officials in the OMB and in Labor's Budget
Office confirmed the equal opportunity staff contention that they had cut the Equal Opportunity or
Investigation and Compliance Office's budget. Indeed,
Barry White, the OMB Budget Office for Labor charged
"that OMB had cut Labor's Title VI budget because
Labor had consistently ranked this office as a low
priority item."[50] White summed up the situation in
this way:

Under the federal government, agency heads,
in submitting their budgets to the Office
of Management and Budget [hereafter noted
OMB] rank programs as either high priority
or low priority items. If a program is
ranked as a high priority item, normally
OMB will not cut that agency's program
budget. On the other hand, if a program
is ranked as a low priority item, there
is a good chance that OMB would cut that
agency's program budget.[51]

White concluded that "Labor had consistently put the
Equal Opportunity Office at the bottom of the pile
and thus OMB had constantly slashed that office's
budget."[52]

Moreover, White stressed that Labor's Title VI
budget had decreased because "public support for
civil rights had declined."[53] According to White, "as
public support for civil rights had declined, so had
funding for Labor's Title VI enforcement program."[54]

1. Legislation. Legislation is another factor
which fosters bureaucratic-legislative contact.
Surely, by enacting legislation, Congress can affect
an agency's performance. This was made quite clear
in Chapter V where it was emphasized that anti-busing
legislation enacted by Congress had hindered HEW from
meeting its Title VI duties, but what about Labor?
In short, has Congress via legislation encouraged or
discouraged Labor from meeting its Title VI responsibilities? The available evidence suggests that
Congress through legislation has encouraged Labor to

fulfill its civil rights obligations under Title VI.
Indeed, by passing the Comprehensive Employment
Training Act of 1973, which forbids discrimination
based on race, color, national origin, sex, religion
or handicap in federally funded employment training
programs, Congress expressed its support for Labor's
efforts to combat various forms of discrimination.

Labor officials, it should be stressed, generally
agreed that "by enacting the Comprehensive Employment
and Training Act, Congress was exhibiting its support
for Labor efforts to end discrimination mandated by
Title VI and other civil rights statutes."[55]

2. Oversight hearings. Congress, as noted in
earlier chapters, can also affect an agency behavior
or performance by conducting oversignt hearings.
Specifically, it was emphasized in Chapters 3, 4, and
5 that Congress via oversight hearings can either
encourage or discourage an agency taking certain
actions. In light of this fact, it seems appropriate
to ask whether Congressional hearings have facilitated
or inhibited Labor from meeting its Title VI duties.
To begin with, however, it should be noted that
Congress has never conducted an oversight hearing
regarding Labor's Title VI operations. Put another
way, Congress has never held hearings to determine
how Labor had undertaken to implement Title VI. Staff
members of Congress's Civil Rights Oversight Committees
emphasized that "they did not know why the committees
on which they served had not investigated Labor's
Title VI performance."[56] Still, it seems reasonable
to speculate that one of the reasons why Congress has
never held an oversight hearing regarding Labor's
Title VI program is that Labor has never applied
stringent Title VI sanctions to penalize Congressional
districts found guilty of violating Title VI.

Two points need to be made here. First, it
should be noted that while Congress has not conducted
any oversight hearings regarding Labor's Title VI
enforcement shop, its (Congress') hearings concerning
fraud, mismanagement and nepotism in Labor's CETA
programs have had an adverse empact on Labor's Title
VI operations. Labor's Title VI enforcers emphasized
repeatedly that "as a result of Congressional oversight
hearings regarding fraud, mismanagement and nepotism
in Labor-funded programs, Labor's undermanned Title
VI office was denied the staff increases it had been

230

allotted by the OMB."57 These officials explained that though the OMB had granted Labor's Title VI office 22 new staff positions, the Equal Opportunity Office had never received these new positions because the Secretary of Labor, responding to Congressional pressure to extirpate fraud and mismanagement in CETA programs, transferred staff positions originally designated to the Title VI office to the General Instpector's Office, which is primarily responsible for eliminating fraud and mismanagement in Labor's programs.

There is indeed evidence to support equal opportunity officers' contention. The Department of Justice, which has conducted a number of studies regarding Labor's Title VI operations, reported in 1979 that Labor's Title VI or equal opportunity office "had been denied staff increases granted it by the Office of Management and Budget because the Secretary of Labor, feeling pressure from Congress to take action against fraud and mismanagement in CETA programs, felt it was more in Labor's interest to increase the staff of the General Inspector's Office"58 (an office which combats fraud in Labor-funded programs) than to increase the staff size of Labor's Title VI office.

The second point that should be stressed is that while Congress has not utilized its powers to legislate and investigate in order to inhibit Labor's enforcement of Title VI, some of its members have taken an interest in Labor's enforcement of Title VI and, on some occasions, have taken actions which have hampered Labor from forcefully implementing this statute. Equal opportunity officers stressed that "whenever they investigated Congressmen's constituents suspected of violating Title VI, these constituents called on their Congressmen to block Labor's Title VI investigations."59 On many occasions, these officials stressed, Congressmen had interfered with Labor's Title VI investigations and had been successful in delaying or halting these investigations. One equal opportunity officer in Labor's regional office in Philadelphia summed up the situation this way:

Every time we investigate a recipient suspected of violating Title VI, that recipient requests that his or her Congressman block our investigation.

Usually responding to these requests,
Congressmen call or write us and stress
that we should not investigate their
constituents. . . .Calls or letters from
Congressmen are perceived by us as forms
of political pressure. Reacting to these
pressures, we usually are not as forceful
as we should be in conducting investigations. For example, investigations may
be delayed because of Congressional pressure. I know this occurred in Westmoreland,
Pennsylvania, when Congressmen sought to
block our investigation.[60]

The Impact of Judicial Activity on Labor's
Title VI Enforcement Operations

This section analyzes the impact of judicial
activity on Labor's Title VI enforcement. Specifically, it evaluates whether court decisions regarding
Labor's implementation of Title VI have helped or
hindered Labor meeting its Title VI responsibilities.
In evaluating the impact of court decisions on Labor's
Title VI enforcement operations, I studied cases that
related specifically to Labor's implementation of
Title VI as well as cases which generally seemed to
have some bearing on Labor's enforcement of this
statute to determine if the courts' actions generally
have encouraged or discouraged Labor from implementing
Title VI. In addition, I conducted interviews with
Labor officials to gain their perceptions of the
impact of court rulings on Labor's Title VI
operations.

By and large, there have been a small number of
cases regarding Labor's Title VI enforcement operations, and the court rulings in these cases are mixed.
In short, some court rulings have encouraged Labor to
forcefully implement Title VI, while other court
rulings have tended to hamper enforcement. First, let
us look at cases that have called for vigorous Title
VI enforcement. Consider, for example, the case of
the NAACP et al. v Brennan, the only case which
specifically pertained to Labor's Title VI program.
In this instance, the NAACP and a group of minority
migrant farmworkers alleged that the Department of
Labor had violated Title VI by approving the program
operations and funding for state employment programs
which discriminated on the basis of race against

232

minority farmworkers both in the referral of jobs and the provisions of employment office service.[61] Specifically, plaintiffs alleged that "Labor violated Title VI by funding state employment offices which denied minority farmworkers the full range of employment services including testing, counseling, job training, and upgrading services."[62]

Labor responded to the plaintiffs' charge by contending that they had neglected to present sufficient evidence to document the allegation that the Department of Labor had violated Title VI.

However, the court disagreed with the Department of Labor argument and sided with the NAACP and minority farmworkers. Indeed, the court took the position that plaintiffs (the NAACP and minority farmworkers) had presented more than sufficient evidence that the Department of Labor had disregarded Title VI when it approved of and funded programs which engaged in discriminatory practices. The court held that Labor should cease funding state employment offices which operated their programs in a discriminatory fashion and should commence Title VI enforcement proceedings against such offices.

The court also ruled that Labor establish a monitor/advocate system. Under this system, Labor officials were to 1) frequently monitor their recipients' programs; 2) investigate complaints immediately upon receiving them; and 3) take corrective action against Labor-funded programs operating in noncompliance with Title VI. Equal opportunity officers asserted that the court ruling in NAACP et al. v Brennan helped Labor's Title VI operations because "it put Labor officials on notice that less than forceful implementation of Title VI would not be tolerated."[63] Also, these officials maintained that the Brennan ruling encouraged Labor to do what it should have been doing all along--take aggressive steps in implementing Title VI.

The case of United Steelworkers of America v Weber, which does not relate to Labor's Title VI enforcement operations per se, is another case which has had a positive impact on Labor's Title VI operations. In this particular case the court ruled that "employers and unions could establish voluntary [affirmative action] programs, including the use of quotas, to aid minorities and women in employment,"[64] even where there is no evidence of previous discrimination by employers.

Labor officials generally agreed that the court's ruling in Weber had a positive impact on Labor's civil rights enforcement efforts. Specifically, these officials pointed out that "as a result of the court's decision in Weber, Labor had re-inserted its affirmative action requirements in its CETA regulations, requirements which had been deleted in response to the court's ruling in Bakke."[65] By placing affirmative action back in CETA regulations, equal opportunity officers asserted, "Labor is showing that it is determined to combat discrimination and is sending potential and current violators of civil rights' laws a clear message, namely that they will pay a cost for violating these laws."[66]

Finally, Fullilove v Klutznick, which does not relate to Labor's Title VI program per se, is also a case which has had a positive affect on Labor's enforcement efforts. In this particular instance, the Supreme Court declared that Congress did not violate the constitutional guarantee of equal protection when it set aside for minority businessmen 10% of federal funds for local public works projects. Civil rights officials at Labor contended that "when the high court endorsed Congress's action to compensate minorities for past discrimination, this created an environment conducive for implementing civil rights laws."[67]

Up to this point, the discussion has revolved around the court rulings which seemingly have encouraged Labor to vigorously implement Title VI. However, these were court rulings which seemingly have discouraged Labor from aggressively enforcing Title VI. For example, Washington v Davis is a case which generally can be viewed as discouraging Labor from vigorously implementing Title VI, in spite of the fact that this particular case does not relate to Labor's Title VI program. As noted in an earlier chapter, the Supreme Court in Washington v Davis held that discriminatory intent must be shown to document acts of discrimination. Put another way, the Court ruled that persons who allege that they are victims of discrimination must provide proof that those parties who have allegedly discriminated against them purposely did so.

Civil rights officers at Labor charged that the Court's ruling in <u>Washington</u> v <u>Davis</u> definitely did not help their Title VI programs. These officials emphasized that "their jobs of documenting discrimination had been made more difficult because proving intentional discrimination is time consuming and nearly impossible."[68]

As mentioned earlier, the <u>Regents of the University of California</u> v <u>Bakke</u> is another case which seemingly discouraged Labor from meeting its Title VI responsibilities. Equal opportunity officers at the Department of Labor contended that top officials at the Department of Labor responded to the <u>Bakke</u> case by dropping affirmative action requirements from the Department's CETA regulations.[69] "This act," officials charged, "reduced already low morale in Labor's civil rights units and may have fostered the impression among Labor recipients that Labor was no longer committed to equal opportunity or the goals of affirmative action."[70]

Interest Group Activities and Labor's Title VI Enforcement Effort

This section identifies the interest groups that have undertaken to affect Labor's Title VI enforcement effort and then focuses on the political strategies or tactics they have employed to accomplish this objective. There are, of course, an array of groups which have endeavored to influence Labor's Title VI enforcement effort, but there have been four groups most active in seeking to accomplish this task. They are the National Association for the Advancement of Colored People, the Leadership Conference on Civil Rights, the Center for National Policy Review, and the Center for Law and Social Policy. Let us take a closer look at the activity of these groups.

The NAACP has continuously used various ways to push for the vigorous implementation of Title VI. Indeed, the evidence shows that the NAACP has sought to influence Labor's Title VI program by assisting victims of discrimination file complaints, by alerting Labor officials to recipients not in compliance with

Title VI, and by taking Labor to court when it believes Labor has neglected to meet its Title VI obligations. For example, it was the "NAACP which aided migrant farmworkers to file the Title VI complaint against Labor-funded programs operating in noncompliance with Title VI; that notified Labor that its recipients were discriminating against minority farmworkers, and that helped minority farmworkers file the suit charging that the Department of Labor had violated Title VI by funding programs blatantly violating the provisions of Title VI."[71]

Similarly, the Leadership Conference on Civil Rights has also endeavored to influence Labor's implementation of Title VI of the Civil Rights Act of 1964 by lobbying the Office of Management and Budget officials and Labor officials responsible for Title VI enforcement. Specifically, the Leadership Conference "has urged officials in the Office of Management and Budget to give Labor and other agencies with Title VI responsibilities more staff and money in order that they might better fulfill their Title VI obligations,"[72] and it has called on Labor officials to "cease relying on voluntary compliance and begin applying stronger Title VI sanctions"[73] such as the termination of funds and the deferral of funds in their efforts to enforce Title VI.

The Center for Law and Social Policy has used litigation as a major weapon to induce governmental agencies to vigorously implement civil rights laws, including Title VI. Indeed, the Center has pledged to file a suit against Labor if its lax enforcement of Title VI continues. For example, in testimony in January 1979 before the Department of Justice and Labor Task Force looking into Labor's Title VI enforcement effort, a spokesman for the Center stated that "the Center's studies showed that Labor was failing to implement Title VI and pledged to file a suit against Labor if it [Labor] neglected to take swift action to improve its Title VI program."[74]

The Center for National Policy Review has undertaken to affect Labor's Title VI program by lobbying officials responsible for implementing Title VI. For example, in testimony in January 1979 before the Departments of Labor and Justice Title VI Task Force, a spokesman for the Center "urged Labor officials to adopt uniform procedures for enforcing Title VI"[75]

236

and stressed that Labor should begin utilizing more stringent Title VI sanctions in its efforts to enforce the nondiscriminatory provisions of Title VI.

As expected, civil rights officers at the Department of Labor contended that interest groups have helped their Title VI enforcement operations. Specifically, these officers pointed out that "interest groups like the NAACP and the National Center for Policy Review had facilitated enforcement of Title VI by alerting them to recipients in noncompliance with Title VI, by aiding victims of discrimination file complaints, and by recommending measures that Labor could adopt to strengthen its Title VI program."[76]

Conclusion

This chapter has examined how the Department of Labor has undertaken to implement Title VI of the Civil Rights Act of 1964. We have shown that though Labor has adopted a number of compliance instruments to secure compliance with Title VI, it has generally been unable to use these instruments effectively because of 1) the competing and conflicting objectives of agency officials, 2) lack of staff, and 3) pressures from Congress. Specifically, we have found that Labor has only utilized the voluntary compliance sanction, disregarding other Title VI sanctions such as the deferral of funds, the termination of funds and the referral of cases to the Justice Department. Voluntary compliance has been the only sanction used by Labor because: 1) Labor's top officials--the Secretary of Labor, the Assistant Secretary for Employment and Training, and the Regional Administrator--believed that voluntary compliance was the · most effective means to deter discrimination in federally assisted programs; 2) it does not clash with Labor's key mission--disbursing grants to employment training programs; 3) it does not get agency officials in trouble with politicians--Mayors, Governors, Congressmen; and 4) it does not adversely affect intended program beneficiaries.

Further, we have found that while in some instances the president has facilitated enforcement of Title VI, in other instances the action of the president has inhibited Title VI implementation. Similarly, the actions of the Congress, the courts,

and interest groups have helped Labor's implementation
of Title VI in some instances, but have hurt it in
others.

[1]U. S., Government Manual--1978 (Washington: Government Printing Office, 1979), p. 280.

[2]Comment, "Title VI of the Civil Rights Act of 1964, Implementation and Impact," George Washington Law Review, 36 (1968), 824.

[3]U. S. Commission on Civil Rights, Last Hired, First Fired: Layoffs and Civil Rights (Washington: Government Printing Office, February 1977), pp. 5-10.

[4]Phillip S. Foner, Organized Labor and the Black Worker (New York: Praeger, 1974), p. 132. See also U. S. Commission of Civil Rights, Last Hired, First Fired, p. 5; U. S. Commission on Civil Rights, Twenty Years after Brown, (Washington: Government Printing Office, December 1975), pp. 65-68; U. S. Commission on Civil Rights, The State of Civil Rights: 1977 (Washington: Government Printing Office, February 1978), p. 2. Here the Commission reports that the "average incomes of black and Hispanic families ($9,242 and $10,259 respectively) were roughly two-thirds that of white families' incomes ($15,537)." Also, this particular report states that "while half of all white men are in professional, managerial, or skilled craft occupations--those paying relatively high wages--less than one fourth of white women and about 30 percent of minority men and 15 percent of minority women are so employed."
For evidence explaining the differences in the socio-economic status of blacks and whites, see Kathleen Long Wolgenmuth, "Woodrow Wilson's Appointment Policy and the Negro," Journal of Southern History,. 24 (November 1958), p. 39. Also see Herbert Aptheker, "Segregation in Federal Government Departments: 1928," Science and Society, p. 130; Peter and David Grabosky and H. Rosenbloom, "Racial and Ethnic Integration in the Federal Service," Social Science Quarterly 56 (June 1975); and K. J. Meier and L. Nigro, "Representative Bureaucracy and Policy Preferences," Public Administrative Review 36 (July/August 1976); David H. Rosenbloom, Federal Equal Employment Opportunity: Politics and Public Personnel Administration (New York: Praeger, 1977), p. 119. Also see Harrell R. Rodgers, Jr., and Charles S. Bullock, III, Law and

Social Change: Civil Rights Laws and Their Consequences (New York: McGraw-Hill, 1972), Chapter 5.

[5]United Steelworkers of America v Weber 99 S. Ct.
2721 (1979).

[6]U. S. Department of Justice, Evaluation of
Labor's Title VI Enforcement Effort (Washington: The
Department of Justice's Federal Programs Section,
December 1975), p. 14.

[7]Ibid.

[8]Ibid.

[9]Statement by Clifford Russell, Equal Opportunity
Officer in Labor's National Office in Washington, in
a personal interview, Washington, D. C., Jan. 16, 1979.

[10]Statement by Carl Kolman, Equal Opportunity
Officer in Labor's National Office in Washington, in
a personal interview, Washington, D. C., January 17,
1979; Lois Snowden, Equal Opportunity Officer in
Labor's National Office in Washington, in a personal
interview, Washington, D. C., March 1, 1979.

[11]Statement by Jim Day, Labor's Regional Administration in Philadelphia, in a telephone interview,
Philadelphia, Pa., February 28, 1979.

[12]U. S., Department of Justice, Evaluation of
Labor's Title VI Enforcement Effort, op. cit.

[13]Statement by Fred Dayton, Equal Opportunity
Specialist in Labor's National Office in Washington,
in a personal interview, Washington, D. C., March 5,
1979; also Clifford Russell and Carl Kolman, op. cit.

[14]Statement by John Lindsey, Equal Opportunity
Officer in Labor's Regional Office in Philadelphia,
in a personal interview, Philadelphia, Pa., February
28, 1979; Portia Dempsey, Equal Opportunity Officer in
Labor's Regional Office in Philadelphia, in a personal
interview, Philadelphia, Pa., February 28, 1979.

[15]Statement by Carl Kolman and Lois Snowden, op.
cit.

[16]U. S., Department of Justice, Evaluation of
Labor's Title VI Enforcement Effort, op. cit.

[17]Statement by Portia Dempsey and John Lindsey, op. cit.

[18]Ibid.

[19]Ibid.

[20]Ibid.

[21]Ibid.

[22]Ibid.

[23]Ibid.

[24]U. S., Department of Justice, Evaluation of Labor's Title VI Enforcement Effort, op. cit., p. 59.

[25]Ibid.

[26]Statement by Portia Dempsey and John Lindsey, op. cit.

[27]U. S.. Department of Justice, Evaluation of Labor's Title VI Enforcement Effort, op. cit., p. 73.

[28]Ibid.

[29]Statement by John Lindsey and Portia Dempsey, op. cit.

[30]Statement by Clifford Russell, op. cit.

[31]Statement by Fred Drayton and Lois Snowden, op cit.

[32]Statement by John Lindsey, Portia Dempsey, Fred Drayton, and Lois Snowden, op. cit.

[33]Ibid.

[34]Ibid.

[35]Ibid., statement by Lois Snowden.

[36]Statement by Portia Dempsey and John Lindsey, op. cit.

[37]Ibid.

241

[38]Statement by Carl Kolman, Fred Drayton, and Lois Snowden, op. cit.

[39]Ibid.

[40]Statement by John Lindsey and Portia Dempsey, op. cit.

[41]Ibid.

[42]Ibid.

[43]Statement by Fred Drayton, Lois Snowden, and Clifford Russell, op. cit.

[44]Statement by Portia Dempsey and John Lindsey, op. cit.

[45]Statement by William Harris, Director of Labor's Investigation and Compliance Office, in a personal interview. Washington, D. C., January 15, 1979.

[46]Statement by Portia Dempsey and John Lindsey, op. cit.

[47]Ibid., statement by John Lindsey.

[48]Statement by Lois Snowden and Fred Drayton, August 12, 1981, op. cit.

[49]Statement by William Harris, op. cit.

[50]Statement by Barry White, Office of Management and Budget, Budget Examiner for Labor, in a telephone interview, Washington, D. C., March 4, 1979.

[51]Ibid.

[52]Ibid.

[53]Ibid.

[54]Ibid.

[55]Statement by Clifford Russell, Lois Snowden, and Carl Kolman, op. cit.

[56]Statement by Katherine Leroy, Staff Member of the House Committee on Civil and Constitutional Rights,

in a telephone interview, Washington, D. C., Feb. 2, 1979; Jeff Williams, Staff Member of the House Committee on Civil and Constitutional Rights, in a telephone interview, Washington, D. C., Feb. 3, 1979.

[57]Statement by Clifford Russell and Fred Drayton, op. cit.

[58]U. S., Department of Justice, Federal Programs Section, Evaluation of Labor's Title VI Enforcement Effort (Washington: The Department of Justice Federal Program Section, October 1978), p. 88.

[59]Statement by Portia Dempsey and John Lindsey, op. cit.

[60]Ibid., statement by John Lindsey.

[61]NAACP v Brennan 360 F. Supp. 1006 (1972).

[62]Ibid.

[63]Ibid.

[64]United Steelworkers of America v Weber 61 L. Ed. 480 (1979).

[65]Statement by John Lindsey, Portia Dempsey, and Carl Kolman, op. cit.

[66]Ibid.

[67]Statement by Lois Snowden and Fred Drayton, op. cit.

[68]Statement by John Lindsey, Portia Long, and Carl Kolman, op. cit.

[69]Ibid.

[70]Ibid.

[71]Statement by Stanley Polypaus, Attorney for the NAACP, in a telephone interview, Washington, D. C., February 23, 1979.

[72]Statement by Glendora Sloane, Chairperson for the Leadership Conference on Civil Rights, in a personal interview, Washington, D. C., Feb., 23, 1979.

243

[73]Ibid.

[74]Statement by Carol Oppenheimer, Representative for the Center for Law and Social Policy, in a personal interview, Washington, D. C., January 18, 1979.

[75]Statement by William Taylor, Director of the Center for National Policy Review, in a personal interview, Washington, D. C., August 15, 1978.

[76]Statement by Portia Dempsey and John Lindsey, op. cit.

CHAPTER VII

POLICY IMPLEMENTATION AND TITLE VI
ENFORCEMENT: SOME CONCLUDING OBSERVATIONS

In this conclusion we discuss what this study suggests for implementation and enforcement of public policy. More specifically, we will focus on what we have learned from this analysis of Title VI enforcement operations. Obviously, of course, we give attention to the validity of the hypotheses suggested in Chapter I. In that chapter we postulated that agency enforcement of Title VI varies because of: 1) the resources (e.g., staff and compliance instruments) agencies have at their disposal; 2) the attitudes and the competing and conflicting objectives of individuals who are responsible for enforcing Title VI; 3) the pressures brought to bear on agencies by the executive, legislative, and judicial branches; and 4) the influence of clientele and outside groups on agencies.

In another part of the chapter, we discuss how the findings of this study related to previous implementation studies. The final section in this chapter considers the implications of our findings for the future enforcement and efficacy of Title VI.

I. The Validity
of the Hypotheses

HUD, HEW and Labor have developed an array of compliance instruments to secure compliance with Title VI. However, they have been unable to utilize these instruments effectively due to a number of factors including the competing and conflicting objectives of agency officials; the absence of standardized procedures for implementing Title VI; lack of staff; and their responsibility to carry out other civil rights obligations. Agency enforcement has also been affected (and hampered) by pressures from mayors, Congressmen, the White House and public and private interest groups.

More specifically, our analysis shows that HUD, HEW, and Labor have employed the voluntary compliance sanction more frequently than any other Title VI sanctions. This sanction has been used because the secretaries of HUD, HEW and Labor generally believed that voluntary compliance was the most effective means to combat discrimination in that its procedures were not protracted and cumbersome, and very importantly, it did not conflict with HUD's, HEW's, and Labor's major missions--disbursing grants to housing programs, to educational institutions and health and welfare organizations, and to employment training programs. Thus, the secretaries reasoned that voluntary compliance did not adversely affect intended program beneficiaries--blacks and other minorities. Another consideration, and a very important one, is that voluntary compliance did not get agency officials in trouble with mayors, governors, Congressmen, or the White House,

Further, we have found that while in some instances the President has facilitated HUD, HEW, and Labor's enforcement of Title VI, in other instances the actions of the President have inhibited Title VI enforcement. Similarly, the actions of the courts as well as interest groups have helped HUD's, HEW's, and Labor's implementation of Title VI in some instances, but have hurt in others. In a somewhat different vein, however, actions of the Congress seem to hurt some agencies more than others. For example, while congressional action severely hindered HEW from meeting its Title VI enforcement operations, such action did not seem to have had the same kind of negative impact on the Title VI enforcement operations of HUD and Labor. Indeed, though in some instances Congressional action impeded HUD's and Labor's Title VI operations, the actions of the Congress in other instances served to facilitate the enforcement of these agencies. Given this situation then, the basic question remains as to why does HEW have a better Title VI enforcement record than HUD and Labor. Or put more generally, our concern focuses on the question of why certain agencies (HEW) can enforce Title VI more vigorously than does other agencies (HUD and Labor).

The standard used to assess which agency has been the more vigorous in its Title VI enforcement efforts is how frequently that particular agency has applied the stringent termination of funds sanction. There are two reasons why I have used the termination of funds sanction as a measure of how effective an agency

246

has been in fulfilling its Title VI responsibilities. First, interviews with Title VI officers at HUD, HEW, and Labor convinced me that the termination of funds sanction was an excellent yardstick for determining the effectiveness of an agency's Title VI program. Indeed, these officials repeatedly emphasized that subtle forms of racial discrimination are still quite prevalent in such areas as education, employment, health, housing and welfare. Hence, they contended the best tool for arresting such discrimination was not voluntary compliance or referring a case to the Department of Justice, but rather invoking the termination of funds sanction. To be sure, some Title VI officers contended that the threat of terminating a noncomplying recipient's funds was indeed a good measure for assessing the aggressiveness and effectiveness of an agency's Title VI enforcement program. But whether or not this particular index is a better means for evaluating an agency's Title VI operation is difficult to determine since none of the agencies under study maintained records indicating how frequently they threatened to terminate the funds of a noncomplying recipient. At any rate, it seems appropriate to note that the data available do show that threatening to terminate the funds of a noncomplying recipient seldom results in that recipient honoring the provisions of Title VI. Consider, for example, the cases of Boston and Chicago.[1] Since 1970, HUD has been warning Boston's public housing officials that if they do not stop discriminating against blacks, their federal assistance would be terminated. Despite this warning and many others, however, Boston housing officials (at least as of January 1980), have disregarded HUD's threats and have continued to operate housing programs in noncompliance with Title VI.

Similarly, since 1965, HEW has been warning Chicago's school officials that if they do not abandon policies which perpetuate racial segregation in the city's public schools, it would cut off that city's federal education grants. In spite of this warning and umpteen others over the years, Chicago school officials have essentially ignored HEW's warnings and threats and continue to operate schools in blatant noncompliance with Title VI.

The second reason why I have used the termination of funds sanction as a measure of the effectiveness of an agency's Title VI program is that both the Civil

Rights Commission and the Department of Justice have
found this particular sanction was an excellent
measure for assessing the effectiveness of an agency's
Title VI operations. Indeed, both the Civil Rights
Commission and the Department of Justice, in their
studies of Title VI agencies, have found that discrimination is very prevalent in education, employment,
health and housing; that Title VI agencies have
inordinately relied on weak sanctions (e.g., voluntary
compliance and referring a case to the Department of
Justice) to end such discrimination; and that the most
effective sanction for halting discrimination in
federally assisted programs is the termination of
funds.[2]

Using the termination of funds measure, then, we
can say that HEW has had the more forceful and effective Title VI program. Specifically, HEW applied the
termination of funds sanction more frequently than HUD
or Labor. Indeed, during the period under study, the
data show that HEW utilized the termination of funds
sanction 200 times. By contrast, HUD has employed
this sanction only one time, and Labor never used it.
Thus, the data clearly show that HEW utilized the
termination of funds sanction more frequently than the
other agencies and consequencly, under our standard,
has enforced Title VI more aggressively than HUD or
Labor. Several reasons might be advanced as to why
HEW has a more forceful Title VI program than HUD or
Labor. These reasons are: 1) the attitudes of HEW's
officials toward the termination of funds sanction;
2) pressures from HEW's constituencies; 3) HEW's Title
VI organizational structure; and 4) HEW's staff.

The fact that HEW's secretaries (prior to 1973)
and civil rights officials believed that the termination of funds sanction was and is the most effective
means for combatting discrimination in federally
assisted programs may be one reason why HEW has a more
aggressive Title VI record than HUD or Labor.[3] While
HUD's and Labor's secretaries and civil rights staffs
contended that the termination of funds sanction was
counterproductive because its usage negatively
affected intended program beneficiaries, HEW's top
officials (prior to 1973) and their Title VI staffs
took opposing viewpoints. They contended that only
when the funds of noncomplying recipients were terminated did such recipients take steps to abide by Title
VI. They emphasized that reports of the Civil Rights

248

Commission and their own civil rights enforcement
experiences convinced them that "voluntary compliance"
and "referral of cases to the Department of Justice"
were ineffective in combatting racial discrimination.
Indeed, HEW officials maintained that only by applying
the termination of funds sanction against Title VI
violators will such violators take steps to comply
with the nondiscriminatory provisions of that statute.
And although these officials conceded that using the
termination of funds sanction would temporarily
disadvantage blacks and other minorities, they believed
that the alternative--to permit discrimination--would
have an even more negative and lasting impact on such
groups. To be sure, the experience of HEW officials
demonstrated that once a noncomplying recipient's
funds were terminated, that recipient immediately took
steps to abide by Title VI. Consequently, HEW officials asserted, minorities who were negatively
affected by the termination of funds sanction were not
hurt for any long period of time.

The major point of the foregoing discussion might
best be summarized as follows: HEW's secretaries and
civil rights officers, unlike such officers at HUD and
Labor, believed that the termination of funds sanction
was and is the most effective tool in deterring
discrimination in federally assisted programs.
Because they (HEW officials) believed this to be the
case, they utilized this sanction more frequently
than HUD and Labor officials. And once the sanction
was used, their experience indicated that compliance
soon followed.

Another reason that might explain why HEW has a
more aggressive Title VI enforcement record than HUD
or Labor might lie in the fact that HEW constituents--
social welfare, educational, women, and civil rights
organizations--exerted more pressure on HEW to enforce
Title VI than did constituents of the other agencies.
Take, for example, litigation as an enforcement
strategy. Labor constituents (e.g., labor unions)
filed one suit to compel it to vigorously implement
Title VI,[4] while HUD constituents (fair housing
groups, homebuilders and realtor organizations) filed
four suits to compel compliance with the anti-
discriminatory provisions of Title VI.[5] By contrast,
HEW constituents have filed over 16 suits to enforce
the provisions of Title VI. Clearly, on the basis of
litigation as an enforcement strategy, HEW has come

under considerably more pressure from its constituents to implement Title VI. Still the question remains as to why HEW has come under more pressure from its constituents than HUD or Labor. To be sure, HEW has come under pressure from its constituents because on many occasions it has neglected to fulfill its Title VI responsibilities, but so have the other agencies. However, perhaps the best explanation as to why HEW, unlike the other agencies, has had to grapple with enormous pressures from its constituents is that its clientele tend to be liberal and more interested in civil rights than are HUD and Labor constituents, e.g. homebuilders, realtors, and labor unions.

HEW's Title VI organizational framework is another factor which may illuminate why its Title VI operations are much better than HUD's or Labor's. Unlike HUD or Labor, HEW does not give program officials (officers whose primary objective is getting funds out as rapidly as possible to recipients) the authority nor multiple opportunities to veto recommendations by civil rights officials (officers whose primary goal is to halt the flow of funds to recipients who violate the provisions of Title VI). With the exceptions of the Secretary and the Reviewing Authority (a board of six lawyers appointed by the Secretary) only civil rights officers at HEW have the authority to determine whether noncomplying recipients' funds should be cut off. Put another way, program officials at HEW have not been granted the authority to overturn civil rights recommendations.

However, an analysis of Title VI organizational structures at HUD and Labor indicates that program officers at these agencies have been granted the authority and multiple chances to veto civil rights officials' recommendations. As noted in Chapters IV and VI, when programs' officials at HUD and Labor have been granted the opportunity to veto actions of civil rights officials taken against Title VI recipients, these program officials have vetoed such actions. This is not surprising in light of the inherent conflict between program officials (officials who are primarily interested in getting the money flowing and keeping it flowing to agency recipients) and civil rights officials (officials who are primarily concerned that federal funds do not flow to agency recipients found in noncompliance with Title VI). The conflict is self-evident. Program officials looked with disfavor on efforts of civil rights officials to halt the flow of funds to recipients who had violated Title VI. Generally, program officials viewed these efforts as diametrically opposed to their interests. But civil rights officials differed sharply with this primary "money flowing" concern of program officials.

The major point for highlighting this controversy is this: having been given the authority to veto efforts of civil rights officials to stop the flow of funds to noncomplying recipients, program officials are disposed to use this authority. Certainly, this has been the case at both HUD and Labor. In general, this has not been the case at HEW.[6] HEW's Title VI enforcement framework does not give program officials the formal authority to veto recommendations of its civil rights officials. The underlying assumption here is that if program officials at HEW had been granted the authority to veto suggestions of civil rights officials for implementing Title VI, its Title VI record would be no better than the record at HUD or Labor.

The size of HEW's Title VI staff may also explain why it has a more aggressive and effective Title VI operation than HUD or Labor. During the time of this study, HEW had a Title VI staff of 1,200, while HUD had a staff of 100 and Labor 73. When placed in the broader context that HEW has 31,000 recipients, HUD 21,000 recipients, and Labor 20,000 recipients, it seems reasonable to conclude that HEW was in a better position than HUD or Labor to meet its Title VI enforcement responsibilities. Even so, however, it seems appropriate to emphasize that all three agencies with Title VI responsibilities were understaffed. Indeed, civil rights officials at HUD, Labor, and HEW repeatedly stressed that limited staff had prevented their enforcement units from forcefully implementing Title VI. This lack-of-staff problem, it should be noted, was not confined to HUD, HEW, and Labor, but generally seems to have been a problem that afflicts all agencies with Title VI responsibilities. A 1979 General Accounting Office Report of the agencies with Title VI duties found that "all agencies with Title VI obligations are understaffed."[7]

II. THE RELATION
TO OTHER STUDIES

In large measure, this study provides support
for previous studies that focus on implementation.
For one thing, our findings support the notion that
groups or politicians that lose at the policy enactment stage seek, and sometimes win, victories at the
policy implementation stage. Specifically, we have
seen how Southern Congressmen who opposed the enactment of Title VI in 1964 have attempted, and in some
ways succeeded, in impeding HEW's enforcement efforts.
For example, in 1965, after HEW published guidelines
for bringing about school desegregation primarily in
the South, Southern legislators called on HEW officials to abandon these guidelines. When HEW officials
ignored such recommendations, the Congressmen in 1966
conducted an oversight hearing regarding HEW's Title
VI program. Essentially, the hearings were designed
to weaken HEW's Title VI guidelines and regulations
which called for integration of Southern schools.
However, this particular tactic proved fruitless.
HEW's civil rights officers continued to press for
Southern desegregation. Consequenly, Southern
Congressmen asked President Johnson to revoke HEW's
guidelines as illegal, arbitrary, and capricious.
But the President was not in a compliant mood. Not
only did he refuse to revoke the guidelines, he went
further and emphasized his support of HEW's efforts
to bring about desegregation in the South.

Despite the setbacks, Southern Congressmen
persisted in their efforts to block HEW's efforts to
implement Title VI. They used a variety of methods
including phone calls, letters, and lobbying the
White House. And they were successful in some of
these efforts. For example, in 1966, Southern legislators convinced the Congress to adopt the Fountain
Amendment (proposed by Congressman Fountain of North
Carolina) which made it more difficult for HEW to cut
off the funds of noncomplying recipients. Prior to
the adoption of this amendment, if HEW found a recipient in violation of Title VI, it would take action
immediately to defer that recipient's funds. However,
under the Fountain Amendment, HEW must now wait ninety
days before it can defer the funds of such recipients.

In spite of this law, however, HEW continued to
push for the enforcement of Title VI. But Southern

legislators likewise remained determined to inhibit
HEW's Title VI enforcement efforts. For example, in
1967 and 1968, the Congressmen used oversight hearings
to obstruct or otherwise frustrate efforts to implement Title VI. Despite these pressures, however, HEW
officers refused to slow down their efforts to bring
about desegregation of Southern schools. But HEW's
efforts to implement Title VI only spurred the
Congressmen to find other ways for obstructing civil
rights enforcement. For example, news reports
suggested that during the presidential campaign of
1968, Southern Congressmen struck a deal with then
presidential candidate, Richard Nixon. The alleged
deal was that if Nixon would slow down the federal
government's civil rights efforts in the South,
Southern Congressmen would support his bid for the
presidency. In the end, some southern legislators
did support candidate Nixon, and upon taking office
in 1969, President Nixon did support the "southern
cause." He openly defied Title VI enforcement by
ordering HEW to fund racially segregated school
districts in Jackson, Mississippi. Moreover, under
the Nixon administration, the Department of Justice,
for the very first time since the 1954 Brown decision,
sought to convince the Supreme Court to grant Southern
school officers additional time to desegregate their
schools. But the Supreme Court rejected the Department of Justice's request and ordered Southern school
officials to desegregate their schools "at once."
But when HEW's Director for Civil Rights, Leon
Panetta, moved to enforce the Court's decision,
Southern Congressmen warned him not to push too
forcefully and too fast. And when Panetta ignored
this warning, Southern legislators urged Nixon to fire
Panetta, and the President did just that.

Despite the fact Nixon and his Southern allies
were able to slow HEW's Title VI enforcement, the
battle was far from over. They still had to grapple
with the Supreme Court Justices who in the 1971 Swann
case mandated that lower courts and HEW could employ
busing to dismantle segregated school systems. As
noted earlier, both President Nixon and Southern
legislators opposed busing as a tool for desegregating
the schools and took steps to stop it. Indeed,
President Nixon threatened to fire civil rights officials at HEW who undertook to use busing as a tool to
integrate the schools, and Southern Congressmen from

253

1971 through 1974 proposed an array of amendments to prohibit HEW from ordering busing to dismantle segregated school districts. But these amendments were defeated, primarily because Northern members of Congress opposed them. However, as the courts and HEW began to order busing in the North, a number of Northern Congressmen joined forces with Southern legislators to oppose busing. This coalition resulted in Congressional adoption of various anti-busing amendments--Byrd (1975), Eagleton-Biden (1976, 1977, 1978, 1979, and 1980. Collectively, these amendments prohibit HEW from using busing as a means of pressuring segregated educational institutions to abide by the anti-discriminatory requirements of Title VI.

Overall, it is apparent that Southern members of Congress who opposed Title VI at the policy enactment level have also opposed it at the policy implementation level. Specifically, the evidence lucidly reveals that these legislators, who opposed the enactment of Title VI, have persisted in their efforts to obstruct HEW from vigorously implementing the statute.

On another dimension, this study has also found support for the notion that multiple actors involved in the implementation process foster delays and militate against the smooth implementation of law.[9] Specifically, we have found that one of the major factors that has inhibited the vigorous enforcement of Title VI has been the inability of Title VI implementors to take immediate action against recipients found guilty of violating this statute. Part of the reason for this delay is that Title VI enforcers cannot take swift actions against noncomplying recipients until they obtain the consent of various top level agency officials including the Secretary of the Department. In addition, enforcement officers must get the consent of Congressmen, the courts, and sometimes even the President of the United States when they undertake to cut off the funds of Title VI violators. Acquiring the consent of these different actors, this study has found, takes time, results in various delays and impedes the vigorous enforcement of Title VI.

Moreover, this study has found that law is not self-executing[10] and that the implementation of law is affected by the interplay of various policy actors including the president, Congress, courts, and agency

officials.[11] Also, we have seen interest group
activity and public opinion may influence the enforcement of law. Specifically, this study illuminates how
(1) the president's posture toward civil rights, the
bureaucracy, and his appointment and removal powers
afford him the opportunity to shape and influence the
implementation of Title VI; (2) Congress's control
over appropriations and its powers to legislate and
conduct oversight hearings can definitely influence
how agencies undertake to meet their Title VI obligations; (3) court decisions can either encourage or
discourage Title VI agencies from meeting their Title
VI duties; (4) attitudes of agency officials responsible for enforcing Title VI may significantly affect
whether or not an agency civil rights unit aggressively
implements the anti-discriminatory requirements of
Title VI; (5) interest groups through lobbying and
propaganda can influence how Title VI will be enforced;
and (6) the public mood toward civil rights may also
have a bearing on how Title VI is enforced.

This study has also come up with some findings of
a more general nature. One finding is that agencies
which have vigorously sought to implement Title VI are
more prone to intense political pressures than agencies
which have not. Put another way, agencies which have
seriously endeavored to meet their Title VI responsibilities are more apt to come under political attack
than agencies which have essentially disregarded their
Title VI duties. For example, HEW, which has applied
the most stringent Title VI sanction (e.g., termination
on funds) more frequently than HUD or Labor, has at
various times come under attack from the White House
and Congress. However, Labor, which has never utilized
the "termination of funds" sanction, has not been subjected to such pressures from either the White House
or Congress. In fact, the evidence reveals that HEW
officials who have attempted to forcefully implement
Title VI have been fired or warned that they would be
fired if they persisted in vigorously implementing
Title VI. Indeed, Leon Panetta, HEW's Director for
Civil Rights, was fired in 1970 by President Nixon over
his efforts to desegregate Southern school districts,
and in August 1972 Nixon threatened to fire other HEW
officers who sought to use busing as a means of integrating the schools.

Nixon, it should be noted, has not been the only
President to discourage HEW from aggressively enforcing

Title VI. To varying extents, Presidents Johnson, Ford, Carter and Reagan have also hindered HEW from meeting its Title VI obligations. President Johnson blocked HEW's attempt to terminate the funds of Chicago's racially segregated schools. Ford vigorously supported legislation to prevent HEW from requiring segregated schools to bus school children for desegregation purposes. Carter overturned HEW's efforts to terminate University of North Carolina funds because that university was not abiding by the provisions of Title VI. And Reagan has cut HEW's civil rights budget to such an extent that it is difficult for HEW officials to implement Title VI, or any other civil rights policies. Likewise, Congress, as noted earlier in this section, has also shown its displeasure with HEW's aggressive enforcement of Title VI.

Unlike HEW, Labor has not made vigorous efforts to enforce Title VI. Nor has it been subjected to much political pressure from the Congress or the White House. In fact, no official at the Department has been fired for enforcing Title VI and no President has interfered with Labor's Title VI enforcement effort. Also, Congress has not enacted any legislation inhibiting Labor from implementing Title VI. Nor has any member of Congress called for an oversight hearing concerning Labor's Title VI operations, despite findings by both the Civil Rights Commission and the Department of Justice that Labor has neglected to enforce the anti-discriminatory requirements of Title VI.

On balance, then, the evidence indicates that an agency which undertakes to enforce Title VI in an aggressive manner is more likely to come under strong political attack than an agency which does not attempt to do so. Agencies which soft-pedal or disregard their Title VI duties apparently do not fear repercussions from pro-civil rights enforcement interests (e. g., NAACP and the Civil Rights Commission), since these interests are politically weak and do not have much influence. For example, although the Civil Rights Commission detects flaws in Title VI agencies programs and recommends ways for rectifying these flaws, it cannot influence agencies to adopt these recommendations. The Civil Rights Commission lacks enforcement powers and political clout and the agencies know it.

On the other hand, this study strongly suggests that if an agency wishes to avoid political trouble, it must refrain from vigorous enforcement of Title VI. In light of this fact, it seems reasonable to infer that the federal government rewards federal agencies which opt not to meet their civil rights duties but penalizes those agencies which seriously seek to fulfill these duties. This behavior strongly suggests the federal government is not genuinely committed to vigorous implementation and enforcement of Title VI.

Another general finding which flows from this study is that political pressures have seemingly had a deleterious impact on the attitudes and behavior of agency civil rights officers at HEW, HUD, and Labor. These officers emphasized repeatedly that when they endeavored to vigorously enforce Title VI and other civil rights statutes, their efforts were often frustrated or blunted by their agency heads, by members of Congress, by a governor or mayor, or even by the President of the United States. This situation led some Title VI officers to state they were "burnt out,"[12] had lost "enthusiasm"[13] and a "sense of purpose"[14] and were "contemplating resignation."[15]

Another major finding which emanates from this study is that assessing an agency enforcement of a law strictly on the basis of whether or not it has developed guidelines for administering that law may be misleading. Other factors--such as the attitudes of enforcement officials, the size of staff, clientele pressures, and the organizational structure of the implementing agency--may be more important considerations in determining whether or not an agency can vigorously implement and enforce a law. Indeed, this study has found that Title VI agencies like HUD or Labor, have developed uniform guidelines for enforcing Title VI but have generally neglected to enforce these guidelines. In stark contrast, HEW has not adopted uniform procedures for implementing Title VI, but it has a better record of implementing this statute than either HUD or Labor. The attitudes of HEW's enforcers, the size and organization of its staff, and pressures from its clientele--all seemingly explain why HEW has a more aggressive Title VI operation than HUD or Labor.

III. The Implications for Future Enforcement of Title VI

Let us now turn attention to the question of what can be done to improve Title VI enforcement. This matter must be considered, however, under circumstances where the federal government's Title VI enforcement effort is apparently declining in effectiveness. This observation is supported by a 1979 Justice Department* study which states:

> Despite past achievements federal enforcement of Title VI is for the most part declining in effectiveness. The past few years have seen the number of groups protected by civil rights statutes increased at the same time as more and longer covered programs are funded. This has resulted in a corresponding increase in agency civil rights compliance workloads. However, the size of agency civil rights staff, when adjusted for inflation, has not changed appreciably. In some agencies, they have actually decreased.[16]

This particular study does not provide support for the contention that all Title VI agencies enforcement operations are declining in effectiveness. It does, however, present evidence which shows that because of political pressures, a lack of resources (staff and money) and competing agency objectives, three of these agencies--HUD, HEW, and Labor--have generally failed to aggressively enforce Title VI. Throughout this study we have found that when HUD, HEW, and Labor have attempted to defer or to terminate the funds of noncomplying recipients, key political actors, including the President, Congress, governors and mayors have put pressure on these agencies not to pull back. And civil rights officials at HUD, HEW, and Labor have responded to these pressures by taking no enforcement action against recipients guilty of

_____

*In December 1980, Drew Days, Assistant Attorney General for Civil Rights in the Carter Administration, observed that the federal government had and is not aggressively enforcing Title VI.

violating the nondiscriminatory provisions of Title VI.
Generally, then, political pressures have obstructed
HUD, HEW, and Labor civil rights officers from meeting
their civil rights obligations.

What can be done to prevent major policy actors
from discouraging Title VI officers from meeting their
Title VI responsibilities? Basically, it seems that
very little can be done because it may be impossible
to depoliticize the Title VI enforcement process.
Indeed, as long as HUD, HEW, and Labor seek to or take
enforcement actions against particular recipients,
these recipients will call on their representatives
in Congress to block these agencies from taking such
actions. And generally, as noted throughout this
study, members of Congress will respond favorably
to such requests because they are essentially interested in pacifying their constituents and in
maximizing votes. Hence, depoliticizing the enforcement process may be impossible. Still, it seems that
some action can be taken to minimize Congressional
interference with agency enforcement of Title VI
programs. For example, if civil rights and other
public interest groups, in particular Congressional
districts, put more pressure on their representatives
to support enforcement of Title VI, this may serve to
counterbalance some of the pressure put on agencies
not to enforce Title VI.

Staff limitations, together with a lack of funds,
have also precluded HUD, HEW, and Labor from meeting
their Title VI responsibilities. Civil rights
officers at these agencies emphasized that limited
staff and funds had prevented them from investigating
Title VI complaints and had made it difficult for
them to monitor whether recipients were abiding by .
the nondiscriminatory provisions of Title VI. To be
sure, more staff and funds would seem to facilitate
vigorous enforcement of Title VI at HUD, HEW, and
Labor, but these resources alone cannot achieve this
objective. For what is needed is a civil rights staff
which is well trained on how to uncover, document, and
combat discrimination based on race, color, or national
origin. Hence, more funds coupled with a larger well-
trained staff may lead to more vigorous implementation
of Title VI and civil rights laws generally.

But more funds and a trained Title VI staff will
not automatically bring about strong enforcement of

259

Title VI, for this will not end the inherent conflict
within agencies between program officers (agency
officials who are primarily interested in keeping
funds flowing to departmental recipients) and civil
rights officers (agency officers who are chiefly concerned with halting the flow of federal funds to
departmental recipients guilty of violating Title VI).
When conflicts between these competing groups have
arisen, the Secretaries of the agencies have resolved
them. And in most instances, particularly at HUD,
HEW, and Labor, the Secretaries have sided with program officials. According to civil rights officers at
these agencies, the Secretaries had behaved in this
manner because they, like program officials, were and
are primarily interested in disbursing federal grants
to departmental (or agency) recipients, not in civil
rights enforcement. Assuming this to be true--and
indeed the Civil Rights Commission and the Department
of Justice findings corroborate this view--the question is what can be done to ensure that recommendations
of civil rights officials that action be taken against
Title VI violators will be adopted.

One thing that can be done to attain this goal is
to create an agency dedicated solely to civil rights
enforcement. The central contention here is that as
long as civil rights is placed under the jurisdiction
of agencies with other major missions, these agencies
will give civil rights second, third, or fourth priority. Certainly, at HUD, HEW, and Labor we have
found that top agency officials, specifically the
Secretaries of the agencies and program officials have
given priority to other agency missions, not civil
rights. Specifically, we found that the Secretaries
of HUD, HEW, and Labor felt that their key goals were
to disburse federal grants to public housing authorities, educational, welfare, and social institutions
and employment training programs, not to enforce civil
rights. Keeping this basic point in mind, it seems
that civil rights will only receive top priority in an
agency dedicated to civil rights enforcement. Surely,
a centralized civil rights agency has its disadvantages. For example, such an agency would be "more
vulnerable to manipulation and political attack as a
result of unpopular enforcement action it might
take."[17] Moreover, the mass movement of civil rights
personnel to a centralized civil rights unit "would
disrupt the administering of existing enforcement
programs."[18]

However, there are definite advantages for creating a centralized Title VI agency. For one thing, "it would eliminate the conflict of interests inherent in having one agency responsible for both program goals and civil rights enforcement."[19] In addition, it would "assure(s) uniform Title VI investigation procedures,"[20] something that is currently nonexistent at many Title VI agencies. No doubt, criticisms will be levelled at these suggestions, but given the advantages and disadvantages of creating a centralized civil rights agency and the current state of civil rights enforcement, the creation of a centralized civil rights unit is definitely preferable to the status quo.

To be sure, the political-social milieu is currently not favorable for creating an agency solely dedicated to civil rights enforcement. The evidence to substantiate this point is overwhelming. Surveys of public opinion show that a majority of Americans, specifically whites, believe that the passage of civil rights laws has solved the "race problem." Indeed, these surveys reveal growing public resentment of the federal government's advocacy of such civil rights policies as affirmative action and busing. President Reagan has seemingly sensed this national mood toward civil rights and has made it crystal clear through his assertions and actions (e.g., agency appointments) that he strongly opposes affirmative action and busing.

And the Congress has likewise responded to this anti-civil rights sentiment. It has enacted anti-busing amendments, refused to delegate HUD the authority to aggressively implement the Open Housing Act of 1968, has passed legislation geared toward cutting back on affirmative action, and has supported President Reagan's budget cuts that have come down especially hard on programs designed to help blacks, minorities and poor people. Moreover, the Supreme Court, which under Chief Justice Warren generally supported civil rights interests, is now much more uncertain and negative in its posture toward civil rights.

Given these circumstances the outlook for civil rights interests is not at all promising. Thus, regardless of its merits, the proposal to create a single civil rights enforcement agency would seem to stand little or no chance of enactment. Indeed, the problem for civil rights interests in the immediate future is not whether to foster new policy initiatives, but rather with <u>how</u> to prevent the deceleration and even obliteration of civil rights gains that have already come about.

[1] The data from these two cases were taken from U. S. Civil Rights Commission, <u>Desegregation of the Nation's Public Schools: A Status Report</u> (Washington: Government Printing Office, February 1979), p. 78; and from interviews with HUD's Title VI officers.

[2] The contention here is supported by various Civil Rights Commission studies. For example, U. S. Commission on Civil Rights, <u>The Federal Rights Enforcement Effort--1974 Volume VI: To Extend Federal Financial Assistance</u> (Washington: Government Printing Office, 1975), Chapters 1, 2, 3, 4; U. S. Commission on Civil Rights, <u>The Federal Civil Rights Enforcement Effort--1974 Volume VII: To Preserve, Protect, and Defend the Constitution</u> (Washington: Government Printing Office, February 1978), pp. 1-26 and 34-36. Furthermore, it seems fitting to note here that in my interview with Theodore Nickens, Assistant Director of the Department of Justice's Federal Program Section, he emphasized repeatedly that the termination of funds sanction was a reasonable measure of the effectiveness of an agency's Title VI program.

[3] While it is true that HEW has used the termination of funds sanction more frequently than HUD and Labor, we should point out here that HEW has not utilized this sanction since 1973. As HEW's civil rights officers put it, this situation has come about because since 1973 HEW's Secretaries, who ultimately decide whether the termination of funds sanction would be employed, have opposed the usage of this sanction in enforcing Title VI, contending that it hurts intended program beneficiaries--blacks and other minorities.

[4] It is important to note here that the one suit filed against Labor to enforce Title VI was brought by a civil rights organization, namely the NAACP.

[5] It should be noted here that the four suits filed against HUD for failing to enforce Title VI were filed by the NAACP and the National Committee Against Discrimination in Housing.

[6] At this point, it seems important to emphasize the fact that simply because HEW's program officials

do not have the authority to veto Civil Rights officials' Title VI recommendations, this does not mean
that these officials have been totally unsuccessful
in preventing Civil Rights officials from carrying out
or implementing Title VI. Indeed, when Civil Rights
officials have recommended that noncomplying recipients' funds be terminated, program officials have
urged the various Secretaries of HEW to reject these
recommendations. In many instances, the Secretaries
have sided with the program officials.

[7]U. S., General Accounting Office, "Survey of
Federal Agency Enforcement of Title VI of the 1964
Civil Rights Act," (unpublished study, February 1979).
Information here was obtained from Arthur Davis,
Analyst for the General Accounting Office in San
Francisco, California. This particular study is
interesting because it presents cogent evidence that
most Title VI agencies are understaffed, underfinanced
and have generally neglected to enforce the anti-
discrimination provisions of Title VI.

[8]Eugene Bardach, The Implementation Game
(Cambridge, Mass.: MIT Press, 1977), p. 56.

[9]Jeffrey L. Pressman and Aaron Wildasky, Implementation (Berkeley: Univ. of California Press, 1973),
p. 79.

[10]Harrell R. Rodgers, Jr., and Charles S.
Bullock, III, Law and Social Change: Civil Rights
Laws and Their Consequences (New York: McGraw-Hill,
1972), p. 211.

[11]Charles O. Jones, An Introduction to the Study
of Public Policy (Mass.: Duxbury Press, 1977),
p. 140.

[12]Statement by Clifford Russell, Equal Opportunity Officer in Labor's National office in Washington, in a personal interview, Washington, D. C.,
January 17, 1979; Lois Snowden, Equal Opportunity
Officer in Labor's National office in Washington, in
a personal interview, Washington, D. C., March 1, 1979.

[13]Ibid.

[14]Ibid.

[15]Statement by Carl Kolman, Equal Opportunity
Officer in Labor's National office in Washington, in
a personal interview, Washington, D. C., January 17,
1979; Zina Greene, Equal Opportunity Specialist at
the Department of Housing and Urban Development, in a
personal interview, Washington, D. C., August 29, 1978.

[16]U. S., Department of Justice, Civil Rights
Division, Title VI Forum, Volume IV, No. 2, Fall 1979,
p. 1.

[17]The recommendations propounded here are not
new; rather, they were originally proposed by President Carter's Task Force on Civil Rights Reorganization. Located with the Office of Management and
Budget, the Task Force's chief objective was to
evaluate and make recommendations for improving civil
rights enforcement. Hence, keep in mind that the
recommendations proposed in this study were actually
those of President Carter's Task Force on Civil
Rights.
     Still, it should be noted that the Task Force
took no action to implement its recommendation when
it disbanded in January 1979.
     For an excellent analysis concerning what to do
to improve federal enforcement of civil rights
statutes, see William Taylor, "Federal Civil Rights
Laws: Can They Be Made to Work?" George Washington
Law Review 39 (1969), 1971.

[18]Ibid., President Carter's Task Force on Civil
Rights.

[19]Ibid.

[20]Ibid.

BIBLIOGRAPHY

Articles

"All The People," The National Journal, July 11, 1981,
    p. 1261.

"Anti-busing Rider Draws Veto of Justice Bill,"
    Congressional Quarterly Almanac, XXXVI, 1980,
    p. 213.

Aptheker, Herbert. "Segregation in Federal Government
    Departments: 1928," Science and Society, 28
    (Winter 1964), 130.

"Budget Cuts Constrain Major Civil Rights Agencies,"
    Washington Post, March 12, 1981, p. 7A.

Comment. "Title VI of the Civil Rights Act of 1964,
    Implementation and Impact," George Washington
    Law Review, 36 (1968), 832.

Freund, William C. "The Politics of Austerity," Time
    Magazine, January 29, 1979.

Grabosky, Peter and David H. Rosenbloom. "Racial and
    Ethnic Integration in the Federal Service,"
    Social Science Quarterly, 56 (June 1975), 110.

"HEW Department Files Affidavit in Federal District
    Court Against Ford Administration," New York
    Times, February 4, 1975, Sec. A, p. 22, col. 4.

Kemp, Den. "The 1981 Budget," Time Magazine,
    March 20, 1978.

Meier, K. J. and L. Nigro. "Representative
    Bureaucracy and Policy Preferences," Public
    Administration Review, 36 (July/August 1976),
    458-69.

"Most of Proposed Budget Cuts in President Ford's
    Final 76 Budget Would Come Out of the Budget of
    HEW," New York Times, Sec. A, p. 21, col. 5.

"NAACP Leaders Express Concerns About Reagan," New
    York Times, November 23, 1980, p. 27.

267

Note. "Enforcing a Congressional Mandate: LEAA and Civil Rights," _Yale Law Journal_, 85 (1976), 721.

President Reagan's Inaugural Address," _Congressional Quarterly_, January 24, 1981, p. 187.

President Reagan's Press Conference Text," _Congressional Quarterly_, January 31, 1981, p. 239.

Proposal to Ease Job Bias Rules," _Washington Post_, August 26, 968, p. 1A.

"Race Issue: Cutting Edge in 80 Elections," _New York Times_, October 10, 1980, Section D, p. 15.

"Reagan Favors Voting Rights Act Extension," _Washington Post_, August 6, 1981, p. 1.

"Reagan Supports Measure to Curb Suits on Busing," _New York Times_, November 19, 1981, pp. 1 and 30.

"Remark by Mrs. Harris Stirs Rift on Politics in Civil Rights Cases," _New York Times_, August 3, 1979, p. 10.

"Safety Net Not Much Help, Critics Charge: What Reagan's Budget Cuts Would Do To The Poor," _Congressional Quarterly_, August 18, 1981, pp. 665-666.

Taylor, William. "Federal Civil Rights Laws: Can They Be Made to Work?" _George Washington Law Review_, 39 (1969), 1971.

"U. S. Changes School, Job Bias Policy," _Washington Post_, May 23, 1981, p. 1A.

"U. S. Easing Rules on Discrimination By Its Contractors," _New York Times_, August 25, 1981, p. 1.

"U. S. Supreme Court Rules 8-0 That Federal Courts Can Order the Construction of Low Cost Housing for Minorities in the Suburbs," _New York Times_, Sec. A, p. 1, col. 8.

Wolgemuth, Kathleen L. "Woodrow Wilson's Appointment Policy and the Negro," _Journal of Southern History_, 24 (November 1958), 457-71.

"110 Years of Voting Rights Legislation," _Congressional Quarterly_, April 11, 1981, pp. 633-636.

Books

Bailey, Stephen and Edith Mosher. ESEA: _The Office of Education Administers a Law_. New York: Syracuse Univ. Press, 1969.

Bailey, Stephen. _Education Interest Groups in the Nation's Capital_. Washington, D. C.: American Council of Education, 1975.

Bardach, Eugene. _The Implementation Game: What Happens After a Bill Becomes Law_. Cambridge, Mass.: MIT Press, 1977.

Barker, Lucius and Jesse McCorry. _Black Americans and the Political System_. 2nd ed. Cambridge, Mass.: Winthrop Publishers, Inc., 1980.

Barker, Lucius and Twiley Barker. _Civil Liberties and the Constitution: Cases and Commentaries_. New Jersey: Prenctice Hall, 1975.

Bell, Derrick. _Race, Racism and Law_. Boston: Little, Brown, 1973.

Bolner, James and Robert Stanley. _Busing: The Political and Judicial Process_. New York: Praeger, 1974.

Bullock, Charles and Harrell Rodgers. _Law and Social Change: Civil Rights Laws and Their Consequences_. New York: McGraw-Hill, 1972.

Center For National Policy Review. _Justice Delayed and Justice Denied_. Washington: Center for National Policy Review, 1975.

Congressional Quarterly. _Nixon: The First Year of His Presidency_. Washington: Congressional Quarterly, Inc., 1978.

_____. Civil Rights Progress Report 1970.
Washington: Congressional Quarterly, Inc., 1975.

_____. Gerald Ford 1974. Washington:
Congressional Quarterly, Inc., 1975.

Davis, George and Fred Donaldson. Blacks in the
United States: A Geographic Perspective.
Boston: Houghton-Miflin, 1975.

Davis, James W. Politics, Programs and Budgets: A
Reader in Government Budgeting. New Jersey:
Prentice Hall, 1969.

_____. An Introduction to Public Administration:
Politics, Policy, and Bureaucracy. New York:
The Free Press, 1974.

Dawson, Richard. Public Opinion and Contemporary
Disarray. New York: Harper and Row, 1973.

Downs, Anthony. Inside Bureaucracy. Boston: Little,
Brown, 1974.

Edelman, Murray. The Symbolic Use of Politics.
Urbana, Ill.: Univ. of Illinois Press, 1964.

Fenno, Richard. The Power of the Purse:
Appropriations Politics in Congress. Boston:
Little, Brown, 1966.

Foner, Phillip S. Organized Labor and the Black
Worker. New York: Praeger, 1974.

Franklin, John H. From Slavery to Freedom: A History
of Negro Americans. 5th ed. New York: Alfred
A. Knopf, 1978.

_____. Reconstruction after the Civil War.
Chicago: Univ. of Chicago Press, 1961.

Gilder, George. Wealth and Poverty. New York.
Basic Books, Inc., Publishers. Chapter 12, 1981.

Hayes, Laurence J. The Negro Federal Government
Worker. Cambridge, Mass.: Harvard Univ. Press,
1941.

Hechlo, Hugh. A Government of Strangers: Executive Politics in Washington. Washington, D. C.: The Brookings Institute, 1977.

Hess, Stephen. Organizing the Presidency. Washington, D. C.: The Brookings Institute, 1976.

Jones, Charles O. An Introduction to the Study of Public Policy. 2nd ed. Mass.: Duxbury Press, 1977.

Kaufman, Herbert. Administrative Feedback: Monitoring Subordinates' Behavior. Washington, D. C.: The Brookings Institute, 1973.

Kearnes, Doris. Lyndon Johnson and the American Dream. New York: Harper and Row, 1976.

Krislow, Samuel. The Negro in Federal Employment. Minneapolis, Minn.: Univ. of Minnesota Press, 1967.

Miles, Rufus. The Department of HEW. Washington, D. C.: Praeger, 1974.

Moran, Charles. Current Biography 1967/1968. New York: H. W. Wilson, 1967.

Morris, Lorenzo and Henry Charles. The Chit'lin Controversy: Race and Public Policy in America. New York: University Press of America, 1978.

Myrdal, Gunnar. An American Dilemma. New York: Harper and Row, 1964.

Nakamura, Robert T. and Frank Smallwood. The Politics of Policy Implementation. New York: St. Martin's Press, 1980.

Nathan, Richard P. The Plot That Failed: Nixon and the Administrative Presidency. New York: John Wiley and Sons, 1975.

Neustadt, Richard E. Presidential Power. New York: John Wiley and Sons, 1960.

Novak, Robert and Rowland Evans. Nixon in the White House: The Institution of Power. New York: Random House, 1971.

Newman, Dorothy et al. Protest, Politics, and Prosperity: Black Americans and White Institutions, 1940-1945. New York: Pantheon Books, 1978.

Olson, Mancur. The Logic of Collective Action. Cambridge, Mass.: Harvard Univ. Press, 1971.

Orfield, Gary. The Reconstruction of Southern Education: The Schools and the 1964 Civil Rights Act. New York: John Wiley and Sons, 1969.

_____. Must We Bus? Washington, D. C.: The Brookings Institute, 1978.

_____. Congressional Power: Congress and Social Change. New York: Harcourt, Brace and Jovanovich, 1975.

Osborn, John. Whitehouse Watch: The Ford Years. Washington, D. C.: New Republic Books, 1977.

Panetta, Leon and Peter Gall. Bring Us Together. New York: Lippincott, 1971.

Parsons, Talcott and Kenneth Clark. The Negro American. Boston: Houghton-Miflin, 1965.

Pfeffer, Jeffrey. Organizational Design. Illinois: AHM Publishing Co., 1978.

Pressman, Jeffrey and Aaron Wildasky. Implementation. Berkeley: Univ. of California Press, 1973.

Radin, Beryl. Implementation, Change and the Federal Bureaucracy: School Desegregation Policy in HEW 1964-1968. New York: Teachers' College Press, 1977.

Ripley, Randal B. and Grace A. Franklin. Congress, the Bureaucracy and Public Policy. Illinois: The Dorsey Press, 1976.

272

Rosenbloom, David H. Federal Equal Employment Opportunity: Politics and Public Personnel Administration. New York: Praeger, 1977.

Rourke, Francis E. Bureaucracy, Politics and Public Policy. Boston: Little, Brown, 1976.

Ruchames, Louis. Race, Jobs and Politics: The Story of FEPC. New York: Columbia Univ. Press, 1953.

Schan, Max. Blacks and American Medical Care. Minn.: Univ. of Minnesota Free Press, 1973.

Siedman, Harold. Politics, Position and Power. New York: Oxford Univ. Press, 1970.

Sundquist, James. Politics and Policy: The Eisenhower, Kennedy and Johnson Years. Washington, D. C.: The Brookings Institute, 1968.

Truman, David. The Governmental Process. New York: Alfred A. Knopf, 1952.

Weinberg, Meyer. A Chance to Learn: The History of Race and Education in the United States. Cambridge and New York: Cambridge Univ. Press, 1977.

Wilson, William J. The Declining Significance of Race. Chicago: University of Chicago Press, 1978.

Wildasky, Aaron. The Politics of the Budgetary Process. 2nd ed. Boston: Little, Brown, 1974.

Wirt, Frederick. The Politics of Southern Equality. New York: Aldine, 1970.

Wolman, Harold. Politics of Federal Housing. New York: Dodd, Mead, 1971.

Cases

Adams v Richardson 35 F. Supp. 636 (1972).

Adams v Richardson 356 F. Supp. 92 (1973).

Adams v Richardson 480 F. 2d., 1159 (1973).

Adams v Califano 430 F. Supp. 118 (D. D. C. 1977).

Alexander v Holmes 396 U. S. 20 (1969).

Board of Public Instruction of Taylor County, Florida
v Finch 414 F. 2d 1068 (1969).

Brown v Califano 455 F. Supp. 837 (1977).

Brown v Weinberger 417 F. Supp. 1215 (1976).

City of Cheyenne v Lynn 420 F. Supp. 1823 (1973).

Columbus Board of Education et al. v Penick 99 S. Ct.
2941 (1979).

Dayton Board of Education et al. v Brinkman 99 S. Ct.
2971 (1979).

Fullilove v Klutznick 65 L. Ed. 902 (1980).

Gautreaux v Romney 326 F. Supp. 480 (1970).

Gautreaux v Chicago Housing Authority 503 F. 2d. 930
(7th Cir. 1974).

Green v County School Board of New Kent County 391
U. S. 430 (1968).

Hicks et al. v Weaver 302 F. Supp. 619 (1969).

Hills v Gautreaux 425 U. S. 284 (1976).

Lau v Nicholls 414 U. S. 563 (1974).

Lee v Macon County 270 F. Supp. (1967).

Memphis v Greene 67 L. Ed. 2d., 769 (1981).

NAACP v Brennan 360 F. Supp. 1006 (1972).

Regents of the University of California v Bakke 98 S.
Ct. 2733 (1978).

Simkins v Moses 218 F. 2d 117 (Fourth Circuit 1948).

United States v Jefferson County Board of Education
372 F. 2d. 836 (1966).

United Steelworkers of America v Weber 61 L. Ed. 2d
480 (1979).

Government Documents

Congressional Quarterly Almanac. Vol. XX. Washington
Congressional Quarterly Inc., 1965.

_____. Vol. XXI. Washington: Congressional
Quarterly Inc., 1966.

_____. Vol. XXII. Washington: Congressional
Quarterly Inc., 1967.

_____. Vol. XXIII. Washington: Congressional
Quarterly Inc., 1968.

_____. Vol. XXIV. Washington: Congressional
Quarterly Inc., 1969.

_____. Vol. XXV. Washington: Congressional
Quarterly Inc., 1970.

_____. Vol. XXVI. Washington: Congressional
Quarterly Inc., 1971.

_____. Vol. XXVII. Washington: Congressional
Quarterly Inc., 1972.

_____. Vol. XXVIII. Washington: Congressional
Quarterly Inc., 1973.

_____. Vol. XXIX. Washington: Congressional
Quarterly Inc., 1974.

_____. Vol. XXX. Washington: Congressional
Quarterly Inc., 1975.

_____. Vol. XXXI. Washington: Congressional
Quarterly Inc., 1976.

_____. Vol. XXXII. Washington: Congressional
Quarterly Inc., 1977.

_____. Vol. XXXIII. Washington: Congressional
Quarterly Inc., 1978.

U. S. Code of Federal Regulations, 45 Public Welfare.
    Washington: Government Printing Office, October,
    1979.

U. S. Commission on Civil Rights. Civil Rights 1963.
    Washington: Government Printing Office, 1963.

_____. The Federal Civil Rights Enforcement
    Effort--1970. Washington: Government Printing
    Office, 1970.

_____. The Federal Civil Rights Enforcement
    Effort: Seven Months Later--May 1971.
    Washington: Government Printing Office, 1971.

_____. Twenty Years After Brown. Washington:
    Government Printing Office. 1974.

_____. The Federal Civil Rights Enforcement
    Effort--1974, Volume IV: To Ensure Equal Educa-
    tional Opportunity. Washington: Government
    Printing Office, January 1975.

_____. The Federal Civil Rights Enforcement
    Effort--1974, Volume VI: To Extend Federal
    Financial Assistance. Washington: Government
    Printing Office, 1975.

_____. Fulfilling the Letter and Spirit of the
    Law: Desegregating the Nation's Public Schools.
    Washington: Government Printing Office, 1976.

_____. Civil Rights Digest - Health Care.
    Washington: Government Printing Office, 1977.

_____. Last Hired, First Fired: Layoffs and
    and Civil Rights. Washington: Government
    Printing Office, January 1977.

_____. The Federal Civil Rights Enforcement
    Effort--1974, Volume VII: To Preserve, Protect,
    and Defend the Constitution. Washington:
    Government Printing Office, June 1977.

_____. Statement on Affirmative Action.
    Washington: Government Printing Office,
    October 1977.

_____. The Federal Government Civil Rights
Enforcement Effort--1977: To Eliminate Employ-
ment Discrimination. Washington: Government
Printing Office, December 1977.

_____. The State of Civil Rights: 1977.
Washington: Government Printing Office,
February 1978.

_____. Civil Rights Digest - Bakke: Slow,
Forward, Neutral and Reverse. Washington:
Government Printing Office, Summer 1978.

_____. Towards Equal Educational Opportunity:
Affirmative Admissions at Law and Medical
Schools. Washington: Government Printing
Office, June 1978.

_____. Civil Rights Update. Washington:
Government Printing Office, January 1979.

_____. Desegregation of the Nation's Public
Schools: A Status Report. Washington:
Government Printing Office, February 1979.

_____. Civil Rights Update. Washington:
Government Printing Office, March 1979.

U. S. Congress. House. Committee on Appropriations,
Subcommittee On Appropriations. Department of
Housing and Urban Development--Independent
Agencies Appropriations for 1971. Hearing, 92nd
Cong., 1st Sess., April 28, 1971. Washington:
Government Printing Office, 1971.

_____. House. Committee on Appropriations,
Subcommittee on Appropriations. Department of
Housing and Urban Development--Independent
Agencies Appropriations for 1974. Hearing, 93rd
Cong., 2nd Sess., March 30, 1974. Washington:
Government Printing Office, 1974.

_____. House. Committee on Appropriations,
Subcommittee on Appropriations. Department of
Housing and Urban Development--Independent
Agencies Appropriations for 1977. Washington:
Government Printing Office, 1977.

_____. House. Committee on Appropriations,
Subcommittee on Appropriations. Department of
Housing and Urban Development--Independent
Agencies Appropriations for 1979. Hearing, 96th
Cong., 1st Sess., March 9, 1979. Washington:
Government Printing Office, 1979.

_____. House. Committee on Appropriations,
Subcommittee on HEW. Departments of Labor and
Health, Education and Welfare for 1979. Hearing,
96th Cong., 1st Sess., March 3, 1979.
Washington: Government Printing Office, 1979.

_____. House. Committee on Appropriations
Subcommittee on Labor. Departments of Labor and
Health, Education and Welfare for 1979. Hearing,
96th Congress., 1st Sess., March 20, 1979.
Washington: Government Printing Office, 1979.

_____. House. Committee on the Judiciary Special
Subcommittee on Civil Rights. Hearing, 89th
Cong., 2nd Sess., on Guidelines for School
Desegregation, December 14, 15, and 16, 1966.
Washington: Government Printing Office, 1966.

_____. Senate. Committee on Appropriations,
Subcommittee on HEW. Departments of Labor and
Health, Education and Welfare, and Related
Agencies Appropriations for 1979. Hearing, 96th
Cong., 2nd Sess., April 8, 1979. Washington:
Government Printing Office, 1979.

_____. Senate. Select Committee on Equal Educa-
tion Opportunity. Equal Educational Opportunity.
Hearing, 91st Cong., 2nd Sess., Part 3A on
Desegregation Under Law. June 15, 16, and 17,
1970. Washington: Government Printing Office,
1970.

_____. Senate. Committee on Labor and Public
Welfare. Oversight Hearing on HEW Enforcement
of School Related Civil Rights Problems, 1975.
Hearing, 94th Cong., 1st Sess., on the Examina-
tion of the Administration and Enforcement of
the Civil Rights Act in the Elementary and
Secondary Areas of Education. April 3, 1975.
Washington: Government Printing Office, 1975.

U. S. Department of Health Education and Welfare.
Washington. Memorandum: Director's Reporting on
Compliance Activities. [Washington: Department
of Health, Education and Welfare's Office for
Civil Rights, November 28, 1978].

_____. Washington. Memorandum: Adams, Brown and
Weal Settlement--To All Regional OCR Staff and
All Headquarters Staff. [Washington: Department
of Health, Education and Welfare's Office for
Civil Rights, January 23, 1978].

_____. Washington. Fall 1978 Elementary and
Secondary School Civil Rights Survey School
System Summary Report: Form OS/CR 101.
[Washington: Department of Health, Education
and Welfare's Office for Civil Rights, 1978].

_____. Washington. This IS HEW. [Washington:
The Department of Health, Education and Welfare's
Public Affairs Office, 1979].

U. S. Department of Housing and Urban Development.
Washington. Compliance and Enforcement Procedures
for Title VI of the Civil Rights Act of 1964.
[Washington: Government Printing Office, 1976].

_____. Washington. Answers to Title VI Question-
naire for the U. S. Commission on Civil Rights.
[Washington: Department of Housing and Urban
Development's Fair Housing Office, 1977].

_____. Washington. Fair Housing and Equal
Opportunities/Checklist Entitlement Application
Review. [Washington: Department of Housing and
Urban Development's Fair Housing Office, January
1978].

_____. Washington. HUD on the Move. [Washington:
Government Printing Office, 1979.

U. S. Department of Justice. Washington. Title VI
Forum Volume II, Winter 1977-1978, No. IV.
[Washington: Department of Justice's Federal
Programs Section, 1977-1978].

_____. Washington. Title VI Forum Volume I, Fall 1976, No. II. [Washington: Department of Justice's Federal Programs Section, 1976].

_____. Washington. Title VI Forum Volume V, Spring/Summer 1979, No. I. [Washington: Department of Justice's Federal Programs Section, 1979].

_____. Washington. Title VI Forum Volume IV, Fall 1979, No. II. [Washington: Department of Justice's Federal Programs Section, 1979].

_____. Washington. Title VI Forum Volume VI, Fall/Winter 1978-1979. [Washington: Department of Justice's Federal Programs Section, 1978-1979].

_____. Washington. The Department of Housing and Urban Development's Title VI Enforcement Effort. [Washington: Department of Justice's Federal Programs Section, August 1975].

_____. Washington. Evaluation of Labor's Title VI Enforcement Effort. [Washington: Department of Justice's Federal Programs Section, 1979].

_____. Washington. Evaluation of Title VI Enforcement in the Manpower Administration's United Employment Service Program. [Washington: Department of Justice's Federal Programs Section, December 1975].

U. S. Department of Labor. Washington. Equal Employment Opportunity Compliance Officer's Handbook. [Washington: Bureau of National Affairs, Inc., 1978].

_____. Washington. ETA Exchange. Volume III, No. 10. [Washington: Department of Labor, 1979].

U. S. General Accounting Office. San Francisco. Survey of Federal Agency Enforcement of Title VI of the 1964 Civil Rights Act. [San Francisco: U. S. General Accounting Office, 1979].

_____. Washington. U. S. Government Manual--1978. [Washington: Government Printing Office, 1979].

U. S. Office of Management and Budget. Washington. Budget of the United States--1978. [Washington: Government Printing Office, 1979].

_____. Washington. Budget of the United States--1977. [Washington: Government Printing Office, 1979].

U. S. President. Public Papers of the Presidents: Lyndon B. Johnson, 1963-1964, Volume I. [Washington: Government Printing Office, 1964].

_____. Public Papers of the Presidents: Lyndon B. Johnson, 1965, Volume II. [Washington: Government Printing Office, 1966].

_____. Public Papers of the Presidents: Richard Nixon, 1969. [Washington: Government Printing Office, 1971].

_____. Public Papers of the Presidents: Richard Nixon, 1971. [Washington: Government Printing Office, 1973].

_____. Public Papers of the Presidents: Richard Nixon, 1972. [Washington: Government Printing Office, 1974].

_____. Public Papers of the Presidents: Gerald R. Ford, 1974. [Washington: Government Printing Office, 1976].

_____. Public Papers of the Presidents: Jimmy Carter, 1977. [Washington: Government Printing Office, 1978].

_____. Weekly Compilation of Presidential Documents. News Conference Volume XIII, No. 31. [Washington: Government Printing Office, 1977].

Interviews

Biddle, Jack. Personal interview. Washington, D. C., March 8, 1979.

Bracerol, Mary. Personal interview. Washington, D. C., March 5, 1979.

Brown, Cynthia. Personal interview. Washington, D. C., December 20, 1978.

Brown, Yvonne. Personal interview. Philadelphia, Pennsylvania, February 25, 1979.

Burke, Timothy. Personal interview. Philadelphia, Pennsylvania, February 25, 1979.

Carey, Harry. Personal interview. Washington, D. C., July 28, 1978.

Carter, Ralph. Personal interview. Washington, D. C., October 2, 1978.

Cheatham, Wilbert. Personal interview. Washington, D. C., January 17, 1979.

Cioffi, Fred. Personal interview. Washington, D. C., March 12, 1979.

Cleaver, Brenda. Personal interview. Philadelphia, Pennsylvania, October 3, 1978.

Cromer, Marie. Personal interview. Washington, D. C., December 20, 1978.

Cunningham, Maxine. Personal interview. Baltimore, Maryland, September 13, 1978.

Davis, Arthur. Telephone interview. San Francisco, California, January 22, 1979.

Davis, Lloyd. Telephone interview. Washington, D. C., August 28, 1978.

Dawson, Frank. Telephone interview. Washington, D. C., March 1, 1979.

Days, Drew. Personal interview. Washington, D. C., January 16, 1979.

Dempsey, Portia. Personal interview. Philadelphia, Pennsylvania, February 28, 1979.

Dodds, Dewey. Personal interview. Philadelphia, Pennsylvania, February 25, 1979.

Drascler, David. Telephone interview. Washington, D. C., March 1, 1979.

Drayton, Fred. Personal interview. Washington, D. C., March 5, 1979.

Ellis, Arthur. Telephone interview. Washington, D. C., April 20, 1979.

Erving, Louis. Personal interview. Washington, D. C., July 19, 1978.

Gilliam, Ron. Personal interview. Philadelphia, Pennsylvania, February 26, 1979.

Greene, Ernest. Telephone interview. Washington, D. C., March 7, 1979.

Greene, Zina. Personal interview. Washington, D. C., August 15, 1978.

Harvey, Robert. Personal interview. Philadelphia, Pennsylvania, February 25, 1978.

Henderson, Lloyd. Personal interview. Washington, D. C., January 17, 1979.

Hess, Stephen. Personal interview. Washington, D. C., October 27, 1978.

Holbert, Kenneth. Personal interview. Washington, D. C., September 5, 1978.

Howell, A. J. Personal interview. Washington, D. C., January 17, 1979.

Kaplan, Peter. Personal interview. Washington, D. C., August 7, 1978.

Keleman, Jack. Telephone interview. Washington, D. C., February 10, 1979.

Kizzie, Fannie. Personal interview. Philadelphia, Pennsylvania, October 3, 1978.

Kolman, Carl. Personal interview. Washington, D. C., January 17, 1979.

Lemming, Clark. Personal interview. Washington, D. C., January 31, 1979.

Leonardis, Victor. Telephone interview. Washington, D. C., January 17, 1979.

Leroy, Katherine. Telelphone interview. Washington, D. C., February 3, 1979.

Lindsey, John. Personal interview. Philadelphia, Pennsylvania, February 28, 1979.

Madison, Waite. Personal interview. Washington, D. C., February 8, 1979.

McGuire, Chester. Personal interview. Washington, D. C., July 26, 1978.

McKinney, Roy. Personal interview. Washington, D. C., April 19, 1979.

Mapp, Richard. Personal interview. Washington, D. C., August 29, 1978.

Morris, William. Personal interview. Washington, D. C., August 23, 1978.

Morse, Mildred. Personal interview. Washington, D. C., August 23, 1978.

Myers, Robert. Personal interview. Philadelphia, Pennsylvania, October 4, 1978.

Newton, Paul. Telephone interview. Washington, D. C., September 20, 1978.

Nickens, Theodore. Personal interview. Washington, D. C., January 16 and 17, 1979.

Nixon, Theodore, Personal interview. Philadelphia, Pennsylvania, February 25 and 26, 1979.

Oppenhiemer, Carol. Personal interview. Washington, D. C., January 16, 1979.

Patterson, Brad. Personal interview. Washington, D. C., October 3, 1978.

Pearl, Lawrence. Personal interview. Washington, D. C., October 26, 1978.

Pinkard, Mary. Personal interview. Washington, D. C., October 20, 1978.

Polypaus, Stan. Personal interview. Washington, D. C., February 23, 1979.

Rauh, Joseph. Telephone interview. Washington, D. C., April 17, 1979.

Russell, Clifford. Personal interview. Washington, D. C., March 5, 1979.

Russell, Jack. Personal interview. Washington, D. C., April 3, 1979.

Saunders, Ben. Personal interview. Washington, D. C., February 9, 1979.

Sheppard, Valida. Personal interview. Washington, D. C., March 12, 1979.

Simmons, Samuel. Personal interview. Washington, D. C., July 28, 1978.

Sloane, Glendora. Personal interview. Washington, D. C., October 13, 1978 and January 17, 1979.

Sloane, Martin. Telephone Interview. Washington, D. C., August 18, 1978.

Snow, Chuck, Telephone interview. Washington, D. C., March 9, 1979.

Snowden, Lois, Personal interview. Washington, D. C., March 1, 1979.

Taylor, William. Personal interview. Washington, D. C., August 15, 1978.

Walker, William. Personal Interview. Washington, D. C., September 11, 1978.

White, Barry. Telephone interview. Washington, D. C., March 4, 1979.

Wilson, Tex. Personal interview. Washington, D. C.,
    August 7, 1978.

n denotes note.

Brown, Yvonne, 194n, 196n, 197n, 201n, 203n, 204n
Bullock, Charles, 115n, 192n, 239n
Bureaucracy,
    power of Title VI officers within, 55-56
    Carter's attitude toward, 34
    Ford's attitude toward, 29-30
    Nixon's attitude toward, 27
    Reagan's attitude toward, 40
Bureaucratic Activity,
    impact on Title VI enforcement, 55-56
Burke, Timothy, 197n, 201n, 203n
Burke, 101, 102
Busing, 28, 32, 36, 44, 48, 50
    anti-busing legislation, 24, 49, 52, 125, 176,
        177, 254, 256
Byrd Amendment, 49, 177, 254
Califano, Joseph, 157, 158, 159, 195n, 200n
Carter, Jimmy, 30, 34, 35, 41, 44n, 49, 90, 95, 98,
        158, 171, 172, 226, 228, 256
    and affirmative action, 30-31
    and busing, 32
    appointment of blacks to federal posts, 34
    attitude toward the bureaucracy, 32
    attitude toward the poor, 33
    civil rights role as perceived by, 30-31
    ethnic purity remark by, 30
    impact on HEW's Title VI operations, 167-168
    impact on HUD's Title VI enforcement machinery, 98
    influence on Labor's Title VI enforcement
        effort, 226
    Title VI memorandum sumbitted to civil rights
        agencies by, 32
Carter, Ralph, 120n
CBS News., 46n
Center for Law and Social Policy, 57, 60, 235
Center for National Policy Review, 57, 59, 157, 198,
        199, 236, 237
CETA Programs, 230
Charlotte, North Carolina, 21-22
Cheyenne, Wyoming, 89, 109
Chicago, Illinois,
    racial segregation in, 29, 98
    segregated schools in, 19, 156-158
Child Nutrition Program, 29
Cioffi, Fred, 198n
Civil Rights Act, 1866, 110-111
Civil Rights Act, 1964, 1, 6, 27, 52, 58, 59, 68, 86,
        93, 124, 154, 180, 189-190, 218-19

288

                                291

Augustus J. Jones, Jr. (Ph.D., Washington University, St. Louis) is an Assistant Professor of Political Science at the University of Florida, Gainesville. In 1978, he received a Research Fellowship from the Brookings Institution.